D0326825

LEGAL EDUCATION IN THE DIGITAL AGE

During the coming decades, the digital revolution that has transformed so much of our world will transform legal education as well. The digital production and distribution of course materials will powerfully affect both their content and the way they are used in the classroom and library. This collection of chapters by leading legal scholars in various fields explores three aspects of this coming transformation. The first set of chapters discusses how digital materials will be created and how they will change concepts of authorship as well as methods of production and distribution. The second set explores the impact of digital materials on law classrooms and law libraries, and the third set considers the potential transformation of the curriculum that digital materials are likely to produce. Taken together, these chapters provide a guide to momentous changes that every law teacher and scholar needs to understand.

Edward Rubin is University Professor of Law and Political Science at Vanderbilt University. After clerking on the U.S. Court of Appeals for Judge Jon Newman, he practiced entertainment law in New York City. He then taught law at the University of California, Berkeley; the University of Pennsylvania; and Vanderbilt, where he served as Dean from 2005 to 2009. He is the author of *Judicial Policy Making and the Modern State: How the Courts Reformed America's Prisons* and *Federalism: Political Identity and Tragic Compromise* (both with Malcolm Feeley) and *Beyond Camelot: Rethinking Politics and Law for the Modern State*. He is also the author of two casebooks: *The Regulatory State* (with Lisa Bressman and Kevin Stack) and *The Payments System* (with Robert Cooter) and the editor of *Minimizing Harm: A New Crime Policy for Modern America*.

Legal Education in the Digital Age

Edited by

EDWARD RUBIN

Vanderbilt University Law School

CAMBRIDGE
UNIVERSITY PRESS

CAMBRIDGE UNIVERSITY PRESS
Cambridge, New York, Melbourne, Madrid, Cape Town,
Singapore, São Paulo, Delhi, Mexico City

Cambridge University Press
32 Avenue of the Americas, New York, NY 10013-2473, USA

www.cambridge.org
Information on this title: www.cambridge.org/9781107012202

First published 2012

Printed in the United States of America

A catalog record for this publication is available from the British Library.

Library of Congress Cataloging in Publication data
Legal education in the digital age / [edited by] Edward Rubin.
    p.   cm.
Includes index.
ISBN 978-1-107-01220-2 (hardback)
1. Law – Study and teaching.   2. Law – Computer-assisted instruction.
I. Rubin, Edward L., 1948–
K100.L45   2012
340.071'1–dc23   2011052728

ISBN 978-1-107-01220-2 Hardback

Contents

Acknowledgments

Matthew T. Bodie (Chapter 2)
I would like to thank Jase Carter for his research assistance on this contribution.

Penny A. Hazelton (Chapter 7)
Many thanks to the library staff at the University of Washington School of Law for continually sending items of interest that inspired my thinking about the future of law libraries. And the editorial assistance of Professors Ron Collins and Ed Rubin greatly improved the final product. Thank you!

John Palfrey (Chapter 5)
I wish to thank my colleague Urs Gasser, co–principal investigator on the youth and media research on which this chapter relies, as well as Sandra Cortesi, Carli Spina, June Casey, the FRIDA team, and all those in the Harvard Law School Library who provided guidance and research support for this work.

R. Anthony Reese (Chapter 3)
Thanks to Ed Rubin for inviting me to participate and for being a patient and thorough editor and to Christopher Leslie, Lisa Payne, and the research staff at the UC Irvine Law Library for their assistance.

Edward Rubin (Introduction and Chapter 9)
I want to thank Ron Collins and David Skover, who began this project and invited me to join; John Berger, for shepherding it through to completion; and all the contributors, who were truly a pleasure to work with.

Gregory Silverman (Chapter 6)
I would like to thank my colleagues, friends, and family for the support and assistance that they provided during the writing of this chapter. In particular, I would like to acknowledge Jan Ainsworth, Mark Chinen, Ron Collins, Sid DeLong, Anne Enquist, Lily Kahng, Jack Kirkwood, John Mitchell, Chris Rideout, Mark Roddy,

Oscar Romero, Michael Rose, Ed Rubin, Veronique Silverman, and David Skover. Above all, I would like to thank my sons, Alexander and Cyril, for their long and tireless efforts in teaching and mentoring me, an initially skeptical student who is game controller–challenged, about the many educational and other virtues of video games and virtual worlds, and the need for educators to take them seriously. But for their influence this chapter would not have been written, and I dedicate it with love and affection to both of them.

David C. Vladeck (Chapter 8)
I would like to thank Ed Rubin for his hard work in spearheading this project, for being unfailingly gracious, and for his top-notch editorial assistance. Thanks as well to Alan Morrison, my former colleague at Public Citizen Litigation Group, and Kathryn Sabbeth, my former Georgetown colleague, for sharing their thoughts about legal education.

Biographical Notes

Matthew T. Bodie

Matt Bodie is professor and associate dean of research and faculty development at Saint Louis University School of Law. He teaches and writes on corporate, contract, employment, and labor law subjects. His articles have been published in *Michigan Law Review, Virginia Law Review, Vanderbilt Law Review, Washington University Law Review, Iowa Law Review, William & Mary Law Review*, and the *Journal of Legal Education*. His article "Information and the Market for Union Representation" was selected for presentation at the Stanford/Yale Junior Faculty Forum and the annual meeting of the American Law & Economics Association. Professor Bodie graduated magna cum laude from Princeton University in 1991. After working for nonprofits in the fields of community investment and land reform, he attended Harvard Law School, where he was an editor and social chair of the *Harvard Law Review* and earned best team and best brief awards in the Ames Moot Court competition. He graduated magna cum laude from Harvard in 1996 and then served as a law clerk to Judge M. Blane Michael of the U.S. Court of Appeals for the Fourth Circuit. He has since worked as a field attorney at the National Labor Relations Board, an acting assistant professor of lawyering at New York University School of Law, and an associate professor at Hofstra University School of Law. He is a reporter for the American Law Institute's Restatement Third of Employment Law and a research Fellow at New York University's Center for Labor and Employment Law. Since 2005 he has been a contributor to PrawfsBlawg, a weblog for legal academics.

Ronald K. L. Collins

Ronald Collins is the Harold S. Shefelman Scholar at the University of Washington School of Law. He specializes in First Amendment law and in constitutional law and is the book editor of SCOTUSblog. Before joining UW in 2010, he was a scholar at the First Amendment Center in Washington, D.C. He received his law degree from Loyola Law School in Los Angeles (law review) and his bachelor's degree from the University of California at Santa Barbara (political philosophy). He clerked for Justice Hans A. Linde on the Oregon Supreme Court and was a Supreme Court Fellow under Chief Justice Warren Burger. After working with the Legal Aid Foundation of Los Angeles and the Legal Aid Society of Orange County, Collins was a teaching Fellow at Stanford Law School. Thereafter, he taught constitutional law and commercial law at several leading schools, including George Washington University Law Center and Temple Law School.

He is the editor of *The Fundamental Holmes: A Free Speech Chronicle and Reader* (Cambridge University Press, 2010) and the coauthor of *We Must Not Be Afraid to Be Free: Stories about Free Speech in America* (Oxford University Press, 2011) and *Dissent* (Cambridge University Press, forthcoming). His other coauthored works include *The Death of Discourse* (2nd ed., 2005) and *The Trials of Lenny Bruce* (2002). He is also the editor of *The Fundamental Hugo Black: A Free Speech Chronicle and Reader* (Cambridge University Press, forthcoming), *The Death of Contract* (1995), and *Constitutional Government in America* (1980). His numerous articles, some fifty-plus, have appeared in a variety of publications, including the *Harvard*, *Stanford*, and *Michigan Law Reviews* and in the *Supreme Court Review*. Collins was selected as a Norman Mailer Fellow in fiction writing with a residence in Provincetown (Winter 2010), in connection with a forthcoming novel and collection of short stories.

Lawrence A. Cunningham

Lawrence A. Cunningham, the Henry St. George Tucker III Research Professor at the George Washington University Law School, teaches and writes about contracts, corporations, and other business-related subjects such as accounting and finance. Books include *Contracts in the Real World: Stories of Popular Contracts and Why They Matter* (Cambridge University Press, 2012); *Introductory Accounting, Finance and Auditing for Lawyers* (West, 2010); and *The Essays of Warren Buffett: Lessons for Corporate America* (Carolina Academic Press, 2009). He has written some 50 articles on those and other subjects, which have appeared in the *Columbia*, *Cornell*, *Iowa*, *Michigan*, *Minnesota*, *UCLA*, *Vanderbilt*, and *Virginia Law Reviews*. Professor Cunningham has also written op-ed pieces for the *National Law Journal*, the *New York Times*, and the *Financial Times* and is a permanent writer for the blog Concurring Opinions.

Before joining George Washington in 2007, Professor Cunningham taught at Boston College Law School, where he served a two-year term as associate dean for academic affairs. From 1992 to 2002, he taught at Benjamin N. Cardozo School of Law, where he served a five-year term as director of the Heyman Center on Corporate Governance and received the Professor of the Year Award in 2000.

Professor Cunningham has been a visiting professor at Vanderbilt University Law School; a lecturer-in-law at Columbia University Law School; and a visiting lecturer at Central European University, Hebrew University of Jerusalem, and University of Navarra. Before entering academia, he practiced corporate law with Cravath, Swaine & Moore in New York.

Peggy Cooper Davis

Peggy Cooper Davis is the John S. R. Shad Professor of Lawyering and Ethics at New York University. Her scholarly work has been influential in the areas of child welfare, constitutional rights of family liberty, and interdisciplinary analysis of legal pedagogy and process. Davis's 1997 book *Neglected Stories: The Constitution and Family Values* illuminates the importance of antislavery traditions as interpretive guides to the meaning of the Fourteenth Amendment. Her recent book, *Enacting Pleasure*, is a collection of essays exploring the social, cultural, psychological, and political implications of Carol Gilligan's relational psychology. For more than ten years, Davis directed New York University's Lawyering Program, a widely acclaimed course of experiential learning that distinguishes the law school's first-year curriculum. She now directs the Experiential Learning Lab, through which she works to develop and test progressive learning strategies and to develop professional education courses that systematically address the interpretive, interactive, ethical, and social dimensions of practice.

Penny A. Hazelton

Professor Penny A. Hazelton is currently associate dean for library and technology services at the University of Washington School of Law, where she has worked since 1985. Her career in law librarianship began after she earned her master of law librarianship from the University of Washington in 1976, following her J.D. from Northwestern School of Law of Lewis and Clark College in 1975. Previous employment includes the University of Maine Law School Library and the Library of the Supreme Court of the United States. In addition to her faculty and administrative responsibilities, Professor Hazelton is the director of the Law Librarianship Program at UW. This very successful program, ranked first by *US News and World Report*, educates and trains lawyers who want to become law librarians. Professor Hazelton's research and teaching interests include law librarianship and legal research. Professor Hazelton has also been active in professional associations such as the Association of American Law Schools and the American Bar Association and has held numerous positions with the American Association of Law Libraries, including serving as its president in 1990/91. She is the recipient of the Frederick C. Hicks Award for Outstanding Contributions to Academic Law Librarianship, the Joseph L. Andrews Bibliographical Award for *Washington Legal Researcher's Deskbook*, 2nd ed., and the Distinguished Alumnus Award from the University of

Washington School of Library and Information Science. She serves as the editor of *Specialized Legal Research*.

John Palfrey

John Palfrey is Henry N. Ess professor of law and vice dean for library and information resources at Harvard Law School. He is the author of *Intellectual Property Strategy* (MIT Press, 2011) and coauthor of *Born Digital: Understanding the First Generation of Digital Natives* (Basic Books, 2008), among other books. He is a faculty codirector of the Berkman Center for Internet & Society at Harvard University and was formerly its executive director. His research is focused on Internet law, intellectual property, and international law. He practiced intellectual property and corporate law at the law firm of Ropes & Gray. Outside Harvard Law School, he is a venture executive at Highland Capital Partners and serves on the board of several technology companies and nonprofits. John served as a special assistant at the U.S. EPA during the Clinton administration. He is a graduate of Harvard College, the University of Cambridge, and Harvard Law School. He writes a blog at http://blogs.law.harvard.edu/palfrey/ and is jpalfrey on Twitter.

R. Anthony Reese

R. Anthony Reese is Chancellor's Professor of Law at the University of California, Irvine. He specializes in copyright, trademark, and Internet aspects of intellectual property law. Before working at Irvine, he spent a decade on the faculty of the University of Texas at Austin, and he has been a visiting professor at New York University School of Law and at Stanford Law School. He has also taught copyright law in international programs organized by the University of Victoria (British Columbia); St. Peter's College, Oxford University; and the University of St. Gallen, Switzerland.

Professor Reese has published numerous articles on copyright law and digital copyright issues in a variety of U.S. and foreign law reviews and edited volumes. He is a coauthor of the casebooks *Copyright, Patent, Trademark and Related State Doctrines* (with Paul Goldstein); *Copyright: Cases & Materials* (with Bob Gorman and Jane Ginsburg); and *Internet Commerce* (with Margaret Jane Radin and John Rothchild).

After receiving his B.A. degree in Russian language and literature from Yale University, Professor Reese worked for several years in international educational exchange, including two years teaching in the People's Republic of China. He earned his J.D. degree with distinction from Stanford University and is a member of the Order of the Coif. He served as a law clerk to the Honorable Betty B. Fletcher of the United States Court of Appeals for the Ninth Circuit. Before entering academia, he practiced law in San Francisco for several years and was a research Fellow for the

Program in Law, Science and Technology at Stanford Law School. Professor Reese is also special counsel to the law firm of Morrison & Foerster LLP.

Edward Rubin

Edward Rubin is University Professor of Law and Political Science at Vanderbilt University. He received his B.A. from Princeton and his J.D. from Yale. After clerking on the U.S. Court of Appeals for Judge Jon Newman and practicing entertainment law in New York City, he joined the law school faculty at the University of California, Berkeley (Boalt Hall), in 1982. There, Rubin served as associate dean at Boalt Hall for two years. In 1998, he moved to the University of Pennsylvania Law School. He became dean of Vanderbilt Law School in 2005 and led an initiative to reform the law school curriculum. Rubin was appointed to his current position in 2009 when his deanship ended. His research focuses on administrative law, modern government, constitutional law, and morality and legal education. He is the author of three books, *Judicial Policy Making and the Modern State: How the Courts Reformed America's Prisons* (Cambridge University, 1998) (with Malcolm Feeley), *Beyond Camelot: Rethinking Politics and Law for the Modern State* (Princeton University, 2005), and *Federalism: Political Identity and Tragic Compromise* (University of Michigan, 2008) (with Malcolm Feeley), and two casebooks, *The Regulatory State* (Aspen, 2010) (with Lisa Bressman and Kevin Stack) and *The Payments System: Cases, Materials and Issues* (West, 2nd ed., 1994) (with Robert Cooter), and is the editor of *Minimizing Harm: A New Crime Policy for Modern America* (Westview, 1999). Rubin has served as a consultant on administrative law to the People's Republic of China and on commercial law to the Russian Federation.

Gregory Silverman

Gregory Silverman is an Associate Professor of Law at Seattle University School of Law, a tribal judge for the Northwest Intertribal Court System, and a fourth-year academic associate at Seattle Psychoanalytic Society and Institute. He received his A.B. from Vassar College and his M.A., M.Phil., and J.D. from Columbia University. He spent a year as a graduate student at the Massachusetts Institute of Technology in the Department of Linguistics and Philosophy and, after law school, was a federal judicial clerk in the United States District Court for the District of Rhode Island. After his clerkship, he was awarded the Max Rheinstein Research Fellowship in Law by the Alexander von Humboldt Foundation and spent two years in Germany as a visiting scholar at the Lehrstuhl für Strafrecht, Strafprozeßrecht und Rechtsphilosophie at the Universität Erlangen-Nürnberg. Before moving to Seattle, he practiced law in Massachusetts for seven years; was chair of the Cape Cod Commission, a regional land use planning and regulatory agency; and taught at the University of

Chicago Law School. More recently, he served as a member of the Washington State Committee for the Study of the Taxation of Electronically Delivered Products. He has published several articles and books on intellectual property, electronic commerce, the law of privacy, public access to court records, and jurisprudence. His current research interests include the intersection of psychoanalysis and law, the use of digital technologies in legal education, and developing formal models of juridical proof and legal reasoning.

David M. Skover

David M. Skover is the Fredric C. Tausend Professor of Law at Seattle University School of Law. He teaches, writes, and lectures in the fields of federal constitutional law, federal jurisdiction, mass communications theory, and the First Amendment. David graduated from the Woodrow Wilson School of International and Domestic Affairs at Princeton University. He received his law degree from Yale Law School, where he was an editor of the *Yale Law Journal*. Thereafter, he served as a law clerk for Judge Jon O. Newman of the U.S. Court of Appeals for the Second Circuit. He has coauthored three books: *The Death of Discourse* (Westview Press, 1996; Carolina Academic Press, 2nd ed., 2005), *The Trials of Lenny Bruce* (Sourcebooks, 2002) (*Los Angeles Times* selection for Best Book of the Year), and *Tactics of Legal Reasoning* (Carolina Academic Press, 1986). In addition, he has authored or coauthored some twenty scholarly pieces in various journals, including the *Supreme Court Review*, *Harvard Law Review*, *Stanford Law Review*, *Michigan Law Review*, *Texas Law Review*, the *Nation* magazine, and the *Yale Bibliographical Dictionary of American Law*. Skover appears frequently on network affiliate television, is heard often in radio interviews, and has been quoted in the national popular press (e.g., *New York Times*, *Wall Street Journal*, *Washington Post*, and *Los Angeles Times*) on a spectrum of issues ranging from First Amendment law to pop media culture and theory. He has three books in progress: *On Dissent* (Cambridge University Press, forthcoming), *The Judge: 26 Machiavellian Lessons*, and *Mania*. For more information, see www.skoveronline.net.

David C. Vladeck

David C. Vladeck is the director of the Federal Trade Commission's Bureau of Consumer Protection. He is on leave from Georgetown Law School, where he teaches courses in civil procedure, federal courts, and administrative law. At Georgetown, he also codirects the Institute for Public Representation, a clinical law program handling a broad array of civil rights, civil liberties, First Amendment, and administrative law litigation. Prior to joining Georgetown's full-time faculty in 2002, Professor Vladeck spent more than twenty-five years with Public Citizen Litigation Group, serving as its director from 1992 to 2002. There he handled and supervised a wide range of complex litigation, including First Amendment, health and safety, civil rights, class action, preemption, and open government cases. He has argued a number of cases before the United States Supreme Court and state courts of last resort, and more than fifty cases before federal courts of appeal. He is a senior Fellow of the Administrative Conference of the United States and an elected member of the American Law Institute. His publications focus on administrative law, the First Amendment, ethics, and access to justice issues.

Introduction

Edward Rubin

Children trudge to elementary school weighed down by heavy hardbound text-books. As they move through the educational process, however, the books get progressively lighter in relative terms, and then in absolute terms as well; by the time they get to college, the now-fully grown students are often flitting to class with a small paperback novel or monograph in hand. Then comes law school, and the process reverses. The books are hardbound and heavy again, and the formidable tomes that are required for each of three or four courses are capable of weighing down even the most robust young adult. The leading constitutional law casebook runs more than thirteen hundred pages and weighs four and a half pounds; one of its competitors is more than two thousand pages in its most recent edition and weighs as much as a healthy human infant.

But the impact of these books on law students' minds is greater than their impact on their vertebrae. In some sense, the casebook defines the traditional – and still dominant – law school course. C. C. Langdell, the originator of the curriculum we still use today, was also the originator of the casebook, and the two are inexorably linked. Despite all the varied tasks that lawyers fulfill in our society – negotiating deals, drafting legislation, gathering facts for litigation, managing institutions, spear-heading social reform – law schools still focus primarily, and in the first year almost exclusively, on teaching students how to read and analyze judicial decisions. These decisions, lots and lots of them, make up the bulk of those bulky law school tomes. The approach that they embody was out of date a hundred years ago, but it continues to weigh down legal education, just as the casebooks weigh down the students.

Although the content of the law school casebook has been outdated for a hundred years, its form remained the best available until quite recently. The print medium was the only way to convey information to students outside, or in preparation for, face-to-face interactions. That has changed, and changed dramatically, in the past two decades. The digital revolution has provided us with personal computers, connected us to the Internet, and given us hard drives, flash drives, and external drives to store the information we receive. Quite commonly, students will be walking around the law school building carrying enough memory capacity to store ten thousand books, and, unlike their casebooks, it weighs almost nothing. Collectively, the students in the school possess greater information storage capacity than the entire print collection of the law library.

These students have already adapted to the promises and possibilities of the digital revolution. They take notes on their laptops, carry out their research on the Internet, and interact with each other – sometimes during class – on the Internet as well. But legal education has been much slower to respond. In the colloquial phrase, we legal educators are still in the horse and buggy era with respect to the digital revolution. To be sure, it is the horse and buggy era of the early 1900s. We know what automobiles are, and we no longer stop and gawk at them when they pass by on the street. We have a sense that they are going to change the way we live, a prospect that we regard with varying degrees of enthusiasm or dismay. Old Jasper and Muffin are still out in the stable, though. We still ride them to work in the morning, go out for the evening in the cabriolet, and use a wagon for transporting goods.

But change is coming. The promise of the new technology is simply too great to ignore. It will enable authors of legal educational materials to do things that they have been unable to do before: to work collaboratively with large, widely dispersed groups; to update their materials on a continuous basis; to provide skills training through the materials themselves; to engage students in interactive problems and exercises; and to develop truly novel pedagogic strategies. It will enable the faculty members who adopt these materials to tailor them in accordance with their own needs and teaching styles, to use them for individualized learning that they could not possibly deliver by themselves, and to supplement or adapt their courses in response to student needs and interests. If the pull of these new possibilities proves insufficient for some law teachers, the push of student demand is likely to move them in the same direction. Law students are increasingly children of the digital age. Within a few years, all but second-career students will have been born after the advent of the Internet. These students are likely to respond with increasing disappointment and frustration if they are handed heavy volumes of material that they can access on their laptops or are subjected to educational approaches that would have struck them as old-fashioned when they were in junior high school.

Digital materials are not simply a new means of delivering educational materials, however. Rather, they represent a new conceptual framework for law schools as institutions. They are likely to change the content of existing courses; the pedagogic techniques of law teachers; the relationships among authors, publishers, and classroom teachers; the relationship between faculty and students; the role of the law library; and any number of other features of the present-day law school. In doing so, these materials may finally release the law school curriculum from Langdell's rigid grip. Will law professors continue to limit their instruction to a small fraction of primary materials that lawyers use when all the other materials are so readily available? Will they continue to underemphasize the vast areas of modern law – regulation, deal making, international transactions, policy making, law reform – that lie outside appellate practice? Will they continue using nineteenth-century pedagogic techniques when twenty-first-century materials and instructions are available at the touch of a keyboard?

For the past hundred years or so, law schools have taken advantage of the fact that they sit astride the path to one of America's most lucrative and prestigious professions. They have refused to change because they have not needed to; the credential they offered was, and remains, of enormous value, regardless of whether it actually prepares the student for the field to which it provides access. But the digital revolution creates an independent force for change. It changes the way the students access information, the way they learn, and the way they think. It changes the way institutions are organized internally and the way they communicate with the world around them. It is not simply a new pedagogic approach, or a new body of material, but a genuine revolution. It will prove impossible for law schools to resist.

This volume emerged from a conference entitled "Workshop on the Future of the Legal Course Book." It was organized by Ronald Collins and David Skover, together with Dean Kellye Testy of Seattle University School of Law and held at the law school on September 27, 2008. Unlike many academic conferences, the workshop did not consist of a series of paper presentations, but rather four discussion sessions: The Status Quo in Content, Competing Delivery Systems, Competing Online Architecture Formats, and Where Do We Go from Here? As the day proceeded, a sense of increasing excitement developed among the participants. We became aware that the digital revolution holds enormous promise for legal education, and for law schools as institutions. But this sense of excitement was accompanied by a parallel sense of concern. Will law schools continue to resist change, as they have for so many years? Will they ignore the promises and possibilities of digital materials until the use of those materials is forced on them by circumstance and thereby only succumb with reluctance to something that they should have welcomed with enthusiasm?

Inspired by the Seattle workshop, this volume is meant to serve as an inspiration and a provocation. We hope to inspire current and potential casebook authors to produce digital materials, law professors to adopt these materials and use them to their fullest potential, and law school administrators to support faculty members in both efforts. We also hope to inspire publishers to produce such materials and casebook authors, law professors, and law school administrators to urge them to do so. And we intend to provoke everyone involved in legal education to question why we are not using twenty-first-century approaches to train twenty-first-century lawyers.

The contributors to this volume have a wide range of backgrounds within legal education. They are theorists, specialists in relevant fields, clinicians, and librarians. They represent a range of views about the advent and effect of the digital revolution, from cautious to enthusiastic, incremental to transformative. But they are unified by their willingness to think, in a sustained and serious manner, about the effects of the digital revolution on the process of legal education and the structure of the law school. They are also unified by their sustained focus on the educational process, on the important task of preparing young people for the profession that we rely upon to organize so much of our society and resolve so many of its conflicts. Although they have given the digital revolution a great deal of serious thought, their commitment, ultimately, is not to electronics but to students.

The volume is divided into three parts. The first part deals with the production of digital materials and contains three chapters. In the first, Ronald Collins and David Skover describe the way that one very basic type of digital course materials, which they call a "conceptions course book," could be created and distributed. They outline the construction stage, the development stage, the access stage, the selection stage, and the delivery stage. In essence, a Conceptions Course Book would begin with a database of hyperlinked primary, secondary, and interdisciplinary materials edited by legal academics and possibly professionals. Law professors who registered with the publisher could then download the materials and adapt them for their own use, omitting some parts and rearranging others, as they felt necessary. Students would then be given a password that would enable them to download the materials, along with any secondary materials they ordered. This process would not only produce new sets of materials but, as Collins and Skover argue, ultimately have major effects on the structure and pedagogy of legal education. Of course, as they note, the Conceptions Course Book is only one way in which digital materials might be produced; there are many others, some of which are described in subsequent contributions. But at the end of their chapter, the reader will have a concrete sense of what it means to say that the basic materials for a law school course can be digitized, and of the process by which that result might be achieved.

In the following chapter, Matthew Bodie discusses the possibility of an open source approach to the production and use of digital materials. He begins by surveying the existing market for law school course books, which has a standard proprietary structure, then contrasts it with the open source model. This model, which is distinctive to the digital world, makes the source code that generates the content for a computer program open to the public. As a result, users can add to or alter the program or take portions of it for their own particular uses. Applied to legal materials, it would create a community of users, where the law teachers who adopt an open source set of course materials could freely adapt these materials for their own purposes, share their ideas about their use with others through discussion sites or blogs, and provide feedback to the community about the effectiveness of various items or approaches. Bodie notes that an open source model seems to run contrary to the incentives that have motivated law professors to produce printed casebooks, most notably prestige and financial remuneration. He then catalogs the conditions that would nevertheless foster the development of open source materials, such as a product that can be divided into modular units, an individual or small group to provide leadership, a larger community of users who can evaluate the product and are willing to contribute to it, and a general willingness of the participants to look past immediate financial gain. The creators and users of legal course materials, he argues, will often meet these criteria. His discussion provides further ways of envisioning the process by which law school materials might be digitized.

With these methods of producing digital materials in mind, the reader can then turn to Anthony Reese's contribution, which analyzes the way that copyright law will affect the production of digital course books, and specifically the use of primary materials not written by the author. Going digital, he notes, creates a number of potential copyright issues; unlike the delimited and easily defined distribution system for printed books, which are produced by a publisher and sold in individual units to the users, providing electronic copies by transmission can involve multiple acts of reproduction, distribution, and even public display. In addition, each professor can adapt or tailor these materials in a way that is impossible with a printed casebook. Thus, the whole process is much more complex, protean, and difficult to control. Reese notes, however, that this will not create any major difficulties for using traditional primary materials such as cases, nor for many new types of materials that might be added, such as statutes, regulations, treaties, legislative hearings, and agency interpretations, because these materials, being produced by the government, are in the public domain. But if authors choose to include other materials that digitization makes readily accessible, copyright problems may arise, problems that are now unfamiliar to most casebook authors. Anyone who wants to produce digital materials or encourage their use will need to pay careful attention to Reese's discussion.

The second part of this book describes the way that digital materials, once they are created, can be used in legal education. Obviously, the four contributions in this section can only be illustrative, not comprehensive. Nonetheless, they raise issues that have broad application to other settings that the digital revolution will affect. The first chapter in this section, by Lawrence Cunningham, provides an in-depth consideration of course books themselves. Taking the contracts casebook as an example, he surveys the history of these books, focusing on the major innovations that their authors carried out since Langdell published the first such book. To provide insight into the way these innovations were perceived at the time, Cunningham discusses the contemporaneous reviews that commented on these casebooks when they were first published. He notes that each approach involved trade-offs related to the purpose of the book (should it emphasize the delivery of knowledge or the stimulation of thought? should the materials be sequenced historically, transactionally, or conceptually?) and its scope (should most of the material be primary sources? or should the book include supplementary information, comparative information, and problems?). Shifting to a digital format will not eliminate the need to make these trade-offs, Cunningham argues; nor will it produce an immediate transformation of the basic pedagogical methods by which they are used. But it will change the balance of considerations that have shaped the present trade-offs; the capacity to include additional material, to rearrange and connect that material, and to revise and update it will all be dramatically increased. Cunningham's chapter explains the immediate effect of digitization, the changes in course materials that will occur as soon as books move into a digital format.

John Palfrey's chapter, which follows, describes further changes in the course book that the digital revolution might produce. In contrast with Cunningham's emphasis on the authors as course book producers, he focuses on the students as course book consumers. He notes that a variety of studies, including one that he and his colleagues carried out, indicate that the digital revolution has produced a generation of young people, including law students, whose thought processes are different in essential ways from those of their predecessors. These digital natives multitask, survey a great deal of information rapidly, pursue topics that catch their interest in depth, and follow up by interacting with the material that they pursue or with each other in connection with that material. A "smarter law school casebook," as Palfrey describes it, should match its users' learning style. It should be technologically advanced; incorporate or link to a wide range of supportive or supplementary material, including visual and audiovisual material; and provide students with the opportunity to interact with this material and with each other in designated note-taking or study groups. Palfrey thus provides a framework for thinking about the long-term changes in course books and teaching styles that the digital revolution will produce, not only through the capabilities it will make available to authors, but through the changes that it will produce in student learning styles.

Further innovations, carrying us entirely beyond the framework of the book, are outlined in the next chapter, by Gregory Silverman. Like Palfrey, he notes that the digital revolution has changed the way that young people think; they multitask, process information quickly, prefer graphic content and immediate feedback, and interact regularly with their peers. This not only places constraints on legal educators, but also creates opportunities to make use of the kinds of learning experiences in which young people already engage. Silverman focuses on video games, which are enormously popular. He notes that these games cannot be dismissed as mere play because play, as biologists, psychologists, and sociologists have documented, serves a crucial role in the learning process. Games, which are play that follows a rule set and yields a definitive outcome, are the mode of play that maximizes learning. Legal educators can make use of this powerful and popular modality. Because of digitization, they can design video games that allow students to interact with each other regarding legal issues, conducting litigation or negotiating transactions that resemble lawyers' real work much more closely than traditional legal education does. Silverman presents a dramatically new approach that leaves the traditional course book far behind, but he focuses securely on teaching law; his chapter provides an idea of the range of new approaches that will become available for that purpose.

The final chapter in the second part, by Penny Hazelton, discusses the future of the law library in the digital era. Many legal educators have yet to envision the possibilities of the digital revolution for teaching materials and techniques, but the idea that the law library will become obsolete as documents are put online seems to be widely accepted. Hazelton argues that this common wisdom is mistaken by focusing on the current roles that law libraries play in the educational process. Provision of printed materials to students, while certainly important, is not the library's primary role; most education is based on course materials, whether print or digital. The library's more crucial roles are, first, to serve as a neutral, academic place where students can gather and study; and, second, to provide staff services that guide students through the complex and varied sources that they will need to access when they practice law. Law libraries will continue to play these roles in the digital era; indeed, the need for them may well increase. They will also continue to serve as repositories of the now-digital information, which needs to be made available to students in inexpensive, readily accessible form. The complex pricing of these materials, their lack of standardization, and their lack of authentication will present challenges that law libraries will need to meet in order to fulfill this role. Their greatest challenge, however, is to continue and strengthen the library's service to students as a meeting place and source of guidance. Hazelton's chapter thus provides a blueprint for the continued relevance of this major unit of contemporary law schools in the coming era.

The third part consists of three chapter that discuss potential effects of the digital revolution on the law school curriculum in general. In doing so, it reiterates and emphasizes a number of the criticisms of contemporary legal education that were raised in the first two parts of the book. David Vladeck's chapter takes a particularly broad approach. The traditional legal curriculum, although not without its virtues, fails to prepare students for modern legal practice. Fortunately, he argues, there is a "serendipitous convergence" between the need to update the curriculum and the advent of digital materials. The pragmatic advantages of digitization are so great that the process will prove impossible to resist. Digital materials are more convenient, cheaper, more ecological, and more readily updated in our rapidly changing legal environment. In addition, they enable law teachers to readily modify prepared materials to serve their individual pedagogic purposes, to incorporate problem sets directly into the course material, and to similarly incorporate audiovisual content. The curricular effects of this inevitable digitalization will greatly improve legal education's ability to prepare students for the practice of law, Vladeck argues. First, it will facilitate direct teaching of legal skills, not as a marginal subject for pass-fail courses or student-run activities, but as a basic element of the curriculum, fully integrated with doctrinal education. Second, it will enable law professors to implement collaborative learning activities that parallel the way law is generally practiced and reflect its basic content. Third, it will allow the incorporation of material dealing with the nature of the legal profession, and with its crucial role in advancing social issues as well as resolving private disputes. Vladeck's chapter provides a road map for curricular reform, a map that all law professors will need as the ineluctable process of digitizing course materials gathers momentum.

My chapter follows up on the themes that Vladeck discusses. I identify three aspects of the traditional curriculum that I regard as outdated, and that the effects of the digital revolution might modernize. These are the heavy emphasis, particularly in first-year courses, on common law and judicial decisions; the failure of law schools to adopt modern pedagogic practices; and the continued reliance on inductive reasoning. Digital materials might expand the range of primary materials, first, to statutes, regulations, and contracts; and, second, to exemplary and supplementary materials, thereby overcoming the excessive focus on judicial decisions. They might also increase the amount of interactivity in legal education, thereby facilitating the experiential learning that contemporary educators recommend and replacing the inductive method with a more modern, hermeneutic approach. I share the concern of many observers that technology can have negative effects, but this concern seems more relevant to natural scenery or historical artifacts than to legal education. Since writing, which includes course books, is already technology, and legal writing is functional, not aesthetic, it seems to me that there is much to be gained and little to be lost from using technology to modernize the curriculum.

The final chapter in this section, by Peggy Davis, focuses on the specific connections between teaching materials and legal pedagogy. Langdell's distinctive contribution to legal pedagogy was to move from the treatise to the casebook; in doing so, he changed its emphasis from the inculcation and recitation of rules to the interpretation and application of legal texts. This, Davis argues, was related to progressive education's emphasis on "learning by doing." Modern casebook authors who have gone beyond the texts of judicial decisions to include questions, problems, and supplementary material have moved legal education still further in this direction. But progress has been limited by a widespread commitment to legal certainty: to the idea that there are definitive answers to legal questions rather than a range of interpretive possibilities. The digital revolution will enable us to move beyond this limitation. By providing students with case files that simulate the uncertain and open-ended character of legal practice, it will enable them to learn from their own experiences, to treat those experiences as the text that provides the real message of their law school education. Such materials redefine not only the process of legal education, but the meaning of the law itself. Davis's chapter thus concludes this volume with a bracing vision of the conceptual vistas that the digitalization of law school teaching materials might reveal.

In the end, this book is an exploratory work, not a conclusive one. Moreover, as anyone with a sense of irony will note, it is presented in traditional print form, still the dominant format for this sort of work, not electronically. Clearly, it can only tell us where we might be headed, not what things will actually look like once we have arrived. What seems clear, however, is that the change process has begun and cannot be reversed. No one, looking back over the technological developments of the last two decades, can possibly maintain that we are not at one of history's great turning points. The digital revolution will affect nearly every aspect of our lives. We, as legal educators, are free to bemoan or celebrate these changes as we wish, but not in the area for which society has given us responsibility. There we are obligated to think seriously about the coming and inevitable changes, and to plan accordingly.

Does history offer us any guidance as we move into a world of unknown possibilities? What did people think when they saw the first printed books or the first industrial factories? We might as well ask what people thought when they saw the first farm or the first wheel. We simply cannot use whatever bewilderment or resistance people in the past felt as an excuse for our behavior in the present. What separates us from them is that we know what revolutions are. We live in an age when they occur frequently enough to teach us, and we possess a mode of thought that validates them as part of history. There is nothing we can do to stop the digital revolution, and no excuse for ignoring it as it occurs. All we can do is decide for ourselves whether we will be its victims or its beneficiaries.

PART I

Creating Digital Course Materials

1

The Digital Path of the Law

Ronald K. L. Collins and David M. Skover

The path of the law is not what it once was. Technology has changed it. The *print way* yields increasingly to the *digital way*.[1] In this environment, the model of the printed casebook that Christopher Columbus Langdell initiated in 1871 is an antiquated vehicle for today's law students who venture down the electronic information highway. And yet more than 140 years later, legal education still lumbers down the horse-and-buggy path paved by the famous dean of the Harvard Law School.

When we consider the ways law is taught, we confront a paradox. On the one hand, the calls for innovative pedagogical reforms are constant; we hear demands for skills-building instruction,[2] transactional approaches,[3] interdisciplinary treatments, multimedia experiences,[4] and the like. In one way or another, all of these aspirations challenge the conventional Langdellian message and methodology. On the other hand, the delivery system for educational content remains basically static; unquestionably, the print casebook still dominates the law school classroom. The most creative and far-reaching educational changes are significantly constrained by the print medium. While pedagogical reforms can and do happen within the print format, their potential pales in comparison to what is possible within the electronic format. For any variety of reasons, we believe that real reform is best served by the marriage of innovative ideas with innovative media.

Today, law students are burdened by the cost, weight, and excess of print casebooks. A typical first-year law student, using some of the more popular texts, could spend up to one thousand dollars for the casebooks alone (sans supplements, secondary materials, outlines, etc.); will haul around weighty books that, all combined, tip the scales at close to thirty pounds; and will typically confront the prospect of more than eight thousand pages in their casebooks.[5] Print publishers have already realized the need to scale back from the dizzying length[6] and exorbitant cost of casebooks.[7] Ironically, while attempting to address the ever-increasing demands of curricular reforms, they compound the students' burdens by issuing a never-ending array of supplemental texts dealing with law stories,[8] transactional problems,[9] theoretical readings,[10] and interdisciplinary lessons,[11] among others – all resulting in increases in prices, pages, and pounds. And though it is true that long overdue pedagogical reforms are surfacing within the print medium,[12] such efforts will not likely change the cost + weight + length equation and are likely to depend on electronic formats for some of their most revolutionary features.

So, why do we cling to the print casebook? There are, of course, institutional constraints to deviating from tradition: the ordained structure of the law school curriculum; the long-practiced methods of teaching, studying, and testing; the industry of tie-in study aids; and the bar examination, among others.

But Marshall McLuhan suggested a more far-seeing answer: We drive into the future with our eyes fixed on the rearview mirror.[13] We prefer the familiar to the unknown; we equate the true with the tried; we give way to inertia rather than expending energy. If legal education remains tethered to print and the case method, if it does not adequately consider interdisciplinary insights, if it ignores the narratives of life and law, if it remains largely oblivious to the way law is practiced, and if it forfeits the advantages of new electronic formats, it does so mainly because we remain bound by our comfortable ways. This, in no small measure, explains why the ghost of Langdell still haunts us. Ever since he cabined the law in his casebook, generations of publishers, professors, and students have made a home there. It is time to move on.

Imagine a book unlike anything that is used in law schools today. It contains all of the classroom materials, primary and secondary, that a student would need for his or her legal education. Its contents are not confined to appellate cases and commentaries but may contain a wide range of skills-building and interdisciplinary educational materials. It has wireless Internet access, hyperlinks, audiovisual experiences, and interactive capacities. Its contents are always current and are custom-tailored by professors for each of the courses they teach. It is as thin as most magazines and weighs less than twelve ounces. And its total cost is a fraction of what a student would otherwise spend for its print-based contents. Unimaginable? Hardly. For you have just imagined something that can be actualized – a "Conceptions Course Book," which is the core topic of this chapter. In all likelihood, it is a book that Dean Langdell would not have endorsed.

A. CHRISTOPHER COLUMBUS (LANGDELL) IN THE NEW (DIGITAL) WORLD

His world is not ours. It is easy to overlook that as one holds on to his legacy. But even as we cling to Langdell's past, we are tugged into the future, where the entire enterprise that gave him fame is changing conceptually, operationally, and economically.

Stepping back in time to his world, we stand to learn how it is vanishing and how a new one is emerging.

When Little, Brown and Company first published Langdell's *A Selection of Cases on the Law of Contracts*,[14] the relationships of the author to his publisher, booksellers, professorial users, and student readers were far different from such relationships today. Those relationships, then and now, are of great pedagogical consequence. For they determine *who* selects content, *what* content is selected, and *how* that content is presented, distributed, and used.

Langdell assumed his mantle of greatness, because he sat at the apex of a hierarchical print publishing model. He could count on his message's going to law students without substantial intervention or dilution. The only likely constraints on content imposed by his publisher were economic ones (e.g., the length of the work). No content constraints were placed on him by the distributional chain (e.g., booksellers).[15] The handful of contracts professors then at Harvard, Yale, Columbia, and elsewhere might have interfered with the transmission of Langdell's contents to his student readers only in a few ways: by assigning select portions of the book, by supplementing the case materials (nowhere as widespread as today), and/or by shaping and shading understanding through their own lectures. Absent such constraints, however, Langdell controlled the message that would reach and influence his student readers. And this with a nod from Oliver Wendell Holmes: "At all events, we advise every student of the law to buy and study the book."[16]

Long before the advent of digitalized information, the potency of the Langdellian model had been diluted. By midpoint in the twentieth century, a single casebook had multiple authors and a single subject had multiple competing casebooks. The texts burgeoned in size[17] as they added excerpts from a diverse assortment of secondary materials. Moreover, they were supplemented by a variety of nutshells, outlines, anthologies, hornbooks, and other such works. All of this invited professors to cherry-pick materials both within and outside the casebook. What ultimately filters down to the modern-day student reader is a far less singular message controlled by a print casebook author. As a practical matter, it is almost impossible for one who stands in Langdell's shoes to leave a similar footprint on the law.

In the near future, we will witness more significant changes in author-publisher, author-distributor, author-professor, and author-student relationships. The old and rigid paradigm will become more elastic and less determinative, more interactive and less dogmatic, more multiexperiential and less textual. Just as the Gutenberg invention overtook scribality, so now the digital invention is poised to overtake print.[18] The advantages of digital content simply cannot be denied. It "is weightless, can be easily searched, linked, and copied, and has no marginal cost of distribution."[19] Within the legal academy, it is already the case that digital research – on LexisNexis, Westlaw, and Google – has largely replaced its print predecessor. Additionally, print casebooks are now supplemented with Internet texts replete with hyperlinks.[20] There are even e-casebooks that can be downloaded and printed. Such hybrid materials, however, leave the Langdellian enterprise mostly intact, though it is surely under siege.

Law has long been text-centric, more so than many other professions that interact with the physical world. And alphabetic text is likely to remain a key medium within legal education. After all, it is difficult to imagine that legal arguments, which typically portray a compendium of facts and sustain a complex and logical line of thought, are not going to depend at all on sustained reading. While the future of the legal course book may still be bright, the same may not be said of its print manifestation.[21] These are times of transition – from print to electronic formats. While that transformation is still incomplete, there are evident signs that the pure print form is clearly inadequate to suit the needs and demands of a generation "born digital."[22]

The real revolution will not occur as long as print publishers are the primary distributors of law school course books, but it is also true that this revolution cannot take place as long as the primary receptacle for reading digital information is the computer as we now know it. It is a truism: Readers read books. They shun reading books on computer screens.[23] But what kind of books will they use if print ones are undesirable and computer ones are unwieldy? Today will become tomorrow once e-readers[24] enter into the equation and enable course book customization and distribution Web sites to realize their full potential. One such Web site, which we propose later, would facilitate the creation, delivery, and use of self-designed law e-books – what we name "Conceptions Course Books" (CCBs).

In one form or another, the CCB model will happen. It is inevitable. And when that time arrives, there will be a turning point in legal education, one just as significant as that ushered in by Christopher Columbus Langdell. To appreciate that turning point it is critical to understand the technology and process that make it possible. In the next section of this chapter, we outline the operational process by which CCBs would be created, and thereafter we explore the theoretical implications of such an endeavor. Having done so, one readily begins to discern the extraordinary transformations that CCBs portend. There will be no turning back.

B. THE CONCEPTIONS COURSE BOOK: PROCESS AND PRODUCT

Basically, a CCB comes into being in the following way: (1) The construction of a course book customization and distribution system owned by a nonprofit corporation, a for-profit corporation, or a consortium (2) on which a database, containing both open-access and restricted-access materials,[25] would be developed by teams of scholars, lawyers, and other professionals (3) that would enable professors to create their own course books by selecting, arranging, and contributing materials and

(4) that would permit students to download the materials to an e-reader or computer. The resulting file constitutes a CCB.

The central idea behind our CCB model is to reinvent the way law school course materials are created with an eye to the following: (1) dramatically expanding the breadth of primary and secondary materials, available within a single database, that may be easily integrated into a custom-designed CCB; (2) significantly enhancing professorial options regarding selection of materials; 3) encouraging professorial interaction with the materials (e.g., as when a professor adds commentaries, questions, or problem exercises to a custom-designed CCB); (4) decreasing student-user costs; (5) increasing student-user options regarding the inclusion of secondary materials (e.g., commercial outlines and nutshells) within a CCB; and (6) furthering pedagogical reform to the degree that professors are open to reconceptualizing the legal course book (e.g., including torts materials or economic analyses in a contracts CCB).

It is important to emphasize that we do not offer CCBs as a panacea. Indeed, certain changes in the consciousness and culture of the legal academy (some major, others minor) would have to precede and then work in tandem with CCBs for path-breaking pedagogical reforms to occur. After all, the CCB is an instrumental means to further educational changes, not the driving force for such changes. Without the innovative professorial mind-set required for real reform, without the institutional support to alter everything from the first-year curriculum to the bar exam, the CCB cannot maximize its potential. What is certain is that the benefits flowing from the use of CCBs will span a spectrum from modest advantages (e.g., CCBs that are glorified casebooks) to moderate gains (e.g., CCBs that redefine subject categories) to momentous ones (e.g., CCBs that include audiovisual interactive role-playing strategy games to teach negotiation skills).

The process by which the CCB system would be implemented can be described as consisting of five distinguishable stages: a construction stage, a development stage, an access stage, a selection stage, and a delivery stage.

1. *The Construction Stage*

- Technological Functions: Although the technical specifics of the CCB system cannot be usefully addressed here, the essential point is that the framework must be constructed for maximum flexibility in the creation, distribution, and use of instructional content. It should accommodate everything from ordinary text files and audiovisual learning objects to interactive exercises and, more imaginatively, multiplayer online role-playing games for legal instruction.[26] Obviously, technologically complex and sophisticated educational contents, which are labor-intensive and expensive to develop, are most likely to be created for commercial purposes. Accordingly, the framework should be built to handle both open-access and restricted-access, or proprietary, formats.

- Design: Here, too, we need not resolve the exact mixture of so-called open-source[27] and proprietary design elements for the system. Whatever the combination, the design should harmonize technical standards and ease operations in all of the system's processes – regarding both the integration of differently formatted learning objects and the compatibility of CCB materials with a student's e-reader or computer. Moreover, if CCBs are to compete with their print counterparts, at the very least they must offer the same degree of integrity and reliability. Hence, while the system should be designed to allow professors to add their own glosses to materials before their CCBs are finalized, it should not permit students who have downloaded those CCBs to modify the contents or copy and distribute them.

- Ownership: There are essentially three models of ownership for the CCB system. It could be constructed, maintained, and operated by a nonprofit corporation, a for-profit corporation, or a consortium of such corporations. A nonprofit entity is more likely to provide materials free of charge, whereas the converse is true for a commercial entity. Nevertheless, for a nonprofit owner to become self-sustaining – that is, without having to rely on government or foundation grants or law school institutional support – it is likely that the CCB system would need to offer both free and for-charge content (and receive a percentage of the proceeds from the latter). As explained more fully later, the richness of a CCB will be increased by the availability of both free and for-pay materials from diverse sources.

2. The Development Stage

- Database Contents: For each core subject matter, there would be a body of hyperlinked[28] primary, secondary, and interdisciplinary materials. These would include cases, annotated constitutions and statutes, legislative histories, administrative regulations, topical overviews, notes and questions, treatise and article excerpts, restatement sections, interdisciplinary readings, historical materials, assorted narratives, transactional problems, audiovisual materials,[29] lectures,[30] interactive practice problems and exams, course outlines, teacher's manuals, and more. To the extent feasible, such materials would be available in both unedited and edited forms (e.g., an entire case or snippets from it).

  Initially, we envision the collection process as mirroring the more traditional topical categories now used in legal education – contracts, torts, civil procedure, and so on. The database will, however, allow professors to mix information among topical categories. For example, a tort CCB might well include materials selected from the database areas relating to contracts, property, evidence, and constitutional law. There could conceivably be prompts at various topical points suggesting such incorporations. For the more imaginative, there would be the option to create their own topical categories (e.g., private harms/public harms) or draw from materials outside legal subject matters (e.g., economics, engineering, medicine, biotech, the environment).

In time, there likely would be competing Web sites with their own databases – different CCB systems or non-CCB Web sites – that might elect to interact with each other in a way profitable to all. The CCB system, for example, might contract with another (free or proprietary) system containing a specialized database entirely dedicated to property law so that CCB users might tap into the rich vein of information that such a particularized database offers.

- Editors: The database contents would be collected and edited by teams of academics and legal professionals.[31] Central to the integrity of the CCB model is the recruitment of learned lead editors and talented assistant editors working under them.

Initially, their selection of materials would mimic existing kinds of course book contents. For any given field of law, they would upload the most widely used cases statutes, regulations, and so forth, to the CCB database. They would then select and upload a variety of secondary materials, consistent with copyright requirements. Thereafter, the teams would design the CCB Web site interface so that all of the materials were arranged in templates by subject matters, topics, and subtopics. Take criminal law, for example. Its template might have Principles of Punishment (Deterrence, Rehabilitation, etc.), Culpability (Requirement of an Act, Strict Liability, etc.), Homicide (Manslaughter, Murder, etc.), and so on. The objective of such templates is to allow professors to select particular topics and discrete materials as the contents of their individualized CCBs.

Alternatively, the editors themselves could create one or more CCBs with prepackaged materials (e.g., *Vladeck on Federal Courts*), which might be adopted by other professors in whole or in part. Yet another option would be for the overseers of the database to arrange with existing law book publishers to license the contents of various course books. The contracts template might include a selection for the entirety of the Schwartz & Riebe casebook[32] or for excerpts from it – all for a designated price.[33] This option would permit professors to select content for the same CCB from different proprietary sources (e.g., Aspen and Carolina Academic Press) and to mix it with open-source materials.

Responding in time to the ever more insistent calls for pedagogical reforms, the editorial teams would strive to enrich the database by including a plethora of nontraditional course contents. Moreover, professors may offer the educational resources that they have created (e.g., text-based or video lectures, interactive quizzes) for posting consideration.

- Licensing of Materials: Whenever necessary, permissions would need to be secured or licensing arrangements made in order to provide use of copyrighted materials. For any public domain resources (e.g., cases, statutes, regulations), of course, no such copyright concerns arise.[34] But propriety materials (e.g., restatement or model code provisions, law review articles, or book excerpts) would be unavailable absent authorization or fair use.[35] The CCB system would be designed so as to compensate copyright holders by way of a pay-per-use structure analogous to I-Tunes.

3. *The Access Stage*

- Password Access: Although the CCB Web site templates (e.g., the table of contents for the trusts and estates materials) could be viewed by anyone, registration would be required for professors who wished to create a CCB or students who wished to download one. Upon registration, professors would be assigned passwords to access the CCB database. Similarly, when a specific CCB was completed, students would be assigned passwords to download that particular CCB and any additional secondary materials that might accompany it.
- Controlled Access: In order to prevent copyright violations and to ensure its own economic viability, the CCB system must contain adequate digital-rights-management safeguards to prevent unauthorized sharing or copying of the CCB.

4. *The Selection Stage*

- General Subject Matter Selection: Professors would first select a subject matter area (e.g., contracts, evidence, corporations, tax). Within that subject area, they might decide to confine a CCB only to certain topics. Someone who picked the law of contracts might limit a CCB only to topics such as the bargaining process, policing the bargain, interpretation, and remedies. By the same measure, someone might not choose the topics of statute of frauds, third-party beneficiaries, and assignment and delegation.

    A similar selection process would occur if a professor opted to use a prepackaged CCB (whether free or proprietary). Assume that Aspen Publishers, for example, licensed the full contents of the latest edition of *Problems in Contract Law: Cases and Materials* by Charles L. Knapp et al. and agreed that the materials could be purchased in full or in part. A professor might decide to select only 60 percent of the casebook and to rearrange its contents. She or he might also add original content and other nonproprietary items from the database.[36] Having done so, the professor might elect to make that CCB available to a colleague at the same or different institution for full or partial adoption consideration. If this second professor decided to adopt the materials, he or she would of course be subject to the licensing rules that applied to the first professor. The same would hold true for a professor who created a largely nonproprietary CCB that contained a few proprietary items.

- Specific Subject Matter Selection: Within each topic (e.g., contract interpretation), different kinds of content might be selected. In order to introduce students to notions of objective and subjective theories of interpretation, a professor might pick *Raffles v. Wichelhaus*[37] followed by selections from Holmes's "The Theory of Legal Interpretation"[38] and excerpts from Grant Gilmore's *The Death of Contract*.[39] This would be an example of mixing nonproprietary and proprietary materials.

- Professorial Input: The CCB system should provide a blank template to allow professors to incorporate within a CCB assigned to their classes any introductory comments, summations, outlines, notes, questions, problems, quizzes, past exams, or other content that they author. There would, of course, have to be a guarantee of indemnification for any breaches of law for which the professor might be responsible.[40]

- Arrangement of Materials: The CCB template must enable a professor to select (i.e., click) the materials desired for inclusion and to arrange the items in whatever order he or she sees fit. A contracts CCB might start with materials on remedies, with the bargaining process or something else. A constitutional law CCB might begin with the text of the federal Constitution, or the Federalist versus Anti-Federalist debate, or judicial review, or congressional commerce powers.

- Teacher's Manual: The CCB database would be designed to permit professors to create a separate CCB for themselves and a slightly different one for their students. The former might contain, among other things, sections of a teacher's manual (or any variety of them) woven into the materials selected; it might also include relevant sections from treatises and lecture notes from other professors as made available on the CCB database.

- Professor as Author/Editor: Before the advent of CCBs, most professors used casebooks such as those prepared by Professors Arthur Corbin (contracts), Gerald Gunther (constitutional law), and William Prosser (torts). Given the CCB system, unless a professor confines selection entirely to prepackaged materials, she or he stands to become an author/contributing editor of his or her CCB. The title page of the CCB might even read something like *Cases and Problems on Torts* by Prosser, Collins, and Skover. Or, depending on the selections and input, the professor might be identified as sole author/editor of the CCB. Some consideration would have to be given, of course, as to how copyright law might affect rights of attribution.

- Order Finalization: The last stage in the professor's creation of a CCB is the finalization of an online order. Professors would know in advance the total pages and cost (if any) for the selections made. Moreover, they would supply information on the law school, the name of the course, and the number of students enrolled.

5. *The Delivery Stage*

- Downloading: Once a CCB order is finalized and professors and students have received their passwords, they can download the CCB with any applicable charges. Before they complete their transactions, however, students might opt to select secondary materials – commercial outlines or study guides, for example – to be incorporated into their CCBs. Such add-ons might be purchased in their entirety and placed at the end of a CCB. Alternatively, if such materials were properly coded, they might be integrated at relevant spots within a CCB. For example, a book excerpt[41] on the history of the *Palsgraf* case[42] could be tagged to that landmark precedent, or a nutshell excerpt[43] on the law of negligence could be situated at the end of the case or topic.
- Receptacle: The student might wish to read, listen to, watch, or otherwise interact with CCB contents on an e-reader,[44] a desktop, a laptop, or some kind of electronic hand-held device. Ideally, wireless e-receptacles should be able to access hyperlinked materials or related information outside the CCB database, and students should be able to highlight, underline, or make marginal notations in the CCB.
- Modifications of CCB: Professors might, for whatever reason, wish to modify or expand a CCB. By following the preceding process, they can revise the CCB file for the current academic year or for a future one. If proprietary information were selected, current students would be charged a modest supplemental fee to download the new file, whereas future students would pay the price, if any, of a new CCB.

As we foresee it, the proposed CCB model would have the following effects: (1) Professorial use would, in a relatively short time, be extensive; younger generations of digital-savvy instructors would not balk at the move away from print publications, and any resistance to change that older, more established teachers might feel would likely be overcome by law school institutional pressures to accommodate student preferences[45] and reduce student costs. (2) Pedagogical reforms would be advanced significantly beyond what is possible in print; without accounting for all of the CCB's capacities, just the individualization of course materials and the interactivity of electronic course books alone would encourage innovative teaching methods that print materials cannot duplicate. 3) Production and student purchase costs would be greatly reduced; although there clearly would be start-up costs to the CCB system, ultimately it would avoid the high expenses associated with print production, delivery, and storage.[46] (4) Publisher profit margins would be sufficient to encourage continued and expansive innovation and licensing of proprietary products; the future for any print content is dismal, as evidenced by the plight of American newspapers.[47] (5) Quality control would be maintained; the gatekeeping function normally performed by print publishers would be continued by the CCB database teams, but their editorial decisions would not be similarly burdened by the costs of production, distribution, and warehousing and the constraints of mass-marketing associated with the print casebook industry.[48] (6) Intellectual property problems, although challenging, would be overcome; we say this because the advantages and potential of CCBs would be so great as to necessitate reconciliation with intellectual property rules.

C. PUTTING PRACTICE INTO THEORY

Admittedly, such pedagogical, institutional, and economic effects are, to a greater or lesser degree, quite practical in character. The CCB model, however, stands to have considerable theoretical and jurisprudential impacts as well. To help illustrate the theoretical dimension of the CCB venture, we begin with the thoughts of two great American judges and then consider the implications of their ideas, and those of others, for pedagogical and jurisprudential purposes.

A dozen or so years after he began his service on the Massachusetts Supreme Judicial Court, Justice Oliver Wendell Holmes gave a lecture to commemorate the opening of a new hall at Boston University School of Law. The address, delivered on January 8, 1897, was titled "The Path of the Law."[49] That lecture, it has been said, "pushed American thought into the twentieth century."[50] Though many of its core ideas traced back to what Holmes had written in *The Common Law* (1881),[51] the lecture was cast in bold strokes. With "The Path of the Law," Holmes brought a provocative blaze into the humdrum world of his life on the bench. Lighting an occasional brushfire to stimulate the legal mind seemed to excite him; it also permitted him to move beyond the pettiness of his work to engage the grandeur of his imagination. By this time, Holmes was also breaking ranks with Langdell, taking exception to the Old Master's belief in, and obsession with, the purported logic inherent in the common law. While Holmes did not discount the role of reason in the judicial decision-making process, he was now far more interested in the role that policy, particularly economic policy, played in that process.

More than a century later, the workings of the legal academy show that Holmes lost the debate, and that his provocative blaze has been quenched by Langdellian convention – or so it seems. Still, Holmes rises, phoenixlike, from the ashes to move the minds of those who are willing to challenge convention. Judge Richard Posner has one such mind. In an insightful article titled "The Speech Market and the Legacy of *Schenck*,"[52] Judge Posner developed certain strands in Holmes's jurisprudence to urge us to rethink much of existing First Amendment doctrine. The result was both creative and provocative, in the same way that Holmes was.

Generally speaking, Posner invited us to take seriously the cost-benefit implications in Holmes's opinions in *Schenck v. United States*[53] and *Abrams v. United States*.[54] Infusing economic analysis into Holmes's clear-and-present-danger standard and his competition-among-ideas maxim, Posner recommended an instrumentalist approach to freedom of speech protection. That approach would permit a legislative or regulatory restriction only if the public benefits secured by the restriction could be convincingly demonstrated by the government to exceed the costs to society in the loss of information plus the administrative costs of regulation. Posner argued that such a "cost-benefit approach, however alien to the characteristically high-flown rhetoric in which lawyers and judges tend to talk about free speech, is consistent with the Amendment's language and history (including its judicial history)."[55] To prove his point, he applied his economic analysis across a broad spectrum of free speech restrictions, including pornography, hate speech, subversive advocacy, commercial advertising, and election campaign finance regulation. Posner then highlighted the implications of his instrumentalist approach for future scholars, who, he suggested, might pursue factual inquiries to determine the real-world benefits and costs of speech restrictions.

Assume that a professor teaching freedom of expression law were frustrated by the fact that all of the leading casebooks treat *Schenck* and *Abrams* in largely identical ways, full of "high-flown rhetoric" and bereft of the kind of instrumentalist thought that Posner recommends. Under the print casebook regime, the most he or she could do, aside from lecturing on the matter in class, would be to offer handouts or direct students to the library to read the article in the book in which it appeared. By contrast, the CCB option would place the professor in the same position as the author of a casebook. In other words, he or she might weave a Posnerian instrumentalist perspective into the course materials at the precise point where it would be most relevant. That might consist of incorporating snippets of the Posner article by way of fair use or arranging with the CCB editors to secure copyright permission for uploading the entire article, which then could be included, in whole or in part, within the course materials. For a law review article such as Posner's, such permission is readily, and often costlessly, obtained. Operationally, this might be done by arranging to have the materials placed on the CCB database as a selection option accompanying the *Schenck* and *Abrams* case choices. The professor might also alert colleagues to this innovation and invite them to adopt those sections for their own CCBs.

Another consideration might come into play. Assume that Judge Posner had elected, in the first instance, to publish his *Schenck* article on the CCB database instead of in a book. He might suppose that his thought would reach a wider and more receptive audience and be more influential in this forum than in a print-based one.[56] Here again, his article would be keyed to the *Schenck* and *Abrams* cases and materials in the database. There is a larger point here: The net effect of such a decision is to transform the CCB system into a publishing entity akin to a law journal, a university or trade press, or the SSRN and other such scholarly databases. We will explore this point further in our subsequent discussion.

To continue our hypothetical, suppose that the professor who incorporated the Posnerian instrumentalist approach to free speech into a CCB read *Law without Values* by Albert Alschuler[57] and becomes convinced that the instrumentalist approach smacks of the type of amorality that Alschuler equates with Holmes.[58] Now, he or she want to revise the course materials to reflect this new thinking. It would be easy to delete Posner's article and all associated references, to supplement it with Alschuler's, or to rewrite the entire discussion to contrast or blend the two approaches.

Implicit in all of this are several observations of theoretical significance. First is the nature of information and knowledge in the digital law school. Law as it is taught need not be bound, static, outdated; these characteristics are associated with the print model of transmitting information. Today's legal educational content can be fluid, malleable, and ever current; these characteristics are associated with the CCB model. It can thus conform to Heracilitus's dictum, certainly applicable to our legal system, that nothing truly endures but change.

Second, the standard notion of authorship is challenged in the CCB domain. Teaching materials no longer need to be hierarchically dictated by the top-down decisions of print casebook authors[59] and publishers. Rather, they can be more democratically designed, with greater control over educational contents granted to the individual professors. As suggested by the earlier hypothetical, once professors become active creators of CCBs, they cease to be mere recipients of packaged information fixed in printed casebooks. Instead, they become developers of unpackaged information selected for customized CCBs. Here again, the CCB process is transformative: Its professorial users become "authors."[60]

Third, the traditional relationships of author-publisher, author-distributor, author-professor, and author-student will likely be changed by the operation of the CCB system. Whereas in the print world, casebook publishers have the final say as to who will or will not be deemed an author, in the CCB world the converse is true; short of breaches of the law, the CCB publisher is willing to allow any professor to be deemed an author and to create his or her own course book. Whereas print casebook publication decisions hinge largely on mass-marketing concerns, the CCB author can publish a course book for a class of five and use it for one time only; the economics of the system would not prohibit such publication. Whereas print authors depended on several middlemen (i.e., warehouses, distributors, and bookstores) to stock and sell their casebooks, the CCB system consolidates all of their functions; in this environment, the law school bookstore may go the way of the phone booth. Whereas the print world clearly demarcated authors from professors who adopted their casebooks, that pronounced demarcation may soon fade considerably; whenever a professor creates a unique CCB, the author-professor dichotomy collapses.[61] And whereas the print author maintains control over the contents that a student user reads within a casebook, the CCB scheme allows some opportunity for students to become, as it were, cocontributors; at a minimum, they would have the option of selecting and integrating certain secondary materials into their assigned CCBs. In sum, on the print stage, the players' roles were fixed and publishing relationships rigid; on the CCB stage, however, roles would begin to merge as relational boundaries increasingly dissolved.

Fourth, the concept of scholarship might be substantially affected. Traditionally, scholarship has been associated with publication in printed books or journal articles, the academic merits of which were evaluated by student editors and outside reviewers. It was this gatekeeping function that primarily validated the purported worth of any published work. By comparison, while the CCB system's gatekeepers make evaluative decisions about the overall contents of the database, they have no interest in the particular work product of a CCB professor. In the future, the intellectual merits of a professor's own contributions to a CCB might be assessed in two different ways. One is by institutional figures, such as the law school dean, advancement committee, professorial colleagues, and outside reviewers.[62] Alternatively some weight might also be given to determinations by the CCB editors when they elected to showcase an outstanding CCB[63] developed by one or more professors whose original contributions were extraordinary. Hence, when scholarship goes from print to digital, its standards may well be reconfigured.

Fifth, the possibilities for pedagogical reforms expand beyond anything yet experienced. As long as book content is determined by the profitability of the print publishing market, meaningful opportunities for diversity and innovation in educational materials are limited. In that market, different jurisprudential movements – everything from law and economics and law and literature, to feminist studies and critical legal studies, to transactional and skills-training approaches – compete for their share of the print-publishing pie. Jurisprudential ideas and educational strategies that deviate from standard approaches are likely to be consigned to snippet add-ons within the text or to supplementary readers. By contrast, the CCB system would more evenhandedly accommodate the preferences of traditionalists who hewed to the casebook line and nontraditionalists who strove to break away from it. In sum, the jurisprudential tent of legal education might be stretched to the limits of our imagination.

The emerging diversity in CCB materials might well clash with certain institutional norms and commercial expectations. For example, insofar as criminal law casebooks are largely uniform, their pedagogical messages are similar. In such printed texts, one can safely find the familiar – the law of homicide, the felony murder rule, the law of voluntary and involuntary manslaughter, the law of conspiracy, and so on. Beyond that, one can also expect to discover the same key cases – *People v. Washington*,[64] *State v. O'Brien*,[65] *Rowland v. State*,[66] and *Griffin v. State*,[67] among others – all edited in much the same way. Casebooks thus set the measure for everything that follows: how courses are taught and tested, how commercial study aids are designed, and how the bar examination is administered. But what happens when many professors in the 200 American Bar Association– (ABA-) accredited law schools begin to experiment with developing their own criminal law CCBs? As the canonical approach to teaching criminal law is contested, those institutional and commercial conventions would be in flux. This is not to say that chaos would reign, for the hold of doctrine is likely to remain mighty. But the print-based norms that govern institutional and commercial perspectives would become less rigid and dogmatic, more elastic and adaptable.

The digital path of the law is both realistic and mysterious. It is a path that traces back in time and arches forward into the future. By traveling it, to draw on Holmes one last time, we may become greater masters of our calling. In a grander sense, the journey may enable us to tap into the "most far-reaching form of power" – "the command of ideas." And to do that, even in ways only partially realized, is to connect our ideas "with the universe" and then, perhaps, to "catch an echo of the infinite."[68] Or so is the hope.

NOTES

1. *See* generally John Palfrey and Urs Gasser, *Born Digital: Understanding the First Generation of Digital Natives* (New York: Basic Books, 2008).
2. *See*, e.g., William M. Sullivan et al., *Educating Lawyers: Preparation for the Profession of Law* (Hoboken, NJ: Jossey-Bass/Carnegie Foundation for the Advancement of Teaching, 2007); Roy Stuckey et al., *Best Practices in Legal Education: A Vision and a Roadmap* (New York: Clinical Legal Education Association, 2007).
3. As one example, the Columbia University Law School offers a skills-based program called the Charles Evans Gerber Transactional Studies Program, which focuses on complex financial transactions. *See* http://www.law. columbia.edu/center_program/deals.

4. Columbia University Law School professor Conrad Johnson argues convincingly: "Connecting doctrine to primary sources, leveraging the 'added value' that many publishers already provide, producing text, graphics, audio, animation, and video that reflect and cater to the multiple learning styles present in our target audience, allows students to learn in multiple ways and to develop analytical and persuasive capacities that are not limited by the over-worn 'top down' approach." Conrad A. Johnson, "Memorandum on Preliminary Thoughts," prepared for the Workshop on the Future of the Legal Course Book (September 2008) (memorandum on file with authors). For example, one could imagine an electronic course book that contained pod-cast minilectures, video interviews of clients, audio clips from depositions and recorded police interrogations, and virtual reality experiences in legal settings. *See* Paula Lustbader, "Memorandum on Preliminary Thoughts," prepared for the Workshop on the Future of the Legal Course Book (September 2008) (memorandum on file with authors). One creative multimedia approach used in Civil Procedure courses is the video documentaries produced by Seattle University Law School professor Marilyn Berger in *Lessons from Woburn*, which are based on Jonathan Harr's book *A Civil Action*. *See* Films for Justice Institute, *Lessons from Woburn*, at http://www.law.seattleu.edu/x1873.xml. Accompanying the videos is a course book that includes research and writing assignments, issues for class discussion, and role-playing exercises. The videos vividly chronicle the story of the *Anderson v. W. R. Grace* case arising from the environmental disaster in Woburn, Massachusetts. *See Anderson v. W. R. Grace & Co.*, 628 F. Supp. 1219 (D. Mass. 1986).

5. These figures represent retail prices plus 7 percent tax for new casebooks that would be required for a typical array of first-year courses, such as the following: Charles Knapp et al., *Problems in Contract Law: Cases and Materials* (New York: Aspen Publishers, 6th ed., 2007) (list price: $138/3.4 lb./1,105 pp.); Joseph Singer, *Property Law: Rules, Policies, and Practices* (New York: Aspen Publishers, 4th ed., 2006) (list price: $139/3.6 lb./1,202 pp.); Richard – Epstein, *Cases and Materials on Torts* (New York: Aspen Publishers, 9th ed., 2008) (list price: $142/4.2 lb./1,402 pp.); John Kaplan et al., *Criminal Law: Cases and Material* (New York: Aspen Publishers, 6th ed., 2008) (list price: $130/4.2 lb./1,144 pp.); Jack Friedenthal et al., *Cases and Materials on Civil Procedure* (Eagen, MN: West, 9th ed., 2005) (list price: $134/4.6 lb./1,295 pp.); Geoffrey Stone et al., *Constitutional Law* (New York: Aspen Publishers, 5th ed., 2005) (list price $142/5.2 lb./1,704 pp.); Laurel Oates et al., *The Legal Writing Handbook: Analysis, Research, and Writing* (New York: Aspen Publishers, 4th ed., 2006) (list price: $78/2.6 lb./914 pp.).

6. How many professors who assign such tomes actually cover the entire text or even a substantial portion of it?

7. *See*, e.g., Jesse Choper et al., *Leading Cases in Constitutional Law* (Eagen, MN: West, 2008) (list price: $94/2.6 lb./912 pp.). The unabridged counterpart costs $146, weighs 5.3 lb., and has 1,745 pages.

8. *See*, e.g., Michael C. Dorf, ed., *Constitutional Law Stories* (Mineola, MN: Foundation Press, 2004).

9. *See*, e.g., Tina L. Stark, *Drafting Contracts: How and Why Lawyers Do What They Do* (New York: Aspen Publishers, 2007).

10. *See*, e.g., John H. Garvey et al., *Modern Constitutional Theory: A Reader* (Eagen, MN: West, 5th ed., 2004).

11. *See*, e.g., Victor Goldberg, *Framing Contract Law: An Economic Perspective* (Cambridge, MA: Harvard University Press, 2007).

12. *See*, e.g., Carolina Academic Press's series Contextual and Practice Casebooks (Michael H. Schwartz, series editor).

13. *See* generally Philip Marchand, *Marshall McLuhan: The Medium and the Messenger* (New York: Ticknor & Fields, 1980), 209.

14. Christopher C. Langdell, *A Selection of Cases on the Law of Contracts: With References and Citations* (Boston, MA: Little, Brown, 1871).

15. Since a printed book could only be sold as a packaged work, there was no opportunity for the bookseller to subdivide its contents and sell them independently. As discussed *infra*, that is no longer the case.

16. Oliver Wendell Holmes, Jr., "Book Review," *American Law Review* 6 (1871): 353, 354 (reviewing Langdell's contracts casebook). Later in his life, Holmes was far less kind toward Langdell's "all for logic" approach to law. *See* G. Edward White, *Justice Oliver Wendell Holmes: Law and the Inner Self* (New York: Oxford University Press, 1993), 197 (10 April 1881 letter from Holmes to Fredrick Pollock).

17. Many of today's casebooks exceed the 1,022 pages of Langdell's 1871 work.

18. *See* generally Ronald K. L. Collins and David M. Skover, "Paratexts," *Stanford Law Review* 44 (1992): 509.

19. Bill McCoy, "Memorandum on Preliminary Thoughts," prepared for the Workshop on the Future of the Legal Course Book (September 2008) (memorandum on file with authors). Following this thought, McCoy, the former general manager of the Digital Publishing Business at Adobe Systems Incorporated, opined: "Institutions that remain paper-centric will be marginalized and their learning experiences devalued by digital-savvy students."

20. One experiment in integrating print casebooks with interactive instruction is being attempted by Thomson-West in its Interactive Casebooks Series. *See* http://interactive-casebook.com/.

21. Bill McCoy predicted a relatively short remaining life for print-based law school texts: "It seems obvious that legal course books, along with most other textbooks, are going to be substantially replaced by digital content, with a significant portion (i.e., well over double-digit percentage) of this replacement occurring within the next five years." McCoy, "Memorandum," *supra*, note 19.

22. This moniker refers to the youth of Generation Y, who "were all born after 1980, when social digital technologies, such as Usenet and bulletin board systems, came online." Palfrey and Gasser, *Born Digital*, 1.

23. Tim O'Reilly, the founder and CEO of the esteemed computer book publishing company O'Reilly Media, has noted a "strong preference of our customers for PDFs" (i.e., portable documents downloadable to e-readers) over either print books or online computer reading. *See* http://radar.oreilly.com/2006/05/gentlemen-prefer-pdfs.html.

24. For current examples, consider the Kindle by Amazon, Barnes & Noble's Nook, the Sony Reader, Apple's IPad, and the Pixelar e-Reader and MReader. As we will later explain, however, all of these e-readers will have to evolve to actualize some of the proposals that we set forth in this chapter. For a provocative, although admittedly dated, chapter on the impact that e-readers may well have on book publishers, authors, readers, and libraries, *see* Steven Levy, "The Future of Reading," *Newsweek*, 26 November 2007, 57.

25. Open-access material is available to all users free of charge, whereas restricted-access material is typically available only for a fee.

26. A pioneering vision for a "virtual learning ecology" offering massively multiplayer online role playing games for legal instruction was offered by Gregory M. Silverman,

"Memorandum on Preliminary Thoughts," prepared for the Workshop on the Future of the Legal Course Book (September 2008) (memorandum on file with authors); *see also* Chapter 6, this volume. In this regard, *see* generally James Paul Gee, *What Video Games Have to Teach Us about Learning and Literacy* (New York: Palgrave Macmillan, 2nd ed., 2007).

27. For a thoughtful article on the possibility of an opensource database for developing electronic course books, *see* Matthew Bodie, "The Future of the Casebook: An Argument for an Open-Source Approach," *Journal of Legal Education* 57 (2007): 10, and Chapter 2, this volume. *See* also Joe Hodnicki, "Professional Reading: Is Open-Source the Future of eBook Legal Publishing?" *Law Librarian Blog*, at http://lawprofessors.typepad.com/law_librarian_blog/2008/01/professional–1.html.

28. For example, links in a Constitutional Law CCB might direct students to SCOTUSBLOG or OYEZ to remain current on developments of the day.

29. *See*, for example, New York Law School's *Visual Persuasion Project*, overseen by Professor Richard Sherwin at www.nyls.edu/pages/2734.asp.

30. A variety of digitally created visual and audio law school lectures could be made available on the CCB database for professor and student use. A professor might want to assign such a video lecture. Imagine, for example, a constitutional law professor who planned to require readings on executive powers but did not wish to cover such readings in class. He or she might assign students to watch a streaming video lecture, available in the CCB, by a noted constitutional scholar.

31. The CCB team might be organized similarly to the structure – e.g., reporters, consultants, editorial revisers, and advisers – used by the American Law Institute for its Restatements.

32. Michael Hunter Schwartz and Denise Riebe, *Contracts: A Context and Practice Casebook* (Durham, NC: Carolina Academic Press, 2009).

33. Assuming technological standardization were achieved, private publishing companies might prefer to maintain proprietary content in their own databases but to develop their Web site systems so as to interact seamlessly with the CCB system.

34. Obviously, if public domain documents were uploaded from commercial databases such as LexisNexis or Westlaw without stripping them of headnotes, hyperlinks, and other features added by the publishers, copyright issues would arise and a licensing arrangement would be required.

35. These and related points are ably discussed in Bodie, "The Future of the Casebook," 28–34.

36. Georgetown Law School professor David Vladeck expressed his eagerness for an electronic course book that would permit him to fuse self-generated instructional materials with portions of a traditional casebook: "My vision is that, at some point, technology will permit publishers … to offer teachers flexibility to adapt their own teaching materials, perhaps by taking a conventional textbook and adding material that the teacher wants to include. For instance, I would be happy to use one of several civil procedure books, provided that I could add a new introduction, set forth my introductory fact-pattern, add a few cases that pose current problems, and include some skills exercises that involve drafting pleadings and discovery. I would also appreciate being able to exclude material that will not be covered in the class. … We all now edit by addition and subtraction, but we're stuck with casebooks that are one-size-fits-all and non-adaptable. My hope is that technology will permit us at some point to use casebooks as menus that offer teachers choices about what to cover; permit us to add and subtract material; and enable us to make the book conform

to our choices about how to teach our students doctrine and how that doctrine is used in law practice." David C. Vladeck, "Memorandum on Preliminary Thoughts," prepared for the Workshop on the Future of the Legal Course Book (September 2008) (memorandum on file with authors).

37. 2 H. & C. 906, 159 Eng. Rep. 375 (1864).

38. *Harvard Law Review* 12 (1899): 417.

39. Grant Gilmore, *The Death of Contract*, ed. Ronald K. L. Collins (Columbus: Ohio State University Press, 1995).

40. Such breaches might include violations of copyright, tort, contract, or obscenity laws.

41. *See, e.g.*, William H. Manz, *The Palsgraf Case: Courts, Law, and Society in 1920s New York* (Newark, NJ: LexisNexis, 2005).

42. *Palsgraf v. Long Island R.R. Co.*, 248 N.Y. 339, 162 N.E. 99 (N.Y. 1928).

43. *See, e.g.*, Edward J. Kionka, *Torts in a Nutshell* (Eagan, MN: West Publishing Co., 2nd ed., 1999).

44. Current examples of such e-readers are mentioned *supra* note 24. To reiterate, our ideas are not confined to the limitations of existing technology. On this point, *see* generally Joe Hodnicki, "Big Screen Kindle Aiming for $5.5 Billion Textbook Market," *Law Librarian Blog*, at http://lawprofessors.typepad.com/law_librarian_blog/2008/07/big-screen-kind.html; Gene Koo, "Kindle Won't Catch Fire in Law Schools," *Law School Innovation/Law Professor Blogs Network*, at http://lsi.typepad.com/lsi/2007/12/kindle-wont-cat.html.

45. Generally speaking, the technological divide between today's law professors and their younger students is significant, in that the latter are far more receptive to electronic alternatives to print casebooks. Regarding this point and digital literacy, *see* Motoko Rich, "Literacy Debate: Online, R. U. Really Reading?" *New York Times*, 27 July 2008, sec. A, p. 1.

46. According to Andrew Kantor: "E-books are a boon for publishers. While the cost of content … remains the same, the cost of production and delivery obviously drops significantly. There's no paper to buy, no shipping charges to pay, no worries about how big a production run should be." Andrew Kantor, "Electronic Ink May Rewrite Book Publishing Industry," *USA Today*, 24 February 2006, at http://www.usatoday.com/tech/columnist/andrewkantor/2006-02-24-e-ink_x.htm. It is already evident that cost savings in electronic book publishing are passed in substantial part down to the reader. For example, Andrew Leigh's *The Wikipedia Revolution* (New York: HarperCollins, 2009) is priced at $25.00 list for the print version and at $10.00 list for the electronic one. *See* http://www.amazon.com/The-Wikipedia-Revolution/dp/B001UQO41Y/ref=kinw_dp_ke. Those cost savings would readily overcome the initial expense that the student would bear for purchasing an e-reader or other receptacle.

47. *See, e.g.*, David Lieberman, "Newspaper Closings Raise Fears about Industry," *USA Today*, 18 March 2009, at http://www.usatoday.com/money/media/2009-03-17-newspapers-downturn_N.htm.

48. Carolina Academic Press CEO Keith Sipe estimates that most law casebook publishers now need to sell between 800 and 1,200 units before it is feasible to publish a casebook. Keith Sipe, interview by authors, 18 March 2009.

49. *Harvard Law Review* 10 (1897): 457.

50. Morton J. Horwitz, *The Transformation of American Law, 1870–1960: The Crisis of Legal Orthodoxy* (New York: Oxford University Press, 1992), 142.

51. Consider G. Edward White, *Justice Oliver Wendell Holmes* (New York: Oxford University Press, 1993), 218 ("the two works have often been contrasted, and the current scholarly view appears to be that Holmes's jurisprudential views evolved considerably between the late 1870s and 1897.").

52. Richard A. Posner, "The Speech Market and the Legacy of *Schenck*," in *Eternally Vigilant: Free Speech in the Modern Era*, eds. Lee C. Bollinger and Geoffrey R. Stone (Chicago: University of Chicago Press, 2002), 121–51.

53. 249 U.S. 47 (1919).

54. 250 U.S. 616, 624 (1919) (Holmes, J., dissenting).

55. Posner, *supra* note 52, 128–9.

56. There may well be warrant for this assumption, as evidenced by the very few professors who seem to know of this seminal article. A recent Lexis search indicates that the article has been cited in legal periodicals a paltry 11 times since its publication seven years ago, and two of those citations were by editors of the book in which the article first appeared. Lexis Search of "The Speech Market and the Legacy of *Schenck*," undertaken 19 March 2009. Should this opportunity to publish within the CCB database become popular, the system might develop a tracking mechanism to calculate how often a particular item was selected for download within CCBs. Moreover, it might be possible – though this is a far more complicated matter – to create a LexisNexis-like function for identifying where an article like Posner's was used or cited in CCBs.

57. Albert W. Alschuler, *Law without Values: The Life, Work, and Legacy of Justice Holmes* (Chicago: University of Chicago Press, 2000).

58. For the record, we are not entering into this philosophical fray.

59. In this regard, Grant Gilmore once described Langdell's casebook project as "dogmatic." *See* Gilmore, *The Death of Contract*, 14.

60. Much as any print casebook author does, CCB authors would, of course, be obliged to give credit to those who wrote the materials they selected for a course book.

61. Naturally, there would be some professors – the less innovative and the novice – who would not be immediately attracted to creating their own CCBs. They would, instead, prefer to order a reliable prepackaged set of materials – either a proprietary package or an already developed CCB made available for selection by the system editors (e.g., our earlier reference to *Vladeck on Federal Courts*). Such professors would rather remain consumers of information than become authors of it.

62. Presumably, such institutional figures make similar decisions today in the case of professors who maintain scholarly blogs, such as Professor Jack Balkin's blog "Balkinization," Professor Eugene Volokh's "The Volokh Conspiracy," or Professor Richard Hasen's "Election Law Blog."

63. Generally speaking, we envision something akin to or approximating the long unpublished but widely copied and distributed 1958 manuscript "The Legal Process," written by Professors Henry Hart, Jr., and Albert Sacks, which has been praised as "the most influential book not produced in movable type since Gutenberg." *See* J. D. Hyman, "Constitutional Jurisprudence and the Teaching of Constitutional Law," *Stanford Law Review* 28 (1976): 1271, 1286 n. 70. More than thirty years after its inception, the uncompleted manuscript was finally published in print. *See* Henry M. Hart, Jr., and Albert M. Sacks, *The Legal Process: Basic Problems in the Making and Application of Law*, eds. William N. Eskridge, Jr., and Philip P. Frickey (New York: Foundation Press, 2001). *See* generally William N. Eskridge, Jr., and Philip P. Frickey, "The Making of *The Legal*

Process," *Harvard Law Review* 107 (1994): 2044. To be sure, the coin of the CCB realm need not be as remarkable as the Hart and Sacks manuscript. Nonetheless, the editorial decision to make a noteworthy CCB available for professorial adoption is analogous to Foundation's publication of *The Legal Process.*

64. 62 Cal.2d 777, 44 Cal. Rptr. 442, 402 P.2d 130 (1965) (felony murder rule).
65. 32 N.J.L. 169 (N.J., 1867) (involuntary manslaughter).
66. 83 Miss. 43, 35 So. 826 (Miss., 1904) (voluntary manslaughter).
67. 455 S.W.2d 882 (Ark., 1970) (conspiracy).
68. The string of quotations in this paragraph is taken from Holmes, "The Path of the Law," 10 *Harvard Law Review* (1897): 466.

2

Open Source and the Reinvention of Legal Education

Matthew T. Bodie

A. INTRODUCTION

Although it is easy and exciting to predict massive, sweeping change in legal education, such change may actually be in store. The accretion of criticisms – too much
focus on the common law, misplaced trust in the Socratic method, failure to prepare
graduates for practice – may have finally led to a moment of systemic reform. In fact,
many of the nation's top schools have already undertaken significant changes to the
structure of their curriculum, their pedagogical methods, or the substance of their
core courses. The changes may stop there; more likely they are heralds of more significant reforms to come.

Now is the time to decide how we will approach the upcoming revolution. If past
practice holds, individual schools will make changes based on their own faculty's
pedagogical preferences. These changes will be made internally, with perhaps a
press release but little else to share with the rest of the academy. Moreover, in all
but the most dramatic of reforms, the course content will be left to individual faculty members. Such has been the way since Christopher C. Langdell: Schools may
develop curriculum, but professors manage their own course materials. And most
professors will outsource this responsibility to casebook authors and the publishers
that support them.

To continue along this path is a mistake. Law schools as well as the legal academy as a whole have the opportunity to play a much greater role in the development of course materials and, by extension, the substance of the courses
themselves. Instead of handing off these crucial pedagogical roles to publishers,
schools should work to establish an "open-source" system for the development of
the next wave of curricular content. This system would provide for both collective planning and individualized tailoring, large contributions and small, massive
restructuring and tinkering around the edges. Although it would be transformative
in its effects, its superstructure would be a fairly modest endeavor. Once it was

created, schools and faculty would be able to work together on curricular puzzles while maintaining separate control over course content. The system is easy to imagine. But – given our propensity to inaction – its actual creation is an uncertain possibility.

In this chapter I trace the outlines of a system of open-source course materials. In Part B, I discuss the traditional means by which course materials are developed, specifically the casebook. Part C sets out the open-source model, as it has developed in the software context, and explores other examples of peer production that have developed along similar principles. In Part D, I briefly discuss the reforms that some of the nation's top law schools have undertaken, and I illustrate the different pedagogical challenges that the different reforms present. I then explore how professors, law schools, and the legal academy as a whole (through the Association of American Law Schools [AALS] or another professional association) could adopt open-source methods of production to reengineer not only course materials but the content of law school itself.

B. THE PRODUCTION OF COURSE MATERIALS

1. *Langdellian Origins*

Although the modern case method is often regarded as a product of Harvard Law School, it is more frequently attributed to the actual man behind the method. Almost immediately upon arriving at Harvard in 1870, Christopher Columbus Langdell introduced the case method to American legal education. Prior to that time, law students had been taught the law primarily through lectures and textbooks that featured legal definitions and rules.[1] Endeavoring to take the approach of a scientist, Langdell focused on actual court opinions and used them to work through the general principles that had been applied to resolve each case. This case method – often called the Socratic method, for its back-and-forth with students as they work through the cases – has remained the primary mode of instruction in legal education.

Of course, in order to use the case method, you need cases. Langdell solved this problem in a very pragmatic way:

> [T]hough it might be practicable, in case of private pupils having free access to a complete library, to refer them directly to the books of reports, such a course was quite out of the question with a large class, all of whom would want the same books at the same time. Nor would such a course be without great drawbacks and inconveniences, even in the case of a single pupil. As he would always have to go where the books were, and could only have access to them there during certain prescribed hours, it would be impossible for him to economize his time or work to

the best advantage; and he would be constantly haunted by the apprehension that he would be spending time, labor, and money in studying cases which would be inaccessible to him in after life.[2]

Langdell self-published his casebook.[3] Given his account, it is interesting to hypothesize what would have happened had our current digital resources been available in his time. He simply wanted to provide his students with access to the opinions. His casebook is, in fact, simply a catalog of cases with no notes or other commentary; he was true to his method. And most professors who adopted Langdell's methods developed their own materials to use in their courses.[4] Prior to 1908, law professors produced at least 171 casebooks; 65 of these were written by Harvard professors.[5]

From the perspective of casebook production, two phenomena from this remarkable period stand out. First was the proliferation of casebooks; the average professor was much more likely to be writing his or her own materials. Second, a law professor of today would be shocked at the level of engagement in the review and critique of others' course materials. During the period between the publication of Langdell's casebook and World War I, one source claims that more than one hundred casebook reviews were written *every year*.[6] And there was much to discuss. The norm that casebooks only contained cases broke down fairly quickly, as other professors moved toward a model of "case and materials," which could include footnotes, short summaries, questions, or problems.[7] Alongside these more technical pedagogical debates were deep divisions over theory, as the formalist-realist debate got into full swing.[8]

Another development of note was the creation of a market for casebooks. From a publisher's perspective, the Langdellian casebook was largely a disaster. It was very long; Langdell's book was more than a thousand pages, as were most books that stuck rigorously to the case method.[9] Moreover, law school enrollments were low; law schools were just becoming a national phenomenon, and there were only about five thousand law students across the country in 1890.[10] And legal publishers could not market the casebook to practitioners as they could the traditional textbook, which resembled a modern treatise in purpose and form. The one asset the Langdellian casebook had going for it was the Langdellian method, which would eventually sweep the country. But even this was a liability at first, as the method was limited to Harvard when it began and was controversial even there.[11]

As a result, although there was a proliferation of titles in the early casebook market, there was little profit to be made by anyone involved. Most schools used local publishers; Harvard authors used both Harvard University Press and the Harvard Law Review Association for their works.[12] As more law schools came online and more professors began using the case method, the market expanded. However, professors continued to use their own materials, as the number of titles suggests. An early effort by a Philadelphia publisher to market casebooks nationally, known as the "Pattee series," met with only limited success. Noting that professors preferred to create their own collection of cases, one commentator reported that "faculty from other schools used Pattee titles not as required classroom reading, but rather to help them produce their own casebooks."[13]

The American Casebook Series, produced by the West Publishing Company, transformed the market. As law schools and the case method both continued their growth, the market for law course materials expanded. West, with its existing set of case reporters, was ideally positioned to take advantage of this market. The publisher had made early forays into the market, with a notable failed effort to purchase the copyright for casebooks by the Harvard faculty.[14] But it was not until the introduction of the American Casebook Series in 1908 that the market truly went national. The series had a standard preface introducing both the series and the case method, and a standard pedagogical approach that blended cases with materials such as summaries, notes, and questions. These books – significantly shorter than the Langdellian originals – became the model for future casebooks.[15]

The nationalization of legal education has had many effects: a standardized curriculum, even in subjects dominated by state common law; mobility for law professors; a national component to the bar exam in almost every state;[16] and nationwide rankings of law schools. Perhaps many if not all of these things would have come to pass without a nationwide casebook system. But a standardized national curriculum is so central to these developments that it is much more likely someone, if not West, would have nationalized the market eventually. Had they not, law schools, and even the practice of law, might have turned out distinctly different from what they are today.

2. *The Modern Market*

The modern national casebook market is dominated by a handful of publishers – Foundation Press, Aspen, West, LexisNexis, and Carolina Press. Most of these publishers are now owned by large information conglomerates: Foundation Press and West by Thomson Reuters; Aspen by Wolters Kluwer; and LexisNexis by Reed Elsevier. As a result, within the last twenty years, the publication of casebooks has migrated from relatively specialized presses to small divisions of much larger corporate entities. The distinctive blue covers of Foundation and red covers of Little Brown live on, but their independent publishers do not.[17] This change in the casebook market is part of the consolidation in publishing more generally. Smaller presses have been gobbled up by larger ones over the last twenty-five years. Law publishers are to some extent simply caught up in the larger societal trends.[18] The result is that law students and law professors are a much smaller part of the company's customer base, and proportionately less important to its bottom line. There are justifiable fears that these companies may not devote the time, resources, or intellectual energy to case-books that more specialized presses could devote in the past.

But despite the increasing size and impersonal character of modern publishers, law professors and law schools have essentially decided to delegate control over the production of course materials to these outside entities. When it comes to legal education, the law school decides which courses will be taught and which students can (or must) take which classes. The school then provides a description of the course, but beyond that it delegates the content of the course to the individual professor who is teaching it. Individual professors, in turn, generally delegate the assembly of course materials to the publishers (and the law professor authors they hire). A small minority of professors choose not to do so and instead create their own course materials, but most use a casebook for at least a chunk of the course. And, of course, students must pay whatever the cost is for the materials the professor chooses.

As a result the market for course materials suffers from a series of imperfections. Because the party choosing the book for purchase is not the party doing the actual purchasing, the choosing party (the professor) does not have the price sensitivity that the purchasing party (the student) has. Not surprisingly, the costs of course materials have tripled since 1986, pacing well ahead of inflation.[19] Ian Ayres has compared the market for casebooks to the market for prescription drugs: In both cases, the choosing party does not really care what price the purchasing party must pay.[20]

Another problem with the market is the "book" part of the casebook itself. Casebooks were ideal for Langdell's students, who had no other access to the cases unless they went to the library. However, law students can now download all cases at any time of day or night through their Westlaw and LexisNexis accounts and increasingly through the courts' own Web sites. Access is no longer an issue. To be sure, casebooks have moved beyond simply reproducing cases; they now provide edited versions of the cases, along with notes, summaries, explanations, questions, and problems. But none of these materials has to be provided in book form. In fact, the book has significant weaknesses with respect to these supplementary materials. It cannot be immediately changed to reflect developments in the law. It cannot link to outside materials that may be recommended but not required. It cannot be edited by the individual professor to exclude certain material and include other. And a casebook is heavy; its physical bulk makes it awkward and even painful to carry around all day.[21]

Of course, the great benefit of the casebook is that it provides a package of materials for the professor to use, free of charge (to the professor). Law professors still need to prepare and develop their classroom approaches to the materials, but they need not spend the time developing the materials themselves. The prepackaged set allows individual professors to benefit from significant economies of scale: Many professors can piggyback on the materials developed by one of their number (or a small group).

The price the students pay is sufficient to provide incentives to both the author(s) and the publishers to produce these prepackaged sets. This system frees up individual professors to pursue independent research rather than compiling cases and other materials. And the price and prestige are enough to keep the market for casebooks replete with a sufficient variety of titles.

Electronic word processing, when combined with the Internet, has dramatically changed the possibilities for all kind of publishing: popular books, trade publications, magazines, newspapers. Course materials should not be left behind. As with the effect of the Linotype on West's production of case reporters, these developments should radically transform the landscape for course materials. The transformation is under way, but just barely. There is still plenty of time to set a course for the right way to develop course materials for law school classes. In my view, the best hope for increased quality and quantity is an open-source approach.

C. THE OPEN-SOURCE MODEL OF PEER PRODUCTION

1. *Open-Source and Computer Software*

"Open source" is a specific approach to the production of computer software. "Source" refers to the source code that lies at the heart of the computer program. Software owned by private companies – referred to as proprietary software – keeps this source code "closed," or secret. Closed code cannot be examined, copied, or changed and thus provides greater protection to the integrity of the program as well as the intellectual property that it represents. Open-source software, on the other hand, leaves its internal source code open to inspection by other programmers and users. Outsiders to the company can access the code for their own use.[22] They can expand upon the code, adapt it for a different purpose, or take of chunk of it and use it in a completely different program.

But "open source" is not only an approach to programming; it is also a movement. In the earliest computers, all programs were freely accessible and adaptable. A computer's software was inextricably linked with its hardware and thus was largely inalienable and useless outside that context.[23] However, as computers grew in importance and interactivity, their internal workings became more standardized and thus more amenable to sharing software. In response, software companies began protecting their software with copyright restrictions. In response to the growth of proprietary software, the hacker and MIT researcher Richard Stallman founded the Free Software Foundation (FSF).[24] Stallman's goal, as he expresses it, was to "spread freedom and cooperation. I want to encourage free software to spread, replacing proprietary software that forbids cooperation, and thus make our society better."[25] The most successful open-source project is the GNU/Linux operating system, which was begun by Linus Torvalds in the early 1990s. GNU/Linux was designed as an open-source competitor to operating systems such as IBM's DOS and Microsoft's Windows. But there are thousands of open-source projects, and many of these have achieved a level of market dominance in certain areas. One example is a type of software known as sendmail, which routes more than 85 percent of e-mails.[26] The GNU/Linux operating system is itself steadily gaining ground and runs on about 30 percent of servers connected to the World Wide Web.[27]

The open-source license has received a fair amount of attention from scholars.[28] Open-source programs are generally designed to be shared, changed, adapted, and passed on from user to user to user. The next user can take a small fragment of code or take a large portion and combine it with another piece to create something new. Under copyright law, a segment of coding could be removed from the pool of open-source code if a programmer took that coding and made a slight adaptation to it. The programmer could then copyright the new program and enforce the copyright against anyone who sought to use that code. In order to prevent this, open-source software has developed a specific type of intellectual property license.[29] This license specifies that others are allowed to use and modify the program, but the new product must remain in the public realm. Perhaps the most well-known license is the GNU GPL (General Public License), which is considered part of all GNU open-source creations. It requires that all derivative works be licensed as a whole without any charge to third parties.[30]

2. *Open Source as Commons-Based Peer Production*

Perhaps the most fascinating aspect of open-source production is the fact that it exists at all. Economic models do not predict that hundreds of programmers would devote their time, energy, and expertise to uncompensated labor that could be (in many cases substantially) compensated in other circumstances. Yet that is what is happening. Sociologists, economists, and law professors struggle to explain why thousands of programmers are so willing, in effect, to donate their time to this endeavor.

In fact, there are other models of production that replicate many of the open-source community's remarkable features. Open source is just one example of what Yochai Benkler has identified as "commons-based peer production."[31] Benkler describes this model of production as "large-scale cooperative efforts in which the thing shared among the participants is their creative effort."[32] More specifically, commons-based production relies on a pool of resources shared generally and equally among participants. The pool grows with each contribution. The participants are peers in the sense of having equal access and (largely) equal control over their production. However, each individual network can tailor its rules to monitor the quality of production, the contributions of individuals, and the overall output.

The most prominent model of commons-based peer production is Wikipedia. It is truly an incredible phenomenon. The Wikipedia project is an effort to create a complete online encyclopedia involving almost anyone who wants to contribute. Operated by the nonprofit Wikimedia Foundation, it is the online infrastructure for a series of entries about people, countries, foods, historical developments, television shows, theories of relativity, and anything else one might find in an encyclopedia. Its growth has been exponential: Entries grew from 30,000 in 2002 to more than 480,000 in 2005 to more than 3.5 million entries in English alone in 2011.[33] As a wiki (an interactive Web site with interlinked Web pages), Wikipedia is open to editing from anyone; all one must do is click on the "edit" button and start typing. One of the keys to the success of the site is its ability to accommodate a wide range of participation. From the hundreds of thousands of people who have made just one edit, to the roughly 40,000 who made five or more edits in one particular month, to the 900 active administrators (as of 2009) who have greater powers to manage the site, the Wikipedia community permits participants to engage with the project at whatever level they feel most comfortable.

Perhaps the most obvious concern with Wikipedia is error: What mechanisms are established to assure that the information on the site is reliable? One method is to maintain a neutral point of view in its entries; Wikipedia seeks to avoid debates or opinions and stick to the facts. Of course, that line is not always clear, particularly when one is writing entries on religion, politics, evolution, or even string theory. Another way of assuring reliability is to police the site's content. Wikipedia employs various ways of policing content while balancing the site's inclusive approach to participation. Wikipedia articles include discussion pages where users can debate the accuracy of the article without changing the actual text. These pages provide "safe space" for users to hash out disagreements. Wikipedia also provides various reputation markers. Users are encouraged to log in before editing; if they do not, their Internet provider (IP) address will be listed beside the edit. Finally, abusive users can be banned from the site. Wikipedia uses a dispute resolution system that progresses through informal conversation to a "request for comment" page, editor assistance, "wikiquette" alerts (an online notice board for complaints), formal mediation, and finally arbitration.[34] Arbitrations are conducted by a committee of elected arbitrators who hold three-year terms. They issue decisions and can impose a variety of sanctions, the most serious being a ban from participating in the site.[35]

Wikipedia needs to have entries that are considered to be factually correct in order for it to be a viable site. This need creates a significant distinction from open-source software, which need not have any agreed-upon "correct" version. Open-source users may congregate around certain instantiations of the software and may reject a particular individual's contribution, but the rejected user can still take that software and use it as he or she wishes. Wikipedia, however, only has one version of its entry for any given entry. Thus, the stakes are much higher when it comes to construction of that entry.[36]

This distinction is what I refer to as the "uniform-variegated" dichotomy for peer-based production models. Uniform peer production may take inputs from dozens, hundreds, or hundreds of thousands of participants, but it requires the participants to agree upon a uniform output. That output may, of course, vary over time, but participants are all essentially working toward one version of the product. Variegated peer production, on the other hand, has a pool of common resources but allows users to draw separately from the pool to create their own versions of the "product." Although groups of users may work together to form their own common creation, that creation can coexist with different versions of the same product type without displacing them. There may be some mechanisms for policing harmful content or providing feedback or ratings for contributions to the pool. But there is no need to agree on a version of the product that must be used by all concerned.

Many of the examples of peer-based production are uniform in nature. The National Aeronautics and Space Administration (NASA) Clickworkers project enlisted volunteers to help map the landscape of Mars. More than 85,000 volunteers, spending as little as five minutes each, helped provide maps that are "virtually indistinguishable from the inputs of a geologist with years of experience."[37] The contributions were highly granular: A worker could spend a few minutes marking a particular crater or hours marking many.[38] The end result was to be a commonly agreed-upon map of Mars. Similarly, the first edition of the *Oxford English Dictionary* relied on tens of thousands of volunteer contributors to send in examples – taken from books, poems, and other sources – of usages for every word in the English language.[39] These projects follow a common approach: Inputs from many contributors are necessary because of the volume of the work, but controls are necessary to maintain the quality of a uniform output.

Variegated peer production, on the other hand, has a lesser need for such controls, as there is not "one" correct version of the final product. Nevertheless, such systems often have some form of quality differentiation, primarily to guide users through the agglomeration of material. Slashdot is an online technology newsletter that posts stories selected by users along with user commentary. There is no uniform end product to the newsletter; all contributions can be posted. To manage these submissions, other Slashdot users provide rankings and additional commentary through a "moderation system."[40] A team of moderators is selected from among the active users and entrusted with the task of ranking others' commentary (on a scale of –1 to –5). There is also a system of "metamoderation" by which the fairness of the moderators is judged as well.[41] Although a variety of opinions proliferate on the site, moderator feedback provides a way for the group as a whole to find the worthier articles more quickly.

This distinction between uniform and variegated peer production is important, because law professors may think of an open-source casebook as a Wikipedia-type venture in which all participants must agree on the final version. In fact, the contrary is true: One of the great strengths of an open-source approach is that it would enable professors to take radically different approaches to the same material. But if they are not collaborating on one product, the question that arises is, What is the use of collaboration? The answer lies in the particular strengths of the open-source approach.

3. *An Open-Source Approach to Casebooks*

What would an "open-source" approach to law school casebooks look like?[42] One immediately thinks of the technical requirements for such an endeavor: namely, wiki- or other database software to establish the structure for file sharing and commentary. Such software would likely include an easily navigable database of files posted by users; a method for posting comments and feedback on these files, perhaps including a ratings system; and a blog or discussion board space for discussing administrative matters, such as recent contributions and developments, as well as deeper issues such as pedagogical theory and interdisciplinary approaches to the subject matter. At minimum, a few managers would be necessary to manage the flow of the site and prevent cyberspam; they may also want to institute some form of username or log-in to protect the site. One (if not more) of the managers would need to be proficient in software development, so the site could keep current with technological advances. Managers might also take a more active role by soliciting certain types of contributions or creating casebook prototypes.

As an illustration, suppose a group of two or three professors decided that they wanted to create an open-source casebook for a first-year Contracts course. They would need a database to which they could upload various pieces of the casebook as they were created. They would likely want to establish some sort of baseline for the size of the pieces: Would they be individual cases or statutes, subsections of a chapter, or whole chapters? Contributions could be in a variety of sizes, but the database would need some sort of labeling system to enable users to see quickly what each piece contained, without the need to download it first. Other professors could then access the site, copy the component parts to their own computer, and assemble them into a textbook. These users could also make changes and post their edited versions back to the site, or they could post their compilations for others to use. A feedback system would allow users to rate each contribution and/or provide short commentary on the contents of the files and their strengths and weaknesses. But variegated production would be the norm: Each professor could take component parts and assemble them as she saw fit.

Would an online commons casebook actually work? In his study on open-source software, the political scientist Steven Weber identified six factors concerning the tasks to be completed and five factors concerning the agents of production that make open source a more effective approach.[43] These factors are, for the most part, all in play when it comes to an open-source approach to casebooks.

a. Factors as to Tasks

1. *Disaggregated contributions that can be derived from knowledge that is accessible under clear, nondiscriminatory conditions.* As Yochai Benkler observes, "Peer production is limited not by the total cost or complexity of a project, but by its modularity, granularity, and the cost of integration."[44] According to these criteria, an open-source approach is ideal for an online casebook. Modularity refers to the extent to which a project can be broken down into smaller components that can be independently produced before they are assembled into a larger product. A professor need only contribute a single edited case, a single hypothetical problem, or a single piece of academic commentary to the commons at any particular time. As Benkler notes, "[a] project that allows highly motivated contributors to carry a heavier load will be able to harness a diversely motivated human capital force more effectively than a project that can receive only standard-sized contributions."[45] Initially, the managers of the casebook database might seek to divvy up the work among participants to ensure proper coverage. Once there is a pool of materials across the subject matter, however, participants need only post whenever they find something interesting or relevant. Thus, these modules also have fine "granularity": There is not a huge amount of time or effort required to make any particular submission. There might be a regression to the easiest form of contribution: For example, there might be many edited cases and fewer discussion sections. On the other hand, it is a lot easier to write an introduction about the Statute of Frauds than it is to write the commentary for an entire casebook, as is currently the level of granularity required. Finally, with regard to the cost of integration, professors need not reach agreement on how to aggregate the materials. Individual professors can assemble their own complete sets, or they can rely on the compilations of others.

2. *A product that is perceived as important and valuable to a critical mass of users.* Casebooks are sometimes seen as lacking in prestige when compared with the production of original scholarship.[46] As a result, many professors do not want to devote their valuable research time to this enterprise. However, casebooks also form the backbone of content for a law school course. All professors have an interest in securing the best possible materials for their students. There

will obviously be network effects to account for, but a well-developed case-book commons would enable law professors to construct their own version of materials in a fraction of the time it would take to produce an entire set of course materials on their own. Most professors, in my view, would value such a product.

3. *A product that benefits from widespread peer attention and review and can improve through creative challenge and error correction.* The online commons casebook would be poised to take advantage of a large group of law professors who would contribute a variety of insights to the material. The professors could provide feedback by commenting on others' work or posting their own edited versions of the material, with the changes that they considered appropriate. Although working in private, individual professors would have access to a wealth of information, ranging from brief commentary about a particular case edit to an online debate about how to structure the course. Moreover, corrections could be made quickly and efficiently. In their current form, casebooks can only be truly updated by a new edition, something that generally happens every three to five years. Online commons casebooks could update their source material instantly and then notify users either on the site or through e-mail. This instant access would not only make error correction more efficient, it would also permit the revision of material that was not originally erroneous but became so as a result of changes in the law.

4. *Strong positive network effects to use of the product.* Casebooks are the way they are because of network effects and path dependency. The advantages of electronic casebooks are so manifest that only past history can explain why the cumbersome print versions are still in use. If law professors were forced to use an online commons to construct their casebooks, a robust database for each course would be up and running within a month. The more professors use such a system, the better. At some point, there may be manageability issues that require stronger monitoring and more definitive feedback mechanisms. But in general, the more professors using the open-source casebook the better.

5. *An individual or small group that can take the lead and generate a substantive core of material.* Given the strong network effects, it may seem that a small group would not be able to get an open-source casebook up and running. But at least for one subject matter category, a small group would be able to post a set of cases and materials that would get other users interested and involved. It is certainly possible for one person to post all the materials, as solo casebook authors are fairly common. In fact, some have already posted materials online for commons use.[47] Properly directed, a small group could readily generate a core of material that others could use and expand upon.

6. *A voluntary community of iterated interaction that can develop around the process of building the product.* As discussed previously, the key to the open-source casebook would be the community that developed around it. Even in its present, printed form, a casebook is not a static thing; it is a constantly evolving and changing product. Law professors are thus accustomed to this process, and those who teach a given course generally have a fairly significant level of commitment to the subject. It is easy to imagine a community of professors, as well as informed and interested practitioners, working together to develop course materials.

b. Factors as to Agents

1. *Ability for contributors to judge with ease the viability of the evolving product.* It might be hard, at first, for users to determine whether the materials at the open-source casebook commons were comparable in quality and breadth to existing casebooks. However, several factors would mitigate this concern. First, the managers could implement feedback mechanisms to provide subjective assessments of the materials by other users. Second, most professors are familiar with the overall shape and contours of existing casebooks for the subjects they teach. It would be relatively easy, for example, for a Contracts professor to survey an open-source Contracts commons to see how the Statute of Frauds, unconscionability, or damages are covered. Moreover, evaluations from other users would provide buzz outside the commons as to the viability of the materials at hand.

2. *Sufficient assurance that user contributions will generate a joint good, rather than be dissipated.* Again, this is simply a question of critical mass. If there is enough content on the site to cover the necessary set of course materials, then users will be encouraged to add their own contributions to keep the content broad and current. The legal field readily meets this requirement. There are some 200 law schools in the United States, and about 17,000 full- and part-time faculty members. For most subjects, therefore, hundreds of professors have a direct interest in contributing to an open-source site for their own pedagogical use. It may be necessary for the database providers and/or content managers to be associated with a reputable institution to combat fears that the system may go offline because of conflicts or funding difficulties. That does not appear to be a problem either, since most law schools are part of well-established, long-lasting universities with secure sources of funding.

3. *Motivations beyond economic gain with longer time horizons.*[48] Law professors are perhaps the perfect contributors when it comes to this category. They have generally traded in the opportunity for a significantly higher salary in

return for reputational benefits. Although law reviews – from highest to low-est ranked – do not pay for publications, law professors spend a great deal of their time and energy writing articles and are generally motivated to seek the highest-ranked journal, using the "expediting" process to leap up the rank-ings. To be sure, casebook authors are used to getting paid for their labors, and these expectations (and monetary rewards) may give professors enough eco-nomic incentive to stick with the current system. But few casebook authors make more than the low five figures, and these authors are only a small per-centage of the legal academy as a whole. An important online contributor would still get recognition and prestige from her peers for her contributions. A well-written piece of commentary might get a newer professor some recog-nition and contacts in the field. No longer would the casebook author reach only those professors and students who used that casebook. Instead, a much broader cross section of scholars and students might read one professor's dis-cussion of, say, the Statute of Frauds, if that discussion were particularly well written and insightful. Overall, whether it be organic or generated by inter-ventions from well-placed law school deans, an open-source casebook com-munity could certainly provide reputational incentives for contributions of robust quality and quantity.

4. *Valuable knowledge gained through participation.* Venturing into the pro-cess of contributing to an open-source casebook would immerse the user in the material while providing commentary and guideposts for the expedition. A professor is much more likely to understand a course's architecture and interior design if she creates her own version of the book through the use of commons materials. As Edward Rubin argues, "it is hard to imagine any better preparation to teach a subject than to write a casebook or treatise on the subject, and the deep knowledge that resulted from this scholarly enter-prise seems likely to produce a variety of collateral benefits for students."[49] Producing one's own casebook would not be a requirement; users could sim-ply take a compiled version that another professor had uploaded. But engage-ment with the process on a macro- and microlevel would provide a much better understanding of the material, the subject, and the overall course.

5. A *positive normative or ethical valence toward the process.* Published casebooks are a compromise, an outsourcing. A professor can assign another's casebook and need not do the work in assembling the materials herself. The students pay the costs; these days, the list price for casebooks is often more than $150. Although I have no empirical data, I would surmise that most professors would love to have more power to manage their casebook materials, either in large or in small measure. An open-source casebook commons would enable professors to create their own materials much more easily than they can do it on their own.

They would be a win-win: The professor would benefit from having materials that fit her own teaching style and course content more closely, and the students would benefit from better materials and no economic rents to third parties. Thus, an open-source approach would make the professor feel more engaged and in control of the subject matter and would be popular with students.[50]

4. So Why Nothing Yet?

To me, an open-source approach to casebooks seems like a no-brainer. It seemed that way in 2005, when I first posted the idea to SSRN;[51] in 2006, when I presented the idea as part of larger open-access package at Lewis & Clark Law School;[52] in 2007, when the paper was published in the *Journal of Legal Education*;[53] and today. And the idea is certainly not mine alone; the eLangdell project was launched to develop a series of online commons casebooks following an open-source or open-access approach. However, as of yet the open-source casebook has only a handful of instantiations. If the idea makes sense, why has it not caught on?

The answer is simple: network effects. A sufficient kernel of content and critical mass of participants are necessary to get any open-source project off the ground. And unlike the actual open-source software, which sprang from a tradition of free and open access to program code, here we have more than 140 years of a market in casebooks. It is simply too easy to stick with a casebook. Even for new professors who have not yet adopted a book, the imprimatur of past success and stability makes it extremely difficult to move away from the traditional source of course materials. Moreover, the casebook allows professors to outsource a big chunk of their teaching responsibilities to other professors without paying any cost. Professors receive performance credit for scholarship, not teaching.[54] Particularly for new professors without teaching experience, a casebook is a lifeboat in strange and forbidding seas.

I would predict that, given more time, open-source casebooks will begin to thrive as an alternative to, if not a replacement for, traditional casebooks. eLangdell or another institution will develop an online open-source framework that encourages creation, participation, and feedback. However, there are institutional players in legal education that should not wait for individual professors to develop their own system. Law schools and their collective institutional representative (AALS) have a strong interest in facilitating an open-source approach to course materials, as discussed further later.

D. CURRICULUM REFORM AND THE OPEN-SOURCE APPROACH

There is good reason to believe we are at the beginning of wholesale changes to the structure of legal education. "Educating Lawyers," a report of the Carnegie

Foundation, has found a receptive audience for many of its reforms.[55] Top-ranked schools have undergone significant changes to their overall curriculum. Perhaps most important, law students are increasingly skeptical about the value of their education. The sharply depressed market for lawyers at present, especially at big firms, may represent a permanent downsizing rather than a temporary shock.[56] With tuitions substantially higher than they were ten or twenty years ago (in current dollars), students are stuck with larger debts and fewer employment opportunities. It is not surprising that they are more likely to question whether law school is a "losing game."[57]

The structural changes in the legal market, combined with intellectual ferment on the legal curriculum, have created a charged atmosphere conducive to real change. The open-source approach is perfectly tailored for such an environment. It would allow for collaboration within and across schools and would enable more successful reforms to be adapted across the board much more quickly. Instead of 200 schools each trying to reinvent the curriculum on its own, these schools could work together in small groups and large. No one answer would be necessary, of course. In fact, the open-source approach would be more likely to allow for a proliferation of different strategies while avoiding costly duplication of efforts or failed experiments.

1. *The Wave of Curricular Reform*

In the past five years, several of the nation's most prominent schools have enacted significant curricular reforms. Here is a brief rundown of some of these changes:

a. Harvard Law School

In 2006, Harvard Law overhauled its first-year curriculum by reducing the credits of existing courses and adding three new sets of courses. The first new course is on legislation and regulation and was designed as an introduction to the legislative process, the administrative state, and statutory interpretation. The legislative/administrative focus would contrast with the traditional reading of appellate court decisions on common law issues in other first-year (1L) courses such as Torts and Contracts. The second addition is a requirement that 1Ls take one of three new international law classes: Public International Law, International Economic Law, or Comparative Law. Finally, first-year students will take a problem-solving course called "Problems and Theories," during winter term, a three-week period between fall and spring semesters. The course is designed to "introduce different theories of law, and ask students to engage in complex problem-solving through teamwork and simulations."[58] Finally, in addition to these new courses, the school developed five suggested paths, called "programs of study," through the upper-level curriculum that include clusters of courses, clinics, cross-registration options, and internship opportunities. Each program of study has an associated group of faculty members, basic and advanced courses, and clinical and research opportunities, and each also provides interdisciplinary perspectives through opportunities in other Harvard schools.[59]

b. Stanford Law School

In contrast to Harvard's introduction of three new courses for 1L students, Stanford kept its first-year curriculum largely intact. However, it has embarked upon a plan to overhaul its upper-level curriculum drastically. The approach, called the "3D" J.D., would provide students with more interdisciplinary training as well as more participatory learning. In addition to making it easier for law students to take courses outside the law school, the school plans on establishing more than twenty joint degree master's and Ph.D. programs. For students who are not seeking joint degrees, the law school is offering "concentration sequences" with particular subject-matter foci. These sequences will include simulation courses: team-oriented problem-solving courses that teach law students to work with graduate students from other university programs. Examples include a course on expert witnesses in which law students and students from the natural sciences work to prepare a witness to testify in a patent infringement case and new negotiation classes that combine students from law, business, and engineering in exercises with simulated clients and opponents.

c. Vanderbilt Law School

Vanderbilt has employed a two-prong approach to its curricular reform. With regard to upper-division courses, the school has sought to establish concentration programs in areas such as International Law and Law and Business. Although concentrations are fairly common at law schools, Vanderbilt has devolved much of its second- and third-year curriculum to the concentration faculty. The faculty groups each have a director and a separate budget, and they manage such functions as conferences, interactions with other university departments on curricular issues, and travel funds for faculty. As for the first-year courses, professors were given the opportunity to apply for teaching relief in order to develop new approaches to existing courses. Three new courses have been approved: a one-week orientation course provided to all students at the start of the first year, a "Regulatory State" course, and a transactional approach to the Contracts course, with other substantial revisions in the planning stages.[60]

d. Washington and Lee University School of Law

Washington and Lee has completely redeveloped its third-year curriculum. Rather than offering a mix of the standard doctrinal and clinical courses, its third-year curriculum is based on experiential learning instruction. The centerpiece of the reforms is a set of new practicum courses, taught by faculty in conjunction with adjunct faculty and professors of the practice. These simulation courses are focused on traditional subject matters but immerse students in a particular role-playing exercise that extends over the semester. Examples include an international law practicum, a climate change litigation practicum, a business planning practicum, and an advanced family law practicum. Each semester students are expected to take two practicum courses, although a clinical or externship course may substitute. In addition, students begin the semester with week-long courses on transactional and dispute resolution practice and will be engaged in a professionalism program during the bulk of the semester.[61]

2. *Open Source and Curricular Reform*

An open-source approach would enable individual law professors to create new sets of casebooks and course materials for existing classes.[62] Open source would work well as a new approach to existing subjects, as it would allow for greater depth and variety of teaching materials and provide for quick and efficient updating to accommodate changes in the law. A successful open-source approach could take over a substantial share of existing casebook markets, as the approach is flexible enough to foster a variety of pedagogical styles and subject-matter coverage beneath its umbrella. Nevertheless, the century-long advantage of publisher casebooks would make open-source adoption a far from settled outcome.

So while there is opportunity for open source to reinvigorate existing courses, open source's greatest potential lies in its ability to serve as a platform for curricular reform. The network effects for existing casebooks are not present for entirely new courses, or even standard courses in new formats. If professors working on a new course funneled their resources into an open-source database that all could use, it would provide a core of materials that would foster various approaches to the development of the course. Working together within an open-source framework would enable cooperation while allowing each participant to follow her own individual plans. Of course, curricular reform can take different forms. The following describe three potential avenues for curricular reform: author-based curricular reform, subject-matter-based curricular reform, and school-based curricular reform. In each of these avenues, open source would be the superior method for exploring the possibilities of reform.

a. Author-Based Curricular Reform

In some instances, the motivation for course reform begins at the individual level. An author or small group of authors may decide to explore new subject matter, develop a narrower course out of a larger traditional one, or drastically overhaul an existing course. These authors may find a publisher, write a manuscript, work with an editor, and finally publish the book along with supporting materials (statutory supplement, teachers' manual, etc.). As an alternative, an author or authors could opt for an open-source approach. These authors would contribute materials to a pool and then draw from the pool to develop their own particular course materials. By starting with an open-source approach, the authors cede any opportunity to profit directly from the work. But the contributions to the field are likely to be much more substantial.

The set of materials related to the Deals course at Columbia Law School provides a glimpse of the open-source approach. Officially called "Deals: The Economic Structure of Transactions and Contracting," the course is the central component of the Transactional Studies Program at Columbia. As described by Victor Fleischer, at the time Columbia's inaugural Research Fellow in Transactional Studies, the Deals course seeks to teach actual transactional skills using fact-intensive case studies.[63] It endeavors to provide students with the theoretical tools necessary to evaluate contractual regimes and then enable them to apply these concepts to actual cases. In a related course called the Deals Workshop, students are given a particular transactional problem and then asked to work together to develop a contractual solution. Faculty members at other schools who wanted to teach similar courses would find them labor-intensive to establish. They would need to develop their own materials essentially from scratch, given the dearth of teaching materials currently provided by the law publishing market. However, Fleischer's article provides a blueprint for them. In addition, Fleischer himself has contributed three case studies that could be used in a deals-oriented course.[64] Other professors have also contributed case studies based on transactions studied in Deals courses.[65] By posting these materials to SSRN, the authors have made them available to academics, students, and practitioners.

The Deals course provides an example of a professor or small group of professors establishing a freely available course road map for others to follow, with course materials also available online. Of course, the Deals materials are only open-source in that they were posted online after they were developed by particular authors. A true open-source approach would allow for multilayer participation at various stages in the process and would facilitate change in the materials over time. Both the Berkman Center for Internet and Society and the Center for Computer-Assisted Learning have developed systems that facilitate such interchange.[66] However, as of this writing, neither has had significant participation by law professors. Perhaps it is only a matter of time,[67] but the network effects of current casebooks may be too strong to make this happen. Instead, the legal academy needs to look beyond the individual author to develop the full potential for open-source and curricular reform.

b. Subject-Based Curricular Reform

The work of an individual author, if pursued through an open-source platform, could blossom into a new open-source casebook that transformed that course across the nation. However, the likelihood of success is much greater if a group of professors leveraged some form of institutional support to embark on a more comprehensive project from the beginning. In fact, there is a group of subject-matter-oriented professors who have successfully worked together within an institutional framework to create a collaborative casebook. Since 1946, members of the Labor Law Group have jointly produced casebooks for labor and employment law.[68] A paper by W. Willard Wirtz served as a springboard for the group, which jointly compiled the casebooks and published them through a series of legal publishers. The money from the sale of the textbooks was placed in a common law trust, which was used to facilitate the group's further projects.[69] In 1970, Wirtz proposed a new casebook made of modules: "each teacher would have the freedom to make his or her own judgment of what should be included, the teacher would notify the publisher, and the magic of modern production techniques would turn out a tailor-made book for that small community."[70] Ultimately, the practical publishing difficulties that prevailed at the time limited the flexibility of this process, and the module approach never achieved the anticipated success.[71] Nevertheless, the Labor Law Group continues to publish a variety of casebooks in the labor and employment area.

Open source will enable professors to collaborate across the country on course materials that all can use. These networks might spring up on their own, but institutional support from AALS sections, Law and Society Association collaborative research networks (CRNs), ABA sections, American Law Institute (ALI) members' consultative groups, or other academic groups oriented around legal subject areas will make these developments much more probable. These institutions can provide some of the funding for the necessary software, conference "space" to discuss the project and identify participants, leaders to take the first steps in establishing the system, reputational benefits and legitimacy, and an ongoing presence to keep the project on track in case the participants happen to wander off course. The combination of institutional backbone with free-ranging participation would create a dynamic but stable open-source project that would have a significantly higher chance of achieving long-term success.

c. School-Based Curricular Reform

As previously discussed, law schools have outsourced large chunks of their education missions – namely, the substance and structure of their courses – to individual professors, who have in turn outsourced course material content to publishers and casebook authors. Although schools have maintained control over course descriptions (broadly written) and curricular requirements, they generally leave the teaching of the course up to the individual professors. And individual professors often have much stronger incentives to work on their research rather than their course materials.[72] However, the recent reforms at Harvard, Stanford, Vanderbilt, and Washington and Lee demonstrate that schools are starting to muscle their way back into the heart of legal education. Each of these schools developed new curricular requirements that included new courses and new programs. Although individual professors may work on these new courses, the school itself has a responsibility for making sure these reforms improve the education of their students. According to this model, schools decide to make the changes – not individual casebook authors, not the ABA or AALS, and not legal publishers.

In the competitive market for legal education, it might seem that schools should seek to capture the gains from their reform efforts by establishing intellectual property protections. Washington and Lee, for example, may not be able to distinguish itself by its innovative third-year curriculum if other schools adopt it. It may seem to make economic sense for schools to develop their own courses and course materials internally, and then keep such advancements to themselves. Or schools might transfer some of the economic gains to their own professors by allowing them to publish casebooks and other course instruments under their own name. In either case, an open-source approach would be against the school's own economic interests; it would forgo an opportunity either to keep innovations internal or to reap the economic rewards of their external use.

There is a competing set of values, however, that support an open-source approach. Although academic research in some disciplines provides profits to professors and/or individual schools, that is generally not the case in law. Law professors are not paid to write law review articles, and in return they can expect their research to find the widest possible audience. This tradition of openness in scholarly exchange supports the open-source approach in law school pedagogy. Professors are accustomed to sharing with each other, and a closed approach by one school would likely trigger reputational damage. Moreover, law has a tradition of using law reviews not only as a basis for scholarly endeavors, but also as a training ground for future lawyers. Integration of research and pedagogy has a distinguished lineage in law.

In addition, an open-source approach would engender more cooperation within the institution. If law professors are working on course materials at different levels of engagement, it may be difficult for them to allocate the economic gains among themselves. The traditional response to such quandaries is to delegate power and profits to a firm. On the other hand, having a school take authorship of the casebook along with the economic rewards associated with authorship would likely frustrate the professors who worked on the materials. Given the tradition of individual or small-group authorship, it would be unusual for professors to assign the benefits of their labors to the school. Professors like to get credit for their work; they would not want this credit to go to their institution. They are generally willing to receive reputational rewards as opposed to economic ones, but this might cease to be the case if their institution reaped unusual economic rewards from their personal efforts. An open-source approach would facilitate exchange internally without concern for the allocation of reputational or economic rewards after the fact.

Finally, the end product is likely to be much better if interschool collaboration is not only allowed but encouraged. It is unusual for casebook authors to work only with other professors at their own school. Given the distribution of academics across the country, one school is not likely to corner the market on the best individual talent for the development of course materials in a particular area. Course materials are likely to be substantially improved if they are opened up to contributions outside the school. And the Internet has only made interschool collaboration that much easier. The gains from improving the course materials, courses, and overall academic experiences available to one's students are likely to outweigh the short-term economic and reputational rents that could be derived from a proprietary approach.

That is not to say that schools should step back and let individual faculty take care of course content. Schools should take the lead on curricular reform – not by staking out protected territory, but rather by establishing principles and facilitating exchange. Washington and Lee, for example, has established a unique approach to their third-year curriculum, with an entirely new set of practicums. By opening up their course materials for these subjects to outside participation and collaboration, they could scale up much more quickly, decrease the pedagogical demands on their own faculty, and arrive at a better product. And by taking the lead, they would cement their reputational gains, even if other schools started using the same approach. Open-source platforms would facilitate this exchange.

In a description of its reforms, Vanderbilt Law indicated an interest in an open approach to its course reform plan. The law school received significant university support for its new approach, and it saw the support as a reason to share their materials with others:

> We realize that university support at this level is extremely rare in American legal education. As a result, we feel that we have an obligation to produce a curricular design that other law schools can adopt. This means that our design must not only provide an up-to-date, effective legal education, but must also be relatively transparent, that it must be flexible enough to be relevant to a wide range of schools, and that it must fit within those schools' existing levels of expenditure. Thus, we are planning to develop and publish materials for our new curriculum and we have issued an open invitation to deans and curriculum planners at other law

schools to visit Vanderbilt at our expense, see what we are doing, and share their own ideas with us.[73]

An open-source approach would engender the sharing of ideas that Vanderbilt's curricular initiative requires. It would allow other schools not only to adopt the reforms much more quickly, but also to play a role in creating and improving the materials at the beginning and on into the future.

Law schools should recapture their roles in legal education. Rather than farming out their educational responsibilities, they should take the initiative on curricular reform and seek to put out the best educational product available. By using an open-source approach, each school could pursue its own vision of reform while enlisting the legal academy as a whole (and potentially practitioners and alumni, too) in perfecting the endeavor. This combination of individualization and collaboration would strike the right balance in creating the best environment for curricular reform to thrive.

E. CONCLUSION

Dean Langdell developed the casebook as the best way of delivering the content that his new form of teaching required. It has been more than 140 years since, and we are still largely using his model. If law schools pour the new materials for the course of future into old wineskins, the results will disappoint. Open-source platforms for the development of new course materials would facilitate innovation, growth, and exchange. These new communities of learning will make the next set of reforms – both now and fifty years hence – that much more likely to succeed.

NOTES

1. Charles Warren, *History of the Harvard Law School and of Early Legal Conditions in America* (New York: Lewis, 1908), 373.
2. Christopher C. Langdell, *A Selection of Cases on the Law of Contracts, with a Summary of the Topics Covered by the Cases* (Boston: Little, Brown, 1871), vii
3. Douglas W. Lind, "An Economic Analysis of Early Casebook Publishing," *Law Library Journal* 96 (2004): 98–9.
4. Lind, "Economic Analysis of Early Casebook Publishing," 98.
5. Lind, "Economic Analysis of Early Casebook Publishing," 102.
6. Albert Ehrenzweig, "The American Casebook: 'Cases and Materials,'" *Georgetown Law Journal* 32 (1944): 224.
7. Ehrenzweig, "American Casebook," 224.
8. An early and foundational example of this debate is Oliver Wendell Holmes, Jr., "Book Notices," *American Law Review* 14: (1880) 233, 244 (reviewing Langdell, *Contracts*).
9. Lind, "Economic Analysis of Early Casebook Publishing," 99.
10. Lind, "Economic Analysis of Early Casebook Publishing," 98.

11. Rosamund Parma, "The Origin, History and Compilation of the Case-Book," *Law Library Journal* 14 (1921): 14.
12. Lind, "Economic Analysis of Early Casebook Publishing," 102–103.
13. Lind, "Economic Analysis of Early Casebook Publishing,"106.
14. Lind, "Economic Analysis of Early Casebook Publishing," 107.
15. Lind, "Economic Analysis of Early Casebook Publishing," 108–10.
16. Currently forty-eight states and the District of Columbia use the MBE. *See* "Jurisdictions Using the MBE," *National Conference of Bar Examiners*, at http://www.ncbex.org/multistate-tests/mbe/mbe-faqs/jurs/.
17. West has recently changed from its traditional brown cover to a more eco-friendly gray and black cover.
18. Overall, five academic publishers put out 80 percent of the textbooks used in college courses. Ian Ayres, "Just What the Professor Ordered," *New York Times*, 16 September 2005.
19. GAO Report, "College Textbooks: Enhanced Offerings Appear to Drive Recent Price Increases," at http://www.gao.gov/new.items/d05806.pdf. (2005).
20. Ayres, "Just What the Professor Ordered."
21. For a more extensive discussion of the weaknesses of casebooks in their current form, *see* Matthew T. Bodie, "The Future of the Casebook: An Argument for an Open Source Approach," *Journal Legal Education* 57 (2007): 10.
22. David S. Evans and Anne Layne-Farrar, "Software Patents and Open Source: The Battle over Intellectual Property Rights," *Virginia Journal of Law & Technology* 9 (2004): *3.
23. Lawrence Lessig, *Free Culture: The Nature and Future of Creativity* (New York: Penguin, 2004), 279.
24. Evans and Layne-Farrar, "Software Patents," *5.
25. Richard Stallman, "Copyleft: Pragmatic Idealism, Free Software Foundation," at http://www.fsf.org/philosophy/pragmatic.html.
26. Yochai Benkler, "Freedom in the Commons: Towards a Political Economy of Information," 52 *Duke Law Journal* 52 (2003): 1245, 1256.
27. Benkler, "Freedom in the Commons,"1257.
28. Steven Weber, *The Success of Open Source* (Cambridge, MA: Harvard University Press, 2004); Benkler, "Freedom in the Commons"; Yochai Benkler, *The Wealth of Networks: How Social Production Transforms Markets and Freedom* (New Haven: Yale University Press, 2006); David McGowan, "Legal Implications of Open-Source Software," *University of Illinois Law Review* (2001): 253–4.
29. McGowan, "Legal Implications of Open-Source Software," 251.
30. McGowan, "Legal Implications of Open-Source Software," 255.
31. Yochai Benkler, "Coase's Penguin, or, Linux and the Nature of the Firm," *Yale Law Journal* 112 (2002): 381–400.
32. Yochai Benkler, "Sharing Nicely: On Shareable Goods and the Emergence of Sharing as a Modality of Economic Production," *Yale Law Journal* 114 (2004): 334. Hoffman and Mehra describe such production communities as "large-scale, altruistic, social production." David A. Hoffman and Salil K. Mehra, "Wikitruth through Wikiorder," *Emory Law Journal* 59 (2009): 157.
33. Benkler, *Coase's Penguin*; Wikipedia, "Welcome to Wikipedia," http://en.wikipedia.org/wiki/Main_Page. Nine of the foreign-language Wikipedias have more than 500,000 entries, and another twenty-three (including Esperanto) have more than 100,000 articles.

34. Hoffman and Mehra, "Wikitruth," 170–5.
35. Hoffman and Mehra, "Wikitruth," 174–5.
36. Reagle, "Good Faith Collaboration," 53–5.
37. NASA, "Clickworkers Results: Crater Marking Activity," http://clickworkers.arc.nasa.gov/documents/crater-marking.pdf.) (3 July 2001).
38. Benkler, "Coase's Penguin," 381–2.
39. Simon Winchester, *The Professor and The Madman* (New York: HarperCollins, 1998); Simon Winchester, *The Meaning of Everything: The Story of the Oxford English Dictionary* (Oxford: Oxford University Press, 2004).
40. Cass Sunstein, *Infotopia: How Many Minds Produce Knowledge* (New York: Oxford University Press, 2006), 191–2.
41. Sunstein, *Infotopia*, 192.
42. For a fuller discussion of this question, *see* Bodie, "Future of the Casebook."
43. Weber, *Success of Open Source*, 271–2.
44. 435.
45. Benkler, "Sharing Nicely," 436.
46. Janet Ainsworth, "Law in (Case)Books, Law (School) in Action: The Case for Casebook Reviews," 20 *Seattle University Law Review* (1997): 272 ("[Y]oung untenured faculty are counseled by their senior colleagues not to waste time working on casebooks."). This is not necessarily a new development. Oliver W. Holmes, Jr., "The Path of the Law," 10 *Harvard Law Review* (1897): 477 ("I have been speaking about the study of the law, and I have said next to nothing of what commonly is talked about in that connection, – textbooks and the case system, and all the machinery with which a student comes most immediately in contact. Nor shall I say anything about them. Theory is my subject, not practical details. The modes of teaching have been improved since my time, no doubt, but ability and industry will master the raw material with any mode.").
47. Gary Neustadter, "Contracts," http://www.scu.edu/law/FacWebPage/Neustadter/e-books/abridged/index.html.
48. Here is Weber's complete characterization: "The agents are driven by motives beyond simple economic gain and have a 'shadow of the future' for rewards (symbolic and otherwise) that is not extremely short." Weber, *Success of Open Source*, 272.
49. Edward Rubin, "Should Law School Support Faculty Research?" *Journal of Contemporary Legal Issues* 17 (2008): 156.
50. Even authors can have moral qualms about certain aspects of their relationships with students. Ayres, "Just What the Professor Ordered."
51. Bodie, "Future of the Casebook"
52. Matthew T. Bodie, "Open Access in Law Teaching: A New Approach to Legal Education," *Lewis & Clark Law Review* 10 (2006): 885.
53. Bodie, "Future of the Casebook."
54. As Rubin states, "All of the earthly rewards that a faculty member can obtain – salary raises, summer grants, chaired professorships, competing offers, speaking engagements, and conference invitations – depend on scholarly production, not teaching." Edward Rubin, "What's Wrong with Langdell's Method, and What to Do about It, *Vanderbilt Law Review* 60 (2007): 614.
55. Carnegie Foundation, *Educating Lawyers* (New York: John Wiley & Sons, 2007).
56. Larry E. Ribstein, "The Death of Big Law," *Wisconsin Law Review* (2010): 749.
57. David Segal, "Is Law School a Losing Game?" *New York Times*, 8 January 2011.

58. Andrea Saenz, Faculty Unanimously Overhauls First-Year Curriculum, *Harvard Law Record*, 12 October 2006, at http://www.hlrecord.org/2.4463/faculty-unanimously-overhauls-first-year-curriculum-1.578496?pagereq=1. *See* also Todd D. Rakoff and Martha Minow, "A Case for Another Case Method," *Vanderbilt Law Review* 60 (2007): 600–2.

59. Elena Kagan, *The Harvard Law School Revisited*, 11 Green Bag 2D 475 (2008), at http://www.greenbag.org/v11n4/v11n4_kagan.pdf.

60. Vanderbilt University Law School, "Vanderbilt Law School's Curricular Reform Initiative," at http://www.aals.org/documents/curriculum/documents/VanderbiltCurricularReform.pdf.

61. Washington and Lee University School of Law, "Washington and Lee's New Third Year of Law School," at http://law.wlu.edu/deptimages/The%20New%20Third%20Year/ThirdYearProgramCommunicationsDocumentfinal.pdf (on file with author).

62. Bodie, "Future of the Casebook."

63. Victor Fleischer, "Deals: Bringing Corporate Transactions into the Law School Classroom," *Columbia Business Law Review* (2002): 475. The paper is also available for free on the Social Science Research Network (SSRN) at http://papers.ssrn.com/sol3/papers.cfm?abstract_id=305340.

64. Victor Fleischer and Geoffrey W. Smith, "Columbia Venture Partners – Medtech, Inc.," at http://papers.ssrn.com/sol3/papers.cfm?abstract_id=417520 (June 2003); Victor Fleischer, Streetwatch, May 2003, at http://papers.ssrn.com/sol3/papers.cfm?abstract_id=407140; Victor Fleischer, Branding the Google IPO (Teaching Case), Feb. 7, 2006, at http://papers.ssrn.com/sol3/papers.cfm?abstract_id=881607.

65. David Millstone and Guhan Subramanian, "*Oracle v. PeopleSoft*: A Case Study," at http://papers.ssrn.com/sol3/papers.cfm?abstract_id=816006 (12 October 2005); Steven M. Davidoff and Kristen Baiardi, "*Accredited Home Lenders v. Lone Star Funds*: A MAC Case Study," at http://papers.ssrn.com/sol3/papers.cfm?abstract_id=1092115.

66. Alexis Madrigal, "Reimagining the Stodgy Law School Casebook for the Digital Age," *Atlantic*, September 2010, at http://www.theatlantic.com/technology/archive/2010/09/reimagining-the-stodgy-law-school-casebook-for-the-digital-age/63290/

67. Bradford and Hautzinger have demonstrated how easy it is for individuals to create digital statutory supplements; they have given their supplement away for free. C. Steven Bradford and Mark Hautzinger, "Digital Statutory Supplements for Legal Education: A Cheaper, Better Way," 59 *Journal of Legal Education* (2010): 515.

68. John E. Dunsford, "In Praise of Casebooks (A Personal Reminiscence)," *St. Louis University Law Journal* 44 (2000): 825.

69. Dunsford, "In Praise of Casebooks," 825.

70. Dunsford, "In Praise of Casebooks," 827.

71. Dunsford, "In Praise of Casebooks," 826–7.

72. Rubin, "What's Wrong with Langdell's Method."

73. Vanderbilt University Law School, "Vanderbilt Law School's Curricular Reform Initiative."

3

Copyright and Innovation in Legal Course Materials

R. Anthony Reese

INTRODUCTION

What will the "casebook of the future" look like? Obviously a great many factors will affect the casebook's development in coming years, as many of the contributions to this volume make clear. This chapter considers how copyright law might influence the directions that authors and publishers of these future coursebooks take.

To understand how copyright might affect future innovation in legal course materials, it is useful to start with an understanding of how copyright affects the preparation of a traditional casebook. To that end, Part A discusses one of the most important facts about copyright and traditional casebooks: that the kinds of materials that authors have generally included in casebooks are mostly in the public domain in the United States. Therefore, authors can freely use these materials without seeking copyright permission or paying license fees. While copyright law generally protects a casebook author's own contributions to her book, the law also leaves that author free to include in her book a great deal of material created by others – including judges, legislators, and regulators.

Parts B and C explore how this lack of copyright in traditional casebook ingredients might affect the future of the casebook in the new technological environment. Part B suggests that authors and publishers may be well positioned to experiment with new methods of distribution, with new ways of allowing users to customize their materials, and with new business models precisely because they will not need to get permission to use the materials in their casebooks in these new ways. Part C then suggests that innovations in adding new and different types of materials to casebooks may occur more slowly because a casebook author may often need to secure permission from copyright owners in order to use those materials. The additional transactions costs that result may make the prospect of adding new types of materials less appealing to authors and publishers.

A. TRADITIONAL LEGAL EDUCATIONAL MATERIALS USE RELATIVELY FEW COPYRIGHTED WORKS BY THIRD PARTIES

Copyright law has long posed fewer obstacles to the creation and dissemination of traditional teaching materials in law than in other fields, at least since the development of the case method and the emergence of the casebook as the basic instructional text in law schools. The main reason for this is that almost all of the crucial components of a traditional law school casebook are in the public domain and free for authors and publishers to use without seeking permission from a copyright owner or paying any license fee.

Following the model developed by C. C. Langdell at Harvard, the traditional casebook relies heavily on primary source materials, with judicial opinions constituting the largest portion of the material. Federal primary legal materials are all squarely in the public domain under U.S. copyright law because the copyright statute provides that any "work of the United States Government" is not protected by copyright.[1] This disqualifies from copyright protection any "work prepared by an officer or employee of the United States Government as part of that person's official duties."[2] The exemption covers an enormous amount of material that may appear in a law school textbook. Because federal officers and employees create federal court opinions in the course of their official duties, the opinions are works of the U.S. government and not protected by copyright.[3] Casebook authors and publishers may therefore freely abridge, excerpt, and reprint these opinions in creating a casebook. But government work status also means that in creating a casebook, an author can freely include federal statutes,[4] agency regulations, administrative decisions, congressional committee hearings and reports, proposed bills, executive orders, presidential signing statements, legal briefs filed by government attorneys, and so on.[5] Consequently, a casebook author who draws on federal legal materials can entirely avoid the transaction costs of identifying and locating copyright owners, contacting them to seek and negotiate permission, and paying for a license to use copyrighted material.

Most state and local primary legal materials are also in the public domain and freely available for casebook writers to use without seeking a copyright owner's permission. At least since the Supreme Court's 1888 decision in *Banks v. Manchester*, state court opinions have not been protected by copyright.[6] As the Court explained in that case,

> [j]udges, as is well understood, receive from the public treasury a stated annual salary, fixed by law, and can themselves have no pecuniary interest or proprietorship, as against the public at large, in the fruits of their judicial labors. This extends to whatever work they perform in their capacity as judges. ... The question is one of

public policy, and there has always been a judicial consensus, from the time of the decision in the case of *Wheaton v. Peters*, 8 Pet. 591, that no copyright could ... be secured in the products of the labor done by judicial officers in the discharge of their judicial duties. The whole work done by the judges constitutes the authentic exposition and interpretation of the law, which, binding every citizen, is free for publication to all.[7]

While there is less case precedent as to state and local statutes, they too have generally been regarded as uncopyrightable and in the public domain.[8] And although questions have been raised in recent years regarding model statutes (such as building codes or the Uniform Commercial Code) authored by private entities and then adopted by particular states or localities, courts have so far held that once such a model statute is enacted by a particular jurisdiction, that enacted statute is in the public domain.[9] So casebook authors who use state and local legal materials, like authors who use federal materials, generally face no permissions costs to do so.

The copyright situation may be somewhat less clear with respect to a variety of international and foreign legal materials, although these have not appeared with great frequency in most traditional casebooks. Treaties signed and ratified by the United States, even though they generally do not meet the definition of U.S. government works, are binding instruments of U.S. law. They would therefore seem to be in the public domain under the principle enunciated in *Banks* regarding judicial opinions and statutes – the principle that statements of law that "bind [] every citizen" are "free for publication to all."[10] As for foreign legal materials, many of these may be in the public domain as well. The Berne Convention, the leading international copyright treaty, leaves each of the 160-plus signatory nations free to choose whether it will extend copyright protection to "official texts of a legislative, administrative and legal nature" as well as "official translations of such texts."[11] Like the United States, many of these nations have chosen not to recognize copyright in their own statutes, judicial opinions, and other primary legal materials, and so there would probably be no claim to copyright in such materials under U.S. law.[12] But some nations do claim copyright under their own laws in legal materials such as statutes and judicial opinions. For example, the primary legal materials in nations of the British Commonwealth are commonly covered by Crown Copyright or Parliamentary Copyright. Whether those nations could claim copyright in their materials in the United States under U.S. copyright law is unclear; there do not appear to be any cases considering such claims.[13] In any event, many nations that recognize a copyright in such primary legal materials generally also allow many educational uses, which might well include excerpts in casebooks.[14] Thus, the international legal materials that seem most clearly subject to copyright protection in the United States are works published by "the United Nations or any of its specialized agencies, or by the Organization of American States," because the current U.S. copyright statute expressly extends copyright protection to those works.[15]

As a result of these various copyright law doctrines, casebook authors can generally use most of the primary legal sources that they wish without even thinking about copyright permission. An author may not have quite as easy a time, though, with respect to secondary materials that she might want to include, such as law review articles, restatements, or uniform or model laws. Those materials are not generally in the public domain, and reprinting or excerpting them may require seeking copyright permission,[16] or at least considering whether copyright permission is needed or whether the proposed use in the casebook would qualify as a fair use beyond the copyright owner's control.[17]

Even with secondary materials, however, the legal casebook author may have an easier time than textbook authors in other fields. The vast majority of legal scholarship is published in law reviews that are run by law students and based in law schools. To the extent that these law reviews hold the copyrights in the articles they publish (or at least have the right to grant permission to reprint them), they seem generally to have been more willing than commercial publishers to grant reprint permission at little or no cost. Indeed, some law reviews have blanket grants of permission that allow free educational uses of their articles, which in some cases might include using excerpts in a casebook. In addition, the arrangements between law reviews and the authors whose articles they publish increasingly seem to allow the author to retain the copyright in her article and thus the ability to authorize a casebook creator to excerpt that article. Under such a copyright arrangement, if a law review for some reason denied a casebook author permission to reprint an excerpt from an article it had published or demanded a price that the casebook author viewed as too high, the casebook author could seek permission directly from the author of the article. And one suspects that the typical academic author in that situation would generally be happy to grant permission to have her work included in a casebook, often at no cost, since authors of law review articles are typically more interested in securing readers than in earning royalties.

Indeed, some law review authors now offer their works under Creative Commons licenses.[18] Creative Commons is a nonprofit organization that has created six standardized licenses that allow a copyright owner to permit any licensee to use her work in ways that copyright would otherwise restrict. The terms of these licenses allow others to use the licensed work as specified in the license without the need to request permission or pay for the use. Whether a casebook author could excerpt in her casebook a Creative Commons licensed law review article would depend on which particular Creative Commons license the article's author had chosen. If the author chose one of the Non-Commercial licenses, then a casebook distributed in the traditional commercial manner would likely be unable to rely on that license to include excerpts. And if the author had chosen one of the No Derivatives licenses, then the casebook author might not be able to abridge the article for the casebook (as opposed to including it in its entirety) without further permission.[19] But the basic Creative Commons license would allow commercial publication of excerpts from, or even the entirety of, the article, with no requirement to seek permission or pay any fee, though it would require attributing the article excerpt to the original author.

For other secondary materials, getting permission may be more difficult or more expensive. For example, the Restatements of the Law and many uniform laws (such as the Uniform Commercial Code) or model laws (such as the Model Penal Code) are authored by the ALI, which asserts copyright in them. Reprinting excerpts from these works may often require obtaining permission from, and paying a fee to, the ALI. Requesting permission may be fairly straightforward – the ALI, for example, has established a permissions mechanism[20] – but the permission fee required may be at least somewhat higher than for the public domain materials that can be included in the casebook for free. But even here, authors may find ways to include such secondary materials without having to obtain or pay for permission. A uniform or model law that has been adopted as the law of a particular jurisdiction could presumably be reprinted from the law of that jurisdiction, at least under the rule of the previously discussed cases involving privately authored model codes.[21] And in many instances, some judicial opinion will likely have quoted the relevant portions of the statute or restatement at issue, so that a casebook author who includes that judicial opinion in the casebook will give readers access to at least to the relevant portions of the underlying materials as well.

On the whole, then, authors and publishers of traditional legal course materials such as casebooks have been free to incorporate in their materials many of the most important preexisting works (or portions of those works), even though other authors created those works, without the need to obtain permission from, or pay license fees to, those other authors. In many other fields, by contrast, authors of course materials face more significant copyright obstacles. Primary and secondary source material in the humanities and social sciences may be far less likely to be in the public domain and therefore less likely to be freely available for use in textbooks or other course material. To be sure, if the textbook focuses solely on works published before 1923, then those works (at least as originally published) will probably be in the public domain and the author can freely include them in her textbook without any permission.[22] More recent works, though, are quite likely to be copyright-protected.[23]

In some fields, even using public domain works may not necessarily be easy. For example, the author of an art history textbook generally needs to include illustrations of many of the works of art she discusses, and those works will often be protected by copyright. Even if the book focuses on older works, which may themselves no longer be copyrighted, the author will generally need a photograph of the work in order to reproduce it in the textbook. And a museum, or its photographer, may well assert copyright in its photograph of the older public domain work. At least one significant judicial decision has concluded that most such photographs are not copyrightable.[24] But even if such assertions of copyright are incorrect, museums may control access to any existing high-quality photographs of the work (as well as controlling the access to the work itself that would be necessary to make any new reproduction-quality photograph).[25] As a result, the author may even have to get permission, and make a payment, to include illustrations of public domain artworks.[26]

To summarize, those who create and publish traditional course materials for law schools have typically been able to include most existing legal materials in their casebooks without needing to get permission from any copyright holder or have faced low hurdles to obtaining the necessary permissions. This may have at least two consequences for casebook innovations in the new technological environment, which Parts B and C of this chapter explore. First, compared to those in other fields, authors and publishers of legal course materials may find it relatively easier to experiment with innovative dissemination mechanisms and business models, because they will generally need permission from few if any other copyright owners in order to do so. At the same time, however, casebook authors may be less likely to experiment as to casebook content, since adding nontraditional types of content to their casebooks may impose unaccustomed copyright clearance burdens that they may not wish to take on.

B. COPYRIGHT AND EXPERIMENTS IN DISSEMINATION METHODS AND BUSINESS MODELS

Technological developments now provide new and different ways to deliver a casebook's content to users beyond the traditional method of printing physical volumes and shipping them to faculty and students. And future developments will likely create even more and as yet unforeseen ways to deliver that content. Because the preexisting legal materials in casebooks can either be used freely (because they are uncopyrighted) or be used with permission that is relatively easy to obtain, casebook authors and publishers may find it easier than authors in many other fields to experiment with new dissemination methods and business models.

1. *Dissemination Mechanisms*

How might the future delivery of course materials change from the physical distribution of printed volumes? For a start, textbooks may be made available in electronic form for download (or other transmission) to a personal computer, to an electronic reader such as a Kindle, or to a tablet device such as an iPad. Or the textbook may be stored as digital files on USB key drives that are physically delivered to users. No doubt other means of dissemination will emerge in coming years.

All of these dissemination mechanisms, though, will require the textbook's publisher to engage in activities beyond the printing and sale of physical volumes. For example, providing electronic copies by transmission such as a download involves (often multiple) acts of reproduction and (at least in the view of some courts) distribution[27] and may involve acts of public display by transmission. Because copyright law generally reserves these activities to the copyright owner, incorporating previously copyrighted material in an innovatively distributed casebook will involve various complexities.

A copyright owner generally has the right to exclude other parties from reproducing, distributing, or publicly displaying her work without her permission.[28] Usually, if a textbook author creates all of the material in her book herself, then the copyright in that material will vest in her, and she will be able to give an innovative publisher all the rights it needs to disseminate the book via new technological means.[29] But if she includes preexisting copyrighted material, she will not be able to grant the publisher permission to reproduce, distribute, or publicly display that material. Instead, the publisher will need to get permission from the other copyright owners in order to engage in its new form of dissemination. While the publisher may be able to get that permission, the cost of identifying and negotiating with the copyright owners and paying any license fees that are agreed upon may increase the book's cost to users. In some instances, moreover, the publisher may be unable to obtain the necessary permission. A copyright owner may not be comfortable with the proposed means of dissemination. He may fear, for example, that making his work available in electronic copies will lead to unauthorized online dissemination that could adversely affect his revenues. He may therefore deny the publisher permission, leaving the publisher in the position of either forgoing the new means of dissemination or convincing the author to remove the material from her book or replace it with material for which permission can be secured (or is not needed).

These potential copyright obstacles to electronic dissemination routes are not limited to newly created works. Those who publish materials that already exist in print form, or perhaps in electronic form on CD or DVD, may already have secured permission to incorporate other parties' copyrighted material in their texts. But many of those existing permissions may well be limited. They may allow the textbook author and publisher to use the material only "in print form" or only on CD or DVD, or they may contain other limitations that would prevent using a new technological method to disseminate the material as part of the textbook.[30] Thus, even authors and publishers who have already obtained copyright permissions for their textbooks may need to renegotiate those permissions in order to be able to adopt a new dissemination model.

As a result of these complexities, authors and publishers of casebooks and other legal course materials may have a significant advantage over other textbook authors in considering and adopting new methods to disseminate their materials. Unlike many of those who write and publish, for example, textbooks in literature, art history, or social sciences, law authors will generally incorporate few, if any, copyrighted third-party works in their materials. The only (or principal) copyright in the casebook will be that of the casebook author (covering both her selection and arrangement of the preexisting materials that are included and also any original textual or other material she has created for the book).[31] The author will thus be able to grant to the publisher all the copyright permission it needs to experiment with new forms of dissemination. And while that scenario may be somewhat oversimplified, since many casebooks will include *some* previously copyrighted material, such as excerpts from law review articles, as discussed earlier it may well be relatively easy to obtain necessary permissions from the owners of the copyright in those materials.

In short, casebook authors and publishers who wish to experiment with new ways to disseminate their materials should find that copyright law poses fewer obstacles to those experiments than it likely poses for authors and publishers of educational materials in many other disciplines.

2. *Customizability*

Casebook authors and publishers may experiment with the manner and form in which their materials reach their users – for example, disseminating a casebook as an electronic file – and they may also want to go further and experiment with how the content of their books is assembled. For example, a publisher might offer casebook content electronically in a modular, customizable format. A professor who adopts the casebook would then be able to choose which chapters or sections she wants to use and in what order. The electronic file containing the casebook for her class, or the volumes printed on demand for her students, would include only those sections, arranged accordingly. More dramatically, the publisher might offer the adopter choices among different materials in the casebook. For example, the adopter might be able to choose one opinion from among several different cases, each of which illustrates the same basic point. Or she might have a choice among several different edited versions of a single opinion, each of which would retain and omit somewhat different portions of the opinion, allowing for different emphases in teaching the case. Again, in accordance with the adopting instructor's choices, the publisher could produce a customized electronic (or printed) version of the casebook for that instructor's course.

Because copyright does not protect most of the preexisting materials included in traditional casebooks, authors and publishers could offer adopting instructors customized versions of the traditional casebook without facing either additional costs to secure copyright permissions to use included materials in these ways or the possibility that copyright permission for such use would be denied entirely. Thus, at least with respect to the copyright issues involved, we might expect to see experiments in customized textbooks emerge more quickly for legal casebooks than for other types of course material.

3. *Business Models*

Textbook authors might also take advantage of new technologies to experiment with new business models for creating and marketing course materials. Here again, casebook authors would likely find such experimentation easier than would authors who write textbooks in other disciplines. For example, casebook authors might offer their materials online for free download, possibly using a Creative Commons license to govern their dissemination. Depending on which license she chose, the author could, for example, allow free noncommercial use of the materials sufficient for any adopting instructor's students to download them (and print them out if they wished) without payment. Or the author might offer the materials for download and suggest (but not require) payment for them, in essence asking users to voluntarily contribute to support the materials' creation and continuing development. At least two casebooks are currently available under this model from Semaphore Press.[32] Or the author might create her casebook and self-publish it using a service such as CreateSpace, which allows authors to sell their books through various online retail outlets as either electronic files or print-on-demand volumes.[33]

If course materials contain a significant number of third-party copyrighted works, the materials' author will likely find these types of business models more difficult to pursue. For example, the owners of copyrights in the included works might not be willing to have excerpts of their works released under a Creative Commons license. Alternatively, they might allow excerpts to be released only under a Creative Commons license that is more restrictive than the one that the textbook author wished to use because of concerns about how Creative Commons licensees would subsequently be able to use those excerpts. And if a textbook author would have to pay third-party copyright owners for permission to incorporate their works into her textbook, then the author might not be willing to release her book under a voluntary contribution model because she might fear that the contributions would not be sufficient to cover her permissions costs. As a result, authors and publishers of traditional casebooks might again find it easier than textbook authors and publishers in the humanities and social sciences to experiment with new business models.

4. *Summary*

Of course, the "copyright advantage" that authors and publishers of legal course materials get by drawing primarily on public domain material in creating their works is only relative, and it is not unique. Other textbook authors may also find themselves using that advantage to experiment with delivery methods, customizability options, and business models. For example, as previously noted, authors of textbooks or anthologies of literature published before 1923 generally do not need copyright permission to reprint their primary source materials. So one might imagine that copyright clearance issues would generally not hinder innovation in creating a customizable anthology of nineteenth-century American verse or in offering downloads of such an anthology for free or for a voluntary contribution.

In other disciplines, at least some course materials are likely created almost entirely by the authors themselves, without including many preexisting copyrighted works (or else using only the facts and ideas in those works, which copyright does not protect).[34] For example, an introductory science textbook might draw heavily on the scientific ideas and data of many people other than the author, but as long as the author and publisher produced the text and illustrations themselves, they would not need copyright permission from others to create and disseminate the textbook. Thus, authors and publishers in those disciplines might have the same kind of freedom (as a matter of copyright law) to experiment with new modes of dissemination. Of course, these authors might find it more difficult than a casebook author to experiment with new business models that might provide lower compensation for their efforts, since the creation of the science textbook from scratch might require more time and effort than the creation of a casebook that draws heavily on preexisting materials and requires the author primarily to abridge, select, and arrange those materials.

Overall, then, those who create and publish legal course materials should find that their decisions about experimenting with new options for delivery, customization, and pricing should be relatively unconstrained by concerns about copyright permissions.

C. COPYRIGHT AND INNOVATION IN CONTENT

Even as casebooks are offered to faculty and students in new ways, copyright issues may hinder innovation in the kinds of materials that appear in the casebook of the future. As just discussed, casebook authors and publishers probably enjoy substantial opportunities to innovate in dissemination methods because traditional course materials generally do not include a substantial number of copyrighted third-party works. But authors might be less likely to experiment by including new kinds of content in their casebooks. Many types of nontraditional content would likely require authors to obtain permission from copyright owners. The relative absence of copyright clearance issues in producing a traditional casebook may have left authors and publishers somewhat unprepared to tackle the copyright issues they will face if they try to add new types of content to their casebooks, or at least somewhat less willing to take on the burden of securing any copyright permission needed to include such new content.

1. *Legal Materials*

As new technologies and new methods of dissemination develop, casebook authors might want to expand the kinds of content that they incorporate in their casebooks. One logical expansion would draw on a greater range of legal documents than most casebooks currently do. In particular, given the current interest in having law schools do more to prepare students to practice law, a casebook author might want to include more practice-related documents.[35] This might include, for example, litigation documents, such as complaints; answers; motions to dismiss; motions for summary judgment; appellate briefs; transcripts of depositions, trial testimony, or oral arguments; settlement agreements; and so on. Many of these documents are more readily available today than in the past, either in proprietary legal research databases (such as Lexis or Westlaw), through court-run services (such as Pacer for the federal courts), or in some instances on the open Web. In other instances the documents can often be obtained from court files. Casebook authors might also seek to include transactional, rather than litigation, documents. Here again, some of these documents might be relatively easily available through public record sources such as the Securities and Exchange Commission's Edgar service or in court files (if a transaction has led to eventual litigation over the documents).

But incorporating such documents, or excerpts from them, into casebooks implicates copyright concerns in ways that including publicly produced materials does not. As previously noted, judicial opinions, statutes, and other legal materials created by government officers are not protected by copyright. But the law is less settled with respect to the copyright status of materials created by private parties as part of the operation of the legal system. Complaints, answers, arguments in support of motions, appellate briefs, and other documents created by private attorneys in the course of litigation seem likely in many cases to be within the scope of copyright protection, because they often contain a sufficient amount of material that was independently created by the authoring attorney and that meets the fairly low minimal creativity standard for copyright protection.[36] And while filing such documents with the court may, in most instances, make them available for public inspection or copying, that filing in the public record likely would not in itself end copyright protection for the works. Similarly, a claim of copyright in a contract or other transactional document would probably not be defeated merely because the contract was filed with the Securities & Exchange Commission and became available online through the Edgar system or because the contract became part of a court record once litigation over the contract ensued.

Indeed, copyright claims by attorneys who have authored litigation documents are not unheard of. In 2002, the law firm Milberg Weiss began placing copyright notices on the class-action complaints it filed and sent cease-and-desist letters to competitor law firms that it believed were infringing on its asserted copyright in its complaints.[37] And some attorneys have complained that legal research services such as Lexis and Westlaw are infringing on the copyright in their briefs when those services make the briefs available online to subscribers.[38]

Few if any courts have considered the question of copyright in privately authored court documents. If the issue is pressed in litigation, courts might decide that, because the public in most circumstances needs to have as complete access as possible to the materials that a court used to make its decision in a case, attorney-authored documents submitted to a court in the course of litigation should not be protected by copyright, or, if they remain copyrighted, should be protected only very narrowly against competing uses and not against uses for educational or informational purposes.

Until courts weigh in on the question, though, the casebook author who wants to incorporate such works into her materials will face uncertainty about whether she can do so without permission. The author and her publisher will have to decide whether (a) to include the works (or portions of them) without permission and take the risk that they can prevail on any copyright infringement claim that might be brought against them; (b) to include the works only after identifying the likely copyright owners, seeking permission, and paying whatever license fees can be agreed upon; or (c) to include none of the works at all. Whichever route is chosen, the possibility of copyright claims in these litigation materials will make it more difficult for authors to include them in their casebooks. For authors unaccustomed to having to obtain permission to include others' works in their casebooks, this copyright hurdle may make them less inclined to experiment with expanding their content to include documents from legal practice. Their natural tendency may be to revert to the largely copyright-free legal materials that have traditionally supplied the majority of casebook content.

In addition, innovative casebook authors might want to use more than just litigation *documents* in their materials. Technology has changed the courtroom as well as the classroom, and litigation today may produce, for example, audio and/or video recordings of depositions, trial proceedings, and appellate arguments. If an author is making her casebook available electronically, that format could easily lend itself to incorporating preexisting works from a variety of media that would have been largely incompatible with the traditional printed casebook, including audio or video recordings. But here again, the copyright status of those nonprint materials will likely be more complicated than the status of judicial opinions and other primary legal materials. For example, C–SPAN recorded its December 2010 broadcast of the Ninth Circuit oral argument in *Perry v. Schwarzenegger*, the case challenging the constitutionality of California's Proposition 8 (which ended the right of gay and lesbian couples in California to marry). Various copyright interests in the content of that video footage might be claimed by C–SPAN and by the attorneys who argued the case.[39] Similar claims might be made for many other privately created audiovisual materials. As with copyright claims in documents written by private attorneys, such claims, however they are ultimately resolved, will make it more difficult for authors to include these materials in their casebooks.

2. *Materials from Other Disciplines*

Authors might also want to expand the scope of their casebook content beyond the traditional judicial, statutory, and regulatory materials by including materials drawn from other disciplines. These materials can offer students a broader set of perspectives, beyond those of the law, on the issues that arise in the area of the casebook's subject. Excerpts from articles or books written by historians, economists, sociologists, anthropologists, psychologists, and other social scientists could add substantial value to casebooks in many areas, from antitrust to trusts and estates.

In many cases, though, the books and articles from which the casebook author would likely draw will have been published by a commercial publisher, and excerpting them will likely require that publisher's permission. Whether the casebook author can include the desired excerpts will thus turn on whether these publishers will grant permission and, if so, at what price. In many cases, the publisher, rather than the author, may hold the copyright in the work, so that even if the author of an article or book would like it to be excerpted in the casebook, she would be unable to grant the casebook author permission, because she had transferred away the copyright. As a result, innovative casebook authors will likely have a more difficult time including works from other disciplines in their books.

3. *Audiovisual Content*

Finally, as noted earlier, some casebook authors may wish to take advantage of new dissemination technologies to incorporate into their casebooks content even further afield from the stuff of traditional casebooks. Going beyond words and static images, an evidence casebook might include clips of courtroom scenes from movies and television shows and ask students to discuss what evidentiary objection might be made on the basis of what happens in the scene, and how a court should rule on the objection. Or a casebook might include excerpts from recordings of congressional committee hearings as background on the various lobbying positions taken as Congress considered a bill that it eventually enacted into law. In many other situations as well, clips of television or radio news coverage might be a valuable supplement to written documents.

Some instructors may already show such audiovisual materials in class, and current copyright law generally allows law professors to play such clips in most circumstances.[40] But new dissemination technologies may allow casebook authors to incorporate these kinds of audiovisual materials directly into their electronic casebook, so that someone who reads the casebook on an electronic device such as a computer or an iPad could use the device to view the clips at the point in the text where they occur. Unlike showing the clips in class, however, incorporating the clips into an electronic casebook is not expressly allowed by current copyright law. So the casebook author and publisher would need permission from the owners of the copyrights in the various clips to be included (unless including the clip constitutes fair use, to be discussed later). As a result, including these nontraditional materials in the casebook of the future may impose transactions costs associated with copyright clearance efforts beyond those typically associated with the traditional casebook, and these costs might either increase the price charged for the casebook or reduce the amount of nontraditional material included.

4. *How Authors Might Innovate*

None of this is to say that copyright issues will necessarily prevent innovation in the content of legal educational materials. Authors and publishers who seek to create materials that they think will be better received than the traditional casebook will have incentives to seek copyright permission from third parties when they think it necessary and proceed without it when they think it is not. And although some copyright owners may be reluctant to grant permission or may demand high license fees, casebook authors may well be able to identify other works that would be more or less equally useful for their pedagogical purposes and whose copyright owners may be amenable to licensing. For example, at least several different court opinions often illustrate a particular legal issue or point of law equally well. If a casebook author wants to go beyond the court opinion and use some of the litigation materials (complaints, briefs, deposition videos, trial transcripts, and so on) associated with one of those cases but cannot get permission to do so, she may be able to get permission to use litigation materials associated with one of the other cases instead. That approach obviously will not work well where a particular case is so fundamental, standard, or unique that no substitutes are likely to be entirely adequate, but in many instances casebook authors will have a substantial choice of subject matter with which to illustrate their points.

Also, if a copyright owner will not give permission for her work to be excerpted or included in a casebook, the casebook author may nonetheless be able to use the work under the fair use doctrine.[41] The Copyright Act provides that use of a copyrighted work that would otherwise be within the scope of a copyright owner's exclusive rights is nonetheless not infringing – and not within the copyright owner's control – if it constitutes "fair use." Unfortunately, determining which uses qualify as fair uses can be difficult, since it requires "case-by-case analysis," which is guided (but not necessarily constrained) by four factors set forth in the statute that must all be considered "and the results weighed together."[42] As a result, whether any particular proposed use in a casebook of a third party's copyrighted material would qualify as fair use may be sufficiently uncertain that publishers may be unwilling to rely on the assertion of fair use as the basis for including such materials in their casebooks. But some authors and publishers will no doubt be able to include in their books as fair use some copyrighted material for which they were unable to obtain permission.

Casebook authors might also experiment by creating some nontraditional materials themselves so that they will not need either to obtain a copyright owner's permission or to rely on the fair use doctrine. Creating even audiovisual materials might be relatively easy, given the proliferation of tools for recording and editing. This approach would obviously not work for actual materials from existing cases or events. But a casebook author could, for example, create her own legal documents and related audiovisual materials as part of a simulation designed to illustrate or explore particular issues or skills. This would at least allow her to include examples of materials that have not generally appeared in casebooks.

So copyright claims in preexisting works that an innovating author might want to incorporate in her new casebook need not necessarily defeat the author's wishes. But including in a casebook content that is more unusual than that traditionally included may require casebook authors or publishers to go to greater lengths to secure copyright permission. These additional copyright hurdles may make it somewhat less likely (a) that casebook authors will pursue innovative content, (b) that if they pursue such content they will also be able to experiment fully with innovative dissemination mechanisms or business models for their casebook, and (c) that if they include significant amounts of innovative content they will be able at the same time to reduce the cost of their casebooks.

D. CONCLUSION

Casebook authors and publishers have generally included in their books a great deal of content created by others without needing to obtain copyright permission, because most primary legal materials are unprotected by U.S. copyright law. Because they have drawn principally on these public domain materials, these authors and publishers may enjoy substantial freedom going forward to innovate in the ways in which they deliver the content of their casebooks to their audience. But innovating as dramatically in the kinds of materials they include in their casebooks may require them to undertake additional efforts in order to obtain copyright clearance for those materials.

NOTES

1. 17 U.S.C. § 105. Section 8 of the predecessor to the current statute, the 1909 Copyright Act, similarly provided that no copyright would subsist "in any publication of the United States Government."
2. 17 U.S.C. § 101 ("work of the United States Government").
3. Long before the statute expressly exempted U.S. government works from copyright protection, the U.S. Supreme Court had unanimously held that federal judicial opinions could not be copyrighted. *Wheaton v. Peters*, 33 U.S. (8 Pet.) 591 (1834).
4. Again, long before the 1976 act's provision on U.S. government works, the Supreme Court recognized (though it did not hold) the principle that "[s]tatutes were never copyrighted." *Wheaton v. Peters*, 33 U.S. (8 Pet.) 591 (1834).
5. These materials all seem likely to meet the statutory definition of a "work of the United States Government," which is defined as "a work prepared by an officer or employee of the United States Government as part of that person's official duties." 17 U.S.C. § 101 ("work of the United States Government").
6. *Banks v. Manchester*, 128 U.S. 244 (1888).
7. 128 U.S. at 253.
8. *See* Paul Goldstein, 1 *Goldstein on Copyright* § 2.5.2.1 (New York: Aspen, 3rd ed., 2005).
9. *See, e.g., Veeck v. Southern Bldg. Code Cong. Internat'l, Inc.*, 293 F.3d 791 (5th Cir. 2002) (en banc); *Building Officials & Code Adm. V. Code Tech, Inc.*, 628 F.2d 730 (1st Cir. 1980).
10. *Banks v. Manchester*, 128 U.S. 244, 253 (1888).
11. Berne Convention for the Protection of Literary and Artistic Works, 9 September 1886, as revised at Paris on 24 July 1971 and amended in 1979, S. TREATY DOC. No. 99–27 (1986), article 2(4).
12. *See* Paul Goldstein and Bernt Hugenholtz, *International Copyright: Principles, Law, and Practice* § 6.1.3.2, at 217–19 (New York: Oxford University Press, 2nd ed., 2010) (noting examples of Germany and Japan).
13. *See, e.g.*, David Vaver, "Copyright and the State in Canada and the United States," *International Property Journal* 10 (1996): 187 ("This is unexplored terrain. It would no doubt be an interesting exercise to discover who in Canadian law qualifies as the author and owner of material that in the US is deemed authorless and ownerless. Who would by US law be judged to have US copyright in works that in Canada are protected only by crown prerogative is an equally interesting point.").
14. *See, e.g.*, Reproduction of Federal Law Order, SI/1997–5 (Can.) ("Anyone may, without charge or request for permission, reproduce enactments and consolidations of

enactments of the Government of Canada, and decisions and reasons for decisions of federally-constituted courts and administrative tribunals, provided due diligence is exercised in ensuring the accuracy of the materials reproduced and the reproduction is not represented as an official version."); §§ 26–27, Copyright Act 1994 (N.Z.) (providing that, notwithstanding the Crown copyright, no copyright exists in New Zealand legislation, regulations, judgments, etc.); *Crown Copyright in the Information Age* (1998), at http://www.opsi.gov.uk/advice/crown-copyright/crown-copyright-in-the-information-age.pdf (noting that Acts of Parliament and Statutory Instruments "may be reproduced freely in a value-added context or for private research and study").

15. 17 U.S.C. § 104(b)(5). *See* Goldstein and Hugenholtz *International Copyright*§ 4.2.2.5, at 154.

16. If permission is necessary, the question of whether the author or the publisher will have to secure it is a matter for negotiation between the parties. It is not uncommon, though, for publishers of course materials to require authors to seek, and pay for, any necessary permissions.

17. *See infra*, text accompanying notes 41–2.

18. For more information on Creative Commons licenses, *see* the organization's Web site at http://creativecommons.org/.

19. Creative Commons, *About the Licenses*, at http://creativecommons.org/licenses/.

20. *See* American Law Institute, *Reprint Permission*, at http://www.ali.org/index.cfm?fuseaction=contact.requestreprintpermission (last visited 31 January 31 2011).

21. *See supra*, text accompanying note 9.

22. Works published before 1923 are now in the public domain in the United States. Robert A. Gorman, Jane C. Ginsburg, and R. Anthony Reese, *Copyright: Cases and Materials* (New York: Foundation Press, 8th ed., 2011), 438.

23. Whether a work published after 1923 is still protected by copyright will depend on, among other things, whether the copyright claimant complied with the formalities for protection required at the time the work was published, whether the work was renewed when renewal was required, and when the work's author died.

24. *Bridgeman Art Library, Ltd. v. Corel Corp.*, 25 F.Supp.2d 421 (S.D.N.Y. 1998), *aff'd on rehearing*, 36 F.Supp.2d. 191 (S.D.N.Y. 1999).

25. *See* R. Anthony Reese, "Photographs of Public Domain Paintings: How, If at All, Should We Protect Them?" *Journal of Corporate Law* 34 (2009): 1035–9.

26. *See, e.g.,* Susan M. Bielstein, *Permissions, a Survival Guide: Blunt Talk about Art as Intellectual Property* (Chicago: University of Chicago Press, 2006), 55–6 (detailing a museum's postpublication demand for payment for permission for including in a book a reproduction of an eighteenth-century print not obtained from the museum).

27. *See, e.g., London-Sire Records v. Doe*, 542 F.Supp.2d 153 (D.Mass. 2008) (holding that transmission of an electronic file constitutes distribution within the copyright owner's exclusive right to distribute copies or phonorecords of her work). *But see* Goldstein, *Goldstein on Copyright* § 7.5.1, at 7:130 (arguing that the current statutory distribution right does not encompass electronic transmissions); R. Anthony Reese, "The Public Display Right: The Copyright Act's Neglected Solution to the Controversy over RAM 'Copies,'" *University of Illinois Law Review* (2001): 125–35.

28. 17 U.S.C. § 106.

29. Indeed, in some cases the publisher may already own the copyright in the casebook, if it is prepared as a work made for hire; in that case, the publisher, as the party that hired the

actual creator of the textbook, would be the author (and initial copyright owner) of the book. 17 U.S.C. § 201(b).

30. Grants of copyright rights made at a particular time often do not encompass, or are ambiguous as to whether they encompass, the right to use the work in media that emerge after the grant was made, and courts have grappled with the so-called new-media problem for decades. *See* Goldstein, *Goldstein on Copyright* § 5.3.3.2.b, 5:77 to 5:84.

31. U.S. copyright law expressly extends protection to an author's compilation of preexisting material. 17 U.S.C. §§ 103(a), 101 ("compilation"). That protection, however, only covers the compilation author's original contribution, which is typically the selection and arrangement of the materials compiled. *Feist Publications, Inc. v. Rural Telephone Service*, 499 U.S. 340 (1991). A casebook author's edited version of a preexisting case, statute, article, etc., may also be protected as a derivative work, though again the copyright will only protect the casebook author's contributions. 17 U.S.C. §§ 103, 101 ("derivative work").

32. *See* http://www.semaphorepress.com/index.html.

33. *See* https://www.createspace.com/.

34. 17 U.S.C. § 102(b) ("In no case does copyright protection for an original work of authorship extend to any idea, procedure, process, system, method of operation, concept, principle, or discovery, regardless of the form in which it is described, explained, illustrated, or embodied in such work.").

35. *See*, e.g., William M. Sullivan et al., *Educating Lawyers: Preparation for the Profession of Law* (San Francisco: Jossey-Bass, 2007).

36. *See Feist Publications, Inc. v. Rural Telephone Service*, 499 U.S. 340, 345 (1991) (holding that work must possess "at least some minimal degree of creativity" to be protected by copyright, but that "the requisite level of creativity is extremely low; even a slight amount will suffice. The vast majority of works make the grade quite easily, as they possess some creative spark, no matter how crude, humble or obvious it might be.") (internal quotation marks and citations omitted).

37. *See*, e.g., Janet L. Conley, "Milberg Weiss Tries to Nail Class Action Imitators," *Fulton County Daily Report*, 20 November 2002; Lisa P. Wang, "The Copyrightability of Legal Complaints," *Boston College Law Review* 45 (2004): 705, http://lawdigitalcommons. bc.edu/bclr/vol45/iss3/5.

38. *See*, e.g., Amy Yarbrough and Laura Ernde, "When Courts Give Legal Briefs to for-Profit Firms," *Daily Journal*, 23 July 2009, 1; Laura Ernde, "Balancing Public Access, for-Profit Interests," *Daily Journal*, 30 October 2009.

39. Presumably the judges who spoke during the argument would not have any claim of copyright in their remarks, which would seem to be U.S. government works ineligible for copyright protection.

40. 17 U.S.C. § 110(1) (exempting from copyright infringement the performance of a work (such as the showing of a film) "by instructors or pupils in the course of face-to-face teaching activities of a nonprofit educational institution, in a classroom or similar place devoted to instruction").

41. 17 U.S.C. § 107.

42. *Campbell v. Acuff–Rose Music, Inc.*, 510 U.S. 569 (1994).

PART II

Teaching with Digital Course Materials

4

Digital Evolution in Law School Course Books

Trade-Offs, Opportunities, and Vigilance

Lawrence A. Cunningham

This chapter considers the future of the law school course book by reflecting on its history, purposes, and promulgation over the seven generations since C. C. Langdell initiated our current mode of legal education in 1870. Some see the future of digital course books as a radical shift, akin to the original revolution of Langdell's Contracts casebook. Others dismiss it as a simple marketing maneuver, the way post-Langdell addition of notes, questions, or problems might be regarded.[1] This look back at casebook history suggests that digital course books are more likely to be something in between, an incremental but meaningful evolution.

Even the most heralded breakthroughs in the design of legal materials were not truly revolutionary, yet the cumulative effect of small shifts is enormous. Today's casebooks, whose transformation took a century, do not remotely resemble those Langdell published. The future of the law teaching book will not be either a radical new turn or a mere gimmick, but something more of a path, as this book's playful title reflects. The transition will present subtle trade-offs, create opportunities in pedagogical leadership, and call for vigilance in production.

Many wonder how this new digital path can be navigated. One approach is to suggest that coordination would be beneficial. Some of our distinguished ancestors likewise worried about a lack of coordination when observing the spontaneous outpouring of so many new casebooks in the early 1900s and again in the 1930s.[2] That concern reappears in contemporary literature and conversation, some even urging coordination within the framework of the open-source movement.[3] In contrast, laissez-faire devotees are content to let the process work spontaneously. They would allow it to take whatever course it may, relying on self-interested, invisible forces to choose the optimal form and content of books implicitly. Again, something in between these two positions seems to be the more effective stance.

What limits identified in the century-plus of using casebooks – and treatises and problems and other apparatus – can an electronic book help to overcome? Put differently, do digital books satisfy a need, as a way to solve an existing problem, or are they an opportunity, a new horizon of possibility not recognized previously? What costs might we incur by using them? The ensuing discussion sheds light on such questions by using the course in contracts as its primary example. One reason for choosing this subject – aside from my own interest in it – is that it is where it all began, with C. C. Langdell, and where big transformations have occurred, with thanks to such professorial luminaries as Lon Fuller.

The chapter proceeds by examining reviews of Contracts casebooks written over the past century and a quarter. Writing book reviews of casebooks was a particularly common professorial activity in the middle of that period. From 1920 to 1950, an average of two Contracts casebook reviews per year appeared in academic law journals. Though this art form has fallen from favor, with only a handful of such reviews written in the past thirty years, there are a sufficient number to provide insight about prevailing practices, needs, and opportunities.

This approach enables us to imagine what our predecessors in the 1920s or 1950s might have done differently if preparing digital teaching books. It also allows us to reflect upon the scores of different teaching books in print today for every first-year course, and many upper-class courses as well. The features of these books vary considerably, stimulating the question whether we need any more variation and how the digital path might influence our assessment. Do we really need more choice? Will that itself be a cost?

Section A takes a brief excursion through the evolution of the course book for Contracts. This history is a sober reminder of the plodding pace of change in American legal education and prepares readers to appreciate trade-offs, opportunities, and risks associated with migration from print to digital books. These are elaborated in three ensuing sections, all animated by the historical perspective and illuminating trade-offs, opportunities, and risks, each stressing a different one of those three implications of the migration from print to digital law books. Section B stresses trade-offs, especially concerning course books' purposes and scope; section C stresses opportunities the digital format offers, highlighting the appeal of digital methods to produce supplements, maintain a work's currency, and facilitate skills training; and section D discusses matters of presentation that creators of print and digital materials alike must address to promote usefulness – and calls for vigilance against associated risks. Section E synthesizes the discussion, concluding that digital course books are important and valuable, but not revolutionary.

A. EVOLUTION OF THE CONTRACTS COURSE BOOK

The closest thing to a revolution in the production of law school materials was Langdell's original Contracts casebook in 1870. But the book was not created parthenogenetically and was not an instant success. Langdell's compilation of cases and instruction using the case method – teaching case after case in a logical order to reveal simple underlying legal ideas and categories – was a response to a long history of grappling with alternative ways to teach law.[4] The principal approaches were the lecture and the treatise, and neither seemed entirely satisfactory. But students had always read cases; Langdell did not invent the idea that they should do so. He did make cases the centerpiece of his system and induce his followers to proselytize effectively for its gradual expansion.[5] Yet Langdell himself did not see the project through, leaving others to build incrementally on his advance.

Ever since Langdell's time, it has been tempting to identify new eras, paradigm shifts, and revolutions in legal pedagogy. But the changes are far rarer and more incremental than the heralds suggest. Perhaps it was not an exaggeration in 1921 for David Amram, when reviewing new casebooks by both Arthur Corbin and Samuel Williston, to pronounce that public policy aspects of their Contract law casebooks portended a huge shift: "That we are at the beginning of a new era of development in our philosophy of social relations is a generally accepted truism."[6] But neither Williston's nor Corbin's book inaugurated any such transformation. They reinforced the Langdellian method that had been solidifying during the intervening fifty years as a result of kindred books by other devotees of the case method such as William Keener.

A new outlook, if not a new era, did emerge the next generation, with the arrival of Edwin Patterson's two-volume Contracts casebook in 1935. This was championed as "the product of a new generation," featuring "new points of view" and "reveal[ing] a tendency to inject into the study economic and sociological data."[7] Others celebrated the achievement as reflecting the scientific advances of the period, especially concerning psychiatry and mental capacity to contract: "In an era of experimentation and change in society at large, and even in law schools, it seems that the entire subject matter of these volumes deserves a place in the curriculum."[8] This was an achievement and the beginning of a shift, but adding scientific perspectives was hardly a new paradigm.

The tendency of the case method's proponents to meet complaints with incremental adaptation is magnificently displayed in Lon Fuller's innovative 1947 casebook. Fuller's book not only included cases for serial examination but also extensive notes, problems, and drafting exercises, together with probing questions about the nature of law. Moreover, Fuller replaced the familiar framework of the Contracts course with a new organization by starting the book with contract remedies instead of contract formation. Contemporaries beheld the work as a masterstroke, blending the case method tradition with new approaches of notable originality. As Malcolm Sharp wrote reviewing the volume, this was "more than a case book."[9] In fact, Fuller's book, rather than Langdell's fossil, is best seen as the true forerunner of contemporary casebooks.

Of course, Fuller's book did not accomplish a revolution either, and there was much left to do. The next milestone was Sharp's 1954 book with Friedrich Kessler, another impressive work combining tradition and innovation. It presented all the great cases along with detailed notes on them, but instead of implying that they formed a coherent doctrine, it revealed glaring tensions, doctrinal contradictions, and the dissolution of the Langdellians' revered ideas and categories, such as the distinction between contracts and torts.[10] This monumental achievement was incompletely realized, however, though a generation later it remained aptly extolled as a "reorganization of the subject" and "a radical and enormously creative innovation."[11] It was left for a future coeditor of the book, Grant Gilmore, to draw out the work's implications in its 1970 edition. These included the expansion of liability in America, the further blurring of the distinction between torts and contracts and the socialization of contracts that Gilmore depicted in his famous text, *The Death of Contract*.

Though momentous, even these accomplishments did not constitute a revolution, as demonstrated by the next major development. Charles Knapp's 1975 casebook not only built on Kessler/Sharp and Gilmore's innovations, but took a turn back toward the doctrinal orientation of the earlier generations' casebooks. Having fused many of these new strands, it then welded them to the traditional doctrinal categories. Strikingly, a reviewer of this work reached end-of-era conclusions that turned out to be unjustified. Karl Klare declared in 1979 that "Knapp's attempt to give students access to the experience of thinking through contracts (and the contracts-torts relationship) as a whole surely signals the impending demise of the casebook method of instruction and of the traditional casebook as a medium of legal scholarship."[12] That would indeed have been a revolution, but it did not occur. The casebook has been thriving ever since and has been endlessly dynamic, though it has been demoted as a vehicle of scholarly inquiry.

This dynamism led to the "law in action" approach epitomized by Stewart Macaulay's 1995 casebook. The casebook drew expressly on Fuller and Kessler/Sharp, putting remedies first and then showing doctrinal contradictions and policy tensions. Its most distinctive feature, however, was its insistence that, in contracting, business reality was more important than legal doctrine, and it implemented this insight by organizing cases by transaction type, rather than according to the familiar doctrinal pattern. Though impressive, this was not entirely novel either, as contract materials had been so arranged in Harold Havighurst's 1950 casebook[13] and Ian Macneil's 1971 book.[14] By developing and extending these earlier efforts, moreover, Macaulay joined critics of the case method who debunked the practice of teaching Contracts using common law appellate opinions, saying that was akin to teaching zoology by focusing on unicorns and dodos.[15] Macaulay's book was influential in altering the Contracts course, but it did not transform it. Books today increasingly concentrate on materials other than appellate opinions, but the casebook still dominates the classroom, and common law appellate opinions remain the mainstay of the Contracts course.

One thing that has changed and is part of a revolution is the use of the masculine pronoun. Before 1975, all casebooks and all reviews of them used the masculine pronoun exclusively. That simply reflected the reality of the worlds of business and law, dominated by men and with women out of sight.[16] Professor Klare applauded Knapp's 1975 effort: "Another attractive feature of the book is its modest but noteworthy effort to respond to the pervasive sexism of American legal culture."[17] As recently as 2001, Lenora Ledwon began her review of the Contracts casebook by Amy Kastely, Deborah Waire Post, and Nancy Ota by noting that when she was a student, she had no casebook edited by a woman.[18] To this day, however, casebooks are edited "overwhelmingly" by "white males whose attention to outsider issues" is equivocal.[19] So even that extraordinary change, as with the other changes chronicled, is not quite a revolution. But neither is it – or any of the other changes made in the century since Langdell – merely a marketing gimmick. The same is true of the digital course book. It will not transform law school, but it does open a new path – the digital path of the law – that is likely to have both familiar and novel features and entail subtle trade-offs of the sort discussed in what follows.

B. TRADE-OFFS TO BALANCE

History's suggestion to expect trade-offs in the migration from print to digital teaching books is verified by considering profound issues concerning the purpose of course books and equally fundamental challenges about their scope. Along with trade-offs come opportunities, of course, but it is worth highlighting explicit examples of how some gains from moving to digital law books will pose potentially high costs.

1. *Purposes*

From long before the casebook's inception, law teachers have debated whether the purpose of legal education is the delivery of knowledge (the transfer of information) or the development of ability (specifically analytical reasoning). Since Langdell, along with his creation of the casebook, ensconced the law school in a graduate level university program, law teachers have also debated whether legal education is professional training or academic exploration. In fact, it is both sides of the two dichotomies in different measures. To find the optimal mix, one must appreciate the vast difference between law school and law practice.[20] Even within the most practice-oriented clinic, students remain students and lawyers are the lawyers. But there is also an intimate connection between law school and practice; even in the most theoretical and abstract seminar, students are becoming lawyers, learning related techniques, developing vocabulary and mooting substantive content. In addition, it seems clear that in both these educational settings, as well as others, the students are acquiring both knowledge and skills.

With respect to the pedagogic purpose in particular settings, digital materials, like printed materials, can be designed well or poorly. The important differences are not the medium as such but the features associated with it – content, principally, plus ease of use and cognitive appeal. It is worth considering how such features may be influenced by the medium, but it is vital to keep the particular pedagogical function in mind. In the simplest world, digital books would be mere electronic copies of existing print books, much as they appear on e-readers such as Kindle and Nook. But the future of the law teaching book may well be different when conceived for development and use electronically. That is the assumption in the discussion that follows.

Aside from its substantive purpose as pedagogy, an important administrative function of the course book is the combination of expertise that goes into it and the centralization of labor it enables. A virtue of editorship, whether books are printed or digital, is efficient production: Better to have one or a few spend the time and effort to locate, edit, organize, and integrate materials than for each teacher to perform all those tasks locally. True, each teacher could create his or her own materials from scratch. That occurred in the 1880s through the early 1900s, despite original casebook promulgation,[21] and is occurring now with digital materials.[22] But it is not efficient. The value of coordination by those suited for the work, by temperament or experience, has long been known.[23] It is particularly valuable to newer teachers. They require the guidance of proven teaching books, and their time is better spent mastering classroom techniques and performing research than finding and formatting materials – points that have been recognized for nearly a century.[24]

To be sure, it is also important that each teacher be able to tailor books made for general use to suit particular preferences or needs. After all, the same subject may be approached differently in many ways, whether as a result of quotidian matters of allocated credit hours or of idiosyncratic points of pedagogical preference. That capacity for tailoring to suit individualized requirements and preferences is held out as one of the most appealing features of the digital course book.[25] This need for balancing central production with tailorability thus creates some preliminary trade-offs between print and digital course books at the basic level of a book's purpose.

With respect to their purely pedagogical purpose, casebooks can serve as references or resources. The earliest casebooks were hailed as offering value not only to students but to practicing lawyers and judges as well. Professors of earlier generations, especially from the 1920s to the 1950s and perhaps as recently as the 1970s, seemed to prize the value of casebooks as scholarship along with their value as teaching materials.[26] They invested considerable effort in producing books that would organize or reconceptualize a field.[27] Famous casebook editors were all recognized in various ways as providing intellectual discoveries, such as Kessler/Sharp's stunning demonstration of doctrinal contradictions through matching pairs of conflicting cases.[28] More recently, Allan Farnsworth and William Young demonstrated the value of a casebook in establishing connections between doctrines,[29] and Robert Hillman and Robert Summers were able to present a layer of general theories of obligation (bargain, reliance, restitution, statute, and so on) as an organizing theme.[30]

One price of such intellectual creativity, however, is that it can limit the tailorability of the materials. The more integrated or layered a casebook, the more difficult it is to assign its components selectively without losing that value. Put those materials in a digital form to increase tailorability and you sacrifice much of the rich scholarly contribution that the work can offer. On the other hand, the days of treating casebooks as a vehicle for such scholarly pursuits – to organize or reconceptualize a field or reveal newly discovered relations – may be numbered.[31] Such efforts to rethink, reorganize, and reshape occur increasingly in articles and scholarly books rather than in teaching materials. If so, digital books may appeal precisely because there is no longer a need for these materials to serve as a path to scholarly discovery, or as a resource or reference. What might have been a disadvantage of an earlier generation's use of digital rather than print books may be a gain today.

On the other hand, there is nothing wrong with attempting to sustain or revive the old tradition of using course books as a form of scholarship, of discovery, and as a reference tool. For those wishing to treat teaching books as a way to develop a field or pursue kindred scholarly undertakings, the switch to digital may be a cost. Those most likely to be interested in doing so are teachers for whom the inherited materials seem most in need of improvement. They would include, for example, teachers promoting more innovative books offering stories of outsider voices and taking a more literary or feminist turn.[32] A shift from print to digital books may both cement the decline of the course book as a scholarly forum and diminish the scholarly significance of such undertakings. If the scholarly casebook innovations of old, from Patterson to Gilmore, may have thrived more in print than in digital form, this shift could be perceived by some to be unfortunate.

A cognate point, in terms of both scholarly value and tailorability, concerns the book's organization or sequencing. The earliest Contracts casebooks sequenced their material historically, showing how case law evolved over time. Arthur Corbin took a transactional approach, presenting materials in the order that they occurred in actual contracting, from formation to discharge.[33] Lon Fuller's 1947 book made the radical departure of putting remedies first, on the grounds that the stakes in Contracts revealed by remedies pervade the entire course.[34] An even bolder reorganization of doctrine appeared in Kessler and Sharp's 1953 book. Doctrines were not isolated into distinct sections for linear examination but woven pervasively, with several topics – such as consideration, excuses, and restitution – reappearing throughout in different guises.[35] Likewise, Ian Macneil's approach of ordering materials according to contract type presented issues more in their social and business context than in legal categories.[36]

Perhaps none of this should matter much for practical purposes, since teachers can assign the casebook's materials in a different sequence to suit their needs or tastes. As Douglas Leslie quipped about Fuller's leadership, anyone can start with remedies using any book: "Just begin the course with Chapter Nine."[37] Rearranging the sequence requires teachers to make a similar investment of thought and time, whether the product is in print or digital format. But unless the print and digital alternatives are mere copies, the execution differs. The sequence and content of print books can be tailored through the syllabus and supplemental print materials. For electronic books, changing the sequencing would mean altering the electronic platform to present the materials in the desired order.

Editors, aware of that prospect, may be tempted to facilitate it – to increase the ease with which teachers can resequence the material in an electronic casebook. That is best done by pursuing a modular approach to the materials, designing chapters, sections, and cases to stand more or less alone so that they can be plugged into just about any sequence a teacher may desire. A format of this sort, however, is the antithesis of the historical achievements that extend from Kessler/Sharp's doctrinal contradictions, through Farnsworth/Young integration and Summers/Hillman layering. Put differently, though tailorability always is valuable, some sequencing choices an editor makes create value that is lost on rearrangement. To the extent that digital books induce greater editorial attention to the virtue of tailorability, and thus to creation of modules, the effect would be to reduce, simplify, and compartmentalize, rather than to reveal contradictions, integrate materials, or conceive layers. At the extreme, course book design would be focused exclusively on teachability and tailorability and not at all on resource or scholarly dimensions.

A final variation on this theme of purpose concerns the interdisciplinary perspectives a course book may offer. Since the 1950s, there have been a few casebooks with a particular interdisciplinary bent, such as realism (then called functionalism) or economics.[38] Today's fashions not only include such interdisciplinary perspectives but also critical theories and viewpoints, especially race, class, sexuality, and gender.[39] These perspectives can even displace doctrine or law as a book's organizing principle.[40] The law and economics perspective seems to have become sufficiently mature to sustain this role, but other perspectives seem less capable of doing so.[41] In any case, critics are increasingly wary of excessive reliance on such perspectives because they can unduly complicate a book.[42] In some discussions, one hears a longing for a return to the purer casebook, a book consisting primarily or exclusively of cases.

It is not easy to predict how migration from print to digital books may affect such discussions or where the resulting equilibrium would reside. On one hand, critics of excess complexity may worry even more that the open-ended character of digital formats compared to the finite boundaries of print risks greater information overload. They would push to curtail multiplying perspectives beyond the prevailing scope in favor of a return to basics. Opposing such nostalgia is the continued press for new perspectives, with stern reminders of the ahistorical, thin, insular flavor of the case-only approach, and championing instead a rich interdisciplinary approach thick with "details of lived experience."[43] In short, it seems less likely that digital materials promise inevitable virtues than that, as with their print cousins, they pose trade-offs that will be difficult for some legal educators to balance.

2. *Scope*

The advent of the digital era generates even greater uncertainty – and opportunity – concerning the scope of the materials that course books contain. Proponents of the pure casebook and case method were content to rely entirely on cases printed in the book as the basis for class discussion, with context and qualification provided by lecture. Early on, editors noticed that some such perspective could be provided more readily in the book, using footnotes, a practice that, in Contracts, Williston began and Corbin continued. But the practice was controversial, with many teachers objecting that the textual footnotes "burdened" the book.[44] Others stressed that, while useful to teachers, the textual materials were "inimical to student interests" because, to recall one side of an old debate, "they do not leave enough to his own initiative."[45] A balance was achieved during the 1930s, reflected in the way books gradually began to be subtitled "Cases and Materials," though they remained overwhelmingly based on cases.[46] Still this "case-text trend"[47] was a step toward equilibrium between Langdell's case method and the treatise/lecture approach of the pre-Langdell period.

Lon Fuller in 1947 rendered the note feature into the form recognized today. No longer footnotes, these rich analytical materials followed the cases and appeared throughout the book with equal prominence.[48] Fuller's notes were so exquisite that they could be classified according to their distinctive contributions to the book and to pedagogy in general. Many gave supplementary facts about the case or provided historical perspective, some presented comparative law contrasts, and others explained the business and economic context of an exchange.[49] Above all, the point was pedagogical: to provide material that prevented students from missing the forest for the trees – something teachers in earlier generations had difficulty doing when assigning books consisting wholly or mostly of case after case, sans context. Those earlier teachers had to provide by lecture the essential material that went beyond the inherent limits of an appellate decision; now the text provided it.

Despite this innovation, the cautions against excess were voiced then and endure now.[50] Law teachers have long argued about the proper pedagogical balance between spoon-feeding students the law and Socratic interrogation more reliant on the technique of "hiding-the-ball." In his 1948 review, Harold Shepherd observed about notes in Fuller's book: "one need not fear an overdose of spoon-feeding, for there is still enough of orthodox case material and problems to satisfy the most ardent case-method teacher."[51] That debate, though it continues, is less pronounced than in earlier eras.[52] The more contemporary concern is that extensive notes can bloat a book, undermining the goal of using notes to reveal the big picture.

It seems doubtful that a shift from print to digital format will directly affect the scope of such analytical materials or that the scope provided in the two settings will directly affect preferences for one medium over the other. But pioneers in the digital realm have the chance to set the standard for whether notes should be curtailed, sustained, or expanded. Digital innovation revives this debate and may alter it. In printed books, space constraints impose caps on the scope and density of notes. Those constraints disappear in digital books, freed from physical limits and enabling links to further material, itself unbound. The universe becomes the limit, opening both a potential world of wonder and the threat of information overload. While notes were first added to maintain the big picture, and lately can obscure it, the digital shift may either enable editors to corral the world for students to focus it on the course or risk drawing them far outside it. Striking the balance will be difficult yet vital. Editors equipped to do so will exploit a promising opportunity while those who try but fail will pay the costs of innovation.

A similar point concerns the inclusion of copious questions in law teaching books, an approach that also raises the issue of too few and too many. The second edition of Arthur Corbin's Contracts casebook in 1933 began the practice of including provocative questions at the end of many cases.[53] These were designed to stoke thought and prepare students for class discussion, deemed better than the practice of springing "on-the-spot hypotheticals" whose details many students miss in the "rapid-fire exercise."[54] Editors gradually found it desirable to add questions following nearly every case for the same purpose: classroom discussion may be "less an impromptu dialectic between student and teacher, in which the latter triumphantly pulls the rabbit from the hat, and more a sustained exploration of implications which are fully sensed in advance."[55]

Debate ensued, and continues, on whether questions should be answered rather than merely posed, raising again the vexing balance between hiding the ball (and insisting that students struggle to work through problems) and spoon-feeding students.[56] Some modern critics worry that editors pose too many questions, potentially defeating the goal of aiding class discussion. Students, who do not know which of a dozen or more questions within a fifteen-page assignment will be posed, may rationally refrain from developing potential answers to any of them.[57] Editors parry that they provide a rich menu from which teachers should assign chosen questions for students to digest in advance. As with the optimal scope of textual notes, on this second matter of scope, the relative appeal of print versus digital books will be influenced by editorial tendencies to produce an ideal number and range of questions. Though in principle it should be possible in either medium, digital pioneers have a chance to set the standard.

In contrast to the problem concerning notes, the digital environment promises one clear advantage when capabilities to provide interactive questioning are considered. Editors of digital books can offer questions seeking electronic answers programmed with follow-up questions calibrated in difficulty according to the quality of previous answers.[58] The challenge in designing an optimal format will shift from numbers and scope of questions to their quality and interactive efficacy. Editors will require not merely the manifest skills of a traditional expositor of legal analysis and interrogation, but expertise in computer-based pedagogy and interactivity.

A related challenge is whether a subject should be taught on the basis of a particular jurisdiction or on general principles. Early casebooks struggled with the proper mix of English and American cases to include. Langdell and his immediate successors drew heavily on English cases, and one important change Corbin inaugurated was to increase the focus on American decisions.[59] Later books struggled with the mix of national and state cases.[60] Today, struggles continue for many courses about whether to focus on local law, on the leading states in a particular field of law, or on national codes.

The multiple sources of law in our system present difficult choices for editors. It is impossible to imagine a print book treating all contending jurisdictions thoroughly. Publishers would not support such a work, which would be lengthy, costly, and rarely adopted. Nor would many editors propose such multijurisdictional treatment because the returns, both economic and academic, are slight. That calculus changes with a digital format, given the vast capacity it offers. The publisher's payoff increases, with a single book providing multiple dimensions of content at low or no incremental cost and increased probability of adoptions. Editors may be more willing to exert the effort for that reason and because it is interesting to compare jurisdictions and juxtapose results. So long as it is readily tailorable, the digital product presenting multiple jurisdictions may be more appealing to teachers than what is available in print.

C. OPPORTUNITIES TO EXPLOIT

Trade-offs create opportunities, with associated costs. While most opportunities entail some costs, a few that digital law book production introduces suggest sizable gains that dwarf negligible costs. These include creating digital supplements, enabling ongoing updating of materials, and promoting skills training, each discussed in turn in this section.

1. *Supplements*

The name "casebook" was entirely apt for what C. C. Langdell and William Keener produced in the late nineteenth century because the primary legal materials were cases, and there was precious little other law included (notes aside). But today, obviously, we no longer live in a common law world. In Contracts, there are the pervasive and vital Uniform Commercial Code, dating to 1952; and more recent statutory or treaty material, such as the Convention on Contracts for the International Sale of Goods, in effect since 1988; and laws on computer contracting and consumer contracting. Besides these newer laws, the Restatements of Contracts (the first from 1932 and the second from 1979) are long-standing formulations of common law resembling statutory text.

The earliest of these noncase materials, the Restatement (First) of Contracts, was rapidly reflected in Contracts casebooks of the 1930s. Early books simply made references to the Restatement,[61] but later ones began reprinting the more important sections in full,[62] and still later ones included tables of Restatement references.[63] The same pattern followed after adoption of the Uniform Commercial Code (UCC), with Grant Gilmore offering an extensive analysis of its relation to general contract law when he joined the Kessler/Sharp book in 1970.[64] More recently, freestanding supplements have been published containing nearly complete texts of the Restatement (Second) of Contracts, the UCC, and other contemporary statutes, regulations, and related materials. Many other law school subjects likewise include both a course book and a "statutory" supplement (whether a true statute such as the Model Penal Code or other positive enactments such as the Federal Rules of Civil Procedure or securities or tax regulations).

Some contemporary teachers believe there is too much statutory material in Contracts course books on the grounds that the UCC warrants full treatment in a separate course.[65] Some think excessive incorporation of the UCC, and especially the Restatement, makes the law seem misleadingly clear and impoverishes engagement with common law opinions and methods.[66] Others insist that an emphasis on statutory and other nonjudicial texts is vital, especially in the first year, because common law appellate opinions are merely fragmentary and residual sources of contemporary law. These points of controversy raise large questions of curricular design and first-year objectives.[67] But they suggest the importance of having materials that offer the full range of treatments regarding common law and statutory enactments.

Digital materials may be more effective than their print counterparts in enabling this inclusive approach. In part, this is simply a matter of scale. Today, the printed statutory supplements for many courses can span hundreds of pages, weigh several pounds, and cost scores of dollars, yet they contain off-the-rack materials requiring little editorial judgment and include laws that are in the public domain. As a result, statutory supplements are the most handily reformatted into digital production.[68] They can be identical copies of the printed version. So prepared, they are readily available for student use, and they are lighter and cheaper. They can be easily accessed and annotated. Early movers in replicating printed statutory supplements in digital form have helped identify and resolve some bugs in the transition, as also occurred during the broader society's movement from print books to e-reader tools.

Another possibility is for editorial pioneers of digital law teaching books to include full statutory materials in course books rather than using a separate supplement. In this context, digital opportunities are tremendous, and the trade-offs and risks scant. That is certainly so with law qua law, such as enacted statutes. But model statutes prepared by organizations such as the American Bar Association, which assert copyright ownership, pose challenges.[69] They cannot simply be captured and distributed digitally but require permission and payment of fees, which can be prohibitively expensive.

2. Currency

A big selling point of any course book from Langdell to today seems to be currency – the advantage and appeal of fresh materials, including new cases. The first edition of Arthur Corbin's Contracts casebook, in 1921, set that pace. Corbin's motivation in the book, for students, teachers, and practitioners alike, was the forward-looking goal of enabling earnest thinking about "What are our American courts going to decide to-morrow?"[70] Reviewers noted with approval that nearly half the cases in the book were decided since 1900.[71] Corbin's creativity was the talk of faculty lounges.[72] Samuel Williston followed in lockstep, with his second edition of the same period featuring more than sixty new cases.[73] This pattern that Corbin and Williston established became the standard practice[74] – one that continues to this day, for all materials, but especially cases.[75]

The purpose has always been pedagogical: to provide "modern factual situations readily understandable by the student"[76] that "will hold the interest of a first year class."[77] But today's classic cases – many of those that Corbin and Williston selected

nearly a century ago – are landmarks that provide intrinsic value, historical illumi-
nation, and a sense of tradition for law and legal education. So throwing out the
classics always provokes regret among teachers,[78] and editors of print books dutifully
apologize ahead of time for the disruption. These editors must make choices, however, about when to eliminate a classic case and how to choose among vying modern ones. True, one option is to relocate removed classics from the printed version to
a teacher's manual.[79] But the digital format promises to eliminate the angst. Any case
removed can simply be placed under a special designated heading (such as optional,
alternative, or archival).

The appeal of the latest cases invites further reflections on how migration from
print to digital course books will change the editors' role and service, especially
concerning dynamic legal developments. Editors of print casebooks tend to keep
a file of new developments as days go by. At year end, they compile the file into a
printed teachers' update; this often is developed into a printed supplement to the
main text released every year or two and culminates in publication of a new edition
of the book itself after a number of years. Under this model, individual teachers in
the interim are responsible for handling new developments – the latest case, statute,
or regulation. It is up to teachers to identify important developments, digest them,
provide them to students, and determine where in the book and course sequence
they will be discussed. For courses taught widely across the country, that means multiplying the costs of covering new developments by the number of teachers inclined
to do so.

This situation opens another area of clear advantage to digital course books.
Editors would no longer be limited to maintaining a daily-developments file for
integration and transmission annually or less often. They could identify important
new cases, statutes, and regulations in real time and incorporate new materials into
the digital course book. In the most intensive real-time scenario, they could use
a compare-type function to show both the original form at the start of a semester and resulting change incorporating the new development. They could commit
to doing this weekly or monthly throughout each semester. Teachers assigning the
book could direct students at the beginning of the term to read updated materials no
earlier than one week before they were to be discussed.

For students and pedagogy in general, the benefits of this are considerable.
Treating current events in the classroom is one of the oldest pedagogical strategies
to engage students. True, if the primary purpose of legal education is to develop the
students' analytical abilities, it matters little whether discussion centers on a classic
pair of vexing cases from the 1870s or 1920s or a pair of cases from last week. But
student engagement and stimulation may be markedly different between cases set
in the alien times of old and those involving the known reality in which students
live. Using cases featuring a hogshead of tobacco, primitive shipping navigation, and

itinerant farming imposes a cognitive tax on developing students' legal skills that disappears when discussing cell phone early termination fees, Internet ticket sales, or a Pepsi television commercial involving a Harrier jet.[80]

3. *Skills Training*

To those only casually acquainted with the history of the case method, contemporary enthusiasm for teaching problems may seem to be a novel pedagogic strategy. But problems have a long and distinguished presence in law teaching, dating back nearly a century. In 1922, the prescient Henry Ballantine stressed the importance of using problems rather than or in addition to cases. They are needed to position law students in the place practice will put them, he wrote, as a "lawyer and investigator … seeking the solution."[81] Ballantine added: "Our case-books and case method of instruction still have undeveloped possibilities."[82]

In a similar spirit, Lon Fuller, father of the contemporary course book, stressed skills training in his 1947 Contracts book. It featured problems throughout to train students in lawyering skills.[83] In two chapters toward the end of the book the exercises intensified, focusing on the dynamic context of conditions and devoting "attention to problems of draftsmanship" and "problems of counseling and negotiation which may arise when a condition has not been fulfilled or when the other party has defaulted." [84] The Fuller book was innovative in its time, and these features that made a "stimulating contribution" to "training in lawyers' skills" show how truly modern it is.

In 1975, two generations later and two generations ago, Charles Knapp's course book contributed similarly valuable materials to build lawyering skills. As described by Karl Klare, Knapp's "doctrinal exposition is organized around a series of skillfully drafted hypotheticals, posing difficult counseling issues."[85] After expressing enthusiastic approval of this approach, Klare opined: "the problem-solving and counseling emphasis is further confirmation of the coming demise of the casebook method of instruction."[86] That prediction overlooked how the problem method and the casebook are not antithetical but complementary – true at least since Fuller's 1947 book. The Knapp book remains such a complementary combination of cases, materials, and problems, through its 2006 sixth edition.[87]

Many are amazed that standard Contracts courses in American law schools do not necessarily involve presenting an actual contract to the class, although fragments may appear via the cases.[88] Of course, many casebooks do present contracts, and many teachers supply them separately. Drafting exercises even occur. But an interest in the more extensive use of transactional materials has emerged in the past generation, building to a widespread movement today. To be sure, this is also not exactly something new under the sun, as it was pioneered by William O. Douglas as early as the 1930s.[89] Many books today lend themselves to a pedagogic approach that stresses the lawyer as counselor, adviser, and deal coordinator, rather than merely as litigator.[90] Even so, print books set limits on these exercises that digital books may overcome.

The great challenge in developing such materials for printed books is space. Materials required for rigorous instruction in contract drafting, as well as negotiation and counseling, may span hundreds of pages for a single transaction – many multiples of the pages required to present a judicial opinion, with its appended notes and questions. But while print formats have finite space, a digital format expands infinitely. Thus, digital course book preparers interested in using transactional materials as a mainstay of the course and course book enjoy a huge advantage over those who rely on printed course books.

As another example, storytelling has become an increasingly popular pedagogic strategy throughout the curriculum in recent years. Evidence includes the *Stories* series edited by Paul Caron and the expanding interest in legal archaeology.[91] Again, this is often seen as more novel than it is. Harold Shepherd in 1948 celebrated Fuller's notes providing additional facts about cases by quipping that the first year is not too soon to let students know that appellate opinions do not provide the full story of a case.[92] Still, storytelling appeals strongly to some scholars and teachers today, particularly those interested in literary, multicultural, or outsider approaches to law. That is epitomized in Contracts by the Kastely/Post/Ota casebook, in which literary excerpts woven throughout the material illuminate the context. Their book is imbued with a humanism that more traditional casebooks eschew.[93] This trait is worthy to provide examples of excellent, persuasive writing to students, regrettably rare in judicial opinions historically afflicted by legalese.

Some of these limits are attributable to "structural restrictions of a casebook."[94] These restrictions require the selection of illustrative cases edited to digestible length. That format necessarily sacrifices parts of the story and can oversimplify and impoverish law's narrative richness. To restore some of the narrative value, literarily inclined editors or teachers may "re-contextualize the cases" by summarizing the "context and the details of lived experience."[95] That may be feasible in print books, as Kastely/Post/Ota attest, but as with handling actual contracts, the digital format offers a wider range of possibilities. A digital course book could incorporate a variety of literary materials for each topic it includes. For example, a Torts casebook discussing product liability may include excerpts from Upton Sinclair's *The Jungle*.[96]

D. PRESENTATION RISKS WARRANTING VIGILANCE

Beyond historically informed comparisons of trade-offs between print and digital books and associated opportunities are a series of matters of presentation to which producers of works in either format must attend. Analogies from history adapted to today's digital realm help identify features that promote a book's usefulness – important whether making print or electronic materials. Discussion surveys matters from size to weight and appearance to apparatus such as tables, indices, and pagination.

Many factors determine what is the right length for a text as well as how crisply delineated its topics are. These include what is required substantively, what fits within the time frame usually allotted to a course, how a subject is divided, and what is fair to ask students to lug around. One question is whether a text should be a single volume or span multiple volumes. Though most Contracts course books have been produced in a single volume, both among the earliest and latest used multiple volumes, C. C. Langdell's 1879 Contracts casebook appeared in two volumes and Stewart Macaulay's editorial team published their 2010 *Contracts Law in Action* in a double volume.[97] A few others in between appeared in multiple volumes, too, including William Keener's 1898 follow-on to Langdell, Samuel Williston's first but not his second book,[98] and Edwin Patterson's 1936 work,[99] later consolidated into a single volume but incorporating George Goble's companion volume.[100]

Such struggles in the print world, however, dissolve in the digital world: there are no volumes in any physical sense. Volumes become just another ordering feature, akin to parts, chapters, sections, headings, and subheadings. But those delineations pose challenges too and have commanded considerable attention throughout casebook history. Early Contracts casebooks took different approaches, dividing the subject between as few as thirteen and as many as sixty-five distinct sub-headings. Teachers did not necessarily prefer one or the other.[101] But it irked some teachers to see an entire topic presented with few or no subheadings, and reviewers praised casebooks that clearly indicated their subdivisions.[102]

Debate hinged on whether the delineation gave away too much to students – that timeworn fight about the balance between hiding-the-ball and spoon-feeding. Critics of the spoon-feeding approach favored fewer headings and less delineation; their opponents stressed the need to give students at least some direction and pointed out that students still miss the guidance even when headings are used meticulously.[103] Editors responded to the critics' message and began assiduously to craft useful headings – a practice that has endured. The practice is likely to continue with digital books as well. If anything, even greater delineation may be called for to account for differences in spatial configuration. For example, screen sizes vary on e-readers while printed books are of uniform page size. Pages are viewed in windows with movement directed by rolling a pointer, rather than flipping back and forth. Greater delineation may be helpful to prevent leaving readers lost in a sea of digits.

If digital content spans more material, whether by incorporating supplements, expanding notes, or producing interactive questions, that expansion would warrant greater delineation compared to print counterparts. Further, the phenomenon of digitization alters reading and learning habits, which law students develop before attending law school. Attention spans shorten and materials must be diced into smaller manageable chunks. Increased headings and subheadings are an appealing device to promote requisite delineation – true for print and electronic books alike in the digital age.

Some of the early casebooks won credit for including one or more indices of material, a feature not appearing in all books at that time.[104] All casebooks have indices now, but the relative granularity, completeness, and accuracy of the index, especially the subject matter index, still matter and vary a great deal. One advantage of a digital arrangement is a search feature that enables electronic identification of a word or phrase anyplace where it appears. That does not dispense with the need for a subject matter index, however, which remains useful as a list of topics in a single place. Further, any search engine must operate comprehensively across a digital book's full text, as opposed to merely covering segments, such as chapters or sections. If material is searchable only within such segments, publishers must create a traditional index in linear form.

Similarly, earlier casebooks did not all have the tables that are customary today. Reviewers applauded innovative casebooks that contained tables separately listing cases or articles[105] and, later, listing Restatement sections.[106] They welcomed technical devices to aid using the tables, such as alternating roman and italic type to distinguish subclasses of items in a list (such as principal cases versus note cases). Reviewers rightly criticized those out of step with prevailing citation practices.[107] Even today, reviewers note related improvements in, such as a list of various sources of contract law pervading a book.[108] It would be a mistake to classify these inventions as peculiar products of the print world to be jettisoned in the digital one. On the contrary, clear guidance on how to find particular materials in a digital book may be more important than in a print book. After all, the entire contents of a print book are physically accessible and in plain view; the opposite is the case for digital books, where content is entirely hidden until successfully accessed.

Vital to all lengthy written expositions are page numbers, a point that seems so obvious and quotidian as to require no mention. It is difficult to imagine using an unpaginated course book, since page numbers are central for myriad purposes, from giving assignments, to referencing passages during class discussion, to citing authority. But lack of page numbers has been a serious initial hurdle in the broader community's switch from print to digital books. Page numbers do not appear in many digital books. That has been an especially serious concern since it disables citation for scholarly purposes. Though in theory digital books do not consist of pages that can be numbered, it does not seem feasible to move the course book from the print tradition to the digital format without providing some form of content numbering.

Early casebooks shunned including images of any sort. Later casebooks added photographs of distinguished judges whose opinions appear or illustrations of the facts in the cases, famously captured by the picture in Torts course books of the railroad platform from the case of *Palsgraf v. Long Island R.R.* Costs are nontrivial, however, since images reduce the room for printed materials and can be expensive to reproduce on paper. Contemporary printed books increasingly provide Internet addresses to access images (as well as other material). Digital books can include the images or links directly, opening up unprecedented possibilities for pedagogical support.

Equally prosaic matters of presentation that people care deeply about abound. For example, it has mattered for more than a century what kind of ink and paper publishers use in printed books.[109] The clarity and legibility of printing are important.[110] People care especially about the amount of white space on a page – the portion covered by type versus left open for marginal notations.[111] Reviewers of early casebooks appreciated the technological capacity to distinguish materials by type size or font;[112] many casebooks today still put footnotes in smaller type than text.[113]

People care about all such presentation features and their electronic analogues in digital books too. In the printed form, paper, ink, and margin features matter because law students underline, highlight, and annotate zealously. Digital books, and the e-readers used for them, must accommodate these habits. Most e-readers offer the opportunity to change font sizes, a plus, but publishers must develop ways to use type size and fonts and other devices to stress and highlight material in different ways. Digital books must have features that enable such exercises and make reading cognitively and physically appealing.[114]

Likewise, people have always cared about the weight and bulk of course books, often a serious problem with print versions.[115] That issue dissolves in the digital realm – probably the most conspicuous advantage. Similarly, binding is a concern – reviewers and students appreciate books that "can stand plenty of hard knocks."[116] Digital books, studied on e-readers, may fit this bill. But other challenges arise despite lighter weight and greater durability. These include memory, battery length, virus risk, and other technological matters whose complexity at least initially appears considerably greater than the problems associated with printed books.

A modern issue that technology poses concerns classroom desk space. When laptop computers first proliferated in the late 1990s, they were large and took up lots of space. That made it tricky for students to include their laptop plus a thick casebook and heavy statutory supplement on classroom desks. Laptops have since shrunk, reducing but not eliminating the physical space problem. In the digital world, books disappear into the laptop, so there may be plenty of room again for coffee and snacks on the classroom desk.

E. SYNTHESIS

A look back at a century-plus of casebook production and review in Contracts evokes the piquant French expression *plus ca change, plus c'est la meme chose*. Prescient among the casebook review authors was Henry Ballantine, who stressed in 1922:

> In a case-book the important thing is to have cases which raise the crucial and vital problems of the subject, in an interesting way, to stimulate thought and discussion. In any argument the first thing to do is to define the issues. It may be suggested that historical materials should be introduced at a point where they will shed light on these crucial questions. They frequently make a poor introduction to a subject because the student cannot appreciate their use and bearing, or what the problem is that they are intended to elucidate. The beginner can often go better from the present to the past than from the dim and uncertain past to the present.[117]

Nearly a century later, those words still resonate, whether the product is prepared in print or digitally.[118] Migration is afoot, though it is more likely to follow a characteristic incremental shift than radical revolution. That is probably desirable to enable resolving associated trade-offs, especially concerning the course book's potential purposes besides the vital one of pedagogy, and finding equilibrium on course book scope, especially concerning notes and questions. It is probably best for experimentation to proceed spontaneously, along with occasional coordination efforts, such as the production of this volume, gathering thought on the subject. That should help assure that the features of digital books work for students and teachers and other constituents, both in taking advantage of opportunities – whether concerning supplements, currency, or skills training – and being vigilant in matters of presentation that promote a book's usefulness.

Nor is there any urgency in racing to any particular destination. After all, in the migration from print to digital books, more important than what legal educators do may be what colleagues in secondary schools and undergraduate programs do. Law students will develop needs and expectations based in part on experience in those levels, and law teachers will have to adapt accordingly. It is not obvious that digital books meet any other particular need of legal education, though they overcome some limits of print books and offer some opportunities to improve pedagogy. They also present more choices, for editors initially, and teachers and students ultimately, meaning both gains and costs. The medium may not be the message, but our predecessors probably would have produced different messages had they prepared their materials in digital not print format, just as we are likely to do. Possibility, not necessity, sometimes is the mother of invention.

NOTES

1. Sidney W. Delong, "An Agnostic's Bible," *Seattle University Law Review* 20 (1997): 295; Michael B. Kelly, "Reflection on Barnett's Contracts, Cases and Doctrine," 20 *Seattle University Law Review* (1997): 343.
2. Karl Llewellyn, "On the Problem of Teaching 'Private Law,'" *Harvard Law Review* 54 (1941): 775; Roscoe Pound, "Taught Law," 37 *Representative of the A.B.A.* (1912): 97.
3. Matthew Bodie, "The Future of the Casebook: An Argument for Open Source Approach," *Journal of Legal Education* 57 (2007): 10.
4. Steve Sheppard, "Casebooks, Commentaries, and Curmudgeons: An Introductory History of Law in the Lecture Hall," *Iowa Law Review* 82 (1997): 547.
5. Bruce A. Kimball, "The Inception of Case Method Teaching in the Classrooms of the Early C. C. Langdell, 1870–1883," *Law & History Review* 17 (1999): 1.
6. David W. Amram, "Book Review," *University of Pennsylvania Law Review* 70 (1922): 373.
7. Harold C. Havighurst, "Book Review," *Iowa Law Review* 21 (1936): 661.
8. Judson A. Crane, "Book Review," *Harvard Law Review* 49 (1936): 512 (referring to the era of scientific discovery reflected in Patterson's materials, especially concerning psychiatry, mental illness, and capacity to contract).
9. Malcolm P. Sharp, "Book Review," *University of Chicago Law Review* 15 (1948): 795.
10. Benjamin Kaplan, "Book Review," *Yale Law Journal* 63 (1954): 1039.
11. Karl Klare, "Contracts Jurisprudence and the First-Year Casebook," *New York University Law Review* 54 (1979): 882.
12. Klare, "Contracts Jurisprudence," 895.
13. Kaplan, "Book Review," 1039 (Havighurst's book "goes immediately to various groups of contracts such as employment contracts, contracts for building and construction, and so forth").
14. See Robert Gordon, "Macaulay, Macneil, and the Discovery of Solidarity Power in Contract Law," *Wisconsin Law Review* (1985): 565.
15. Lawrence Friedman, *Contract Law in America: A Social and Economic Case Study* (Madison: University of Wisconsin Press, 1965).
16. See Mary Joe Frug, "Re-Reading Contracts: A Feminist Analysis of a Contracts Casebook," *American Law Review* 34 (1985): 1065.
17. Klare, "Contracts Jurisprudence," 896.
18. Lenora Ledwon, "Storytelling and Contracts," *Yale Law Journal of Law & Feminism* 13 (2001): 117.
19. Ledwon, "Storytelling and Contracts," 11.
20. [Oliver Wendell Holmes, Jr.], "Book Review," *American Law Review* 14 (1880).
21. Sheppard, "Casebooks, Commentaries, and Curmudgeons" 615, n. 365.
22. A fine-tuned search of the Internet for electronic course books in law schools will reveal a number of course books prepared by individual teachers and offered to their classes.
23. E.g., Herman Oliphant, "Book Review," *University of Illinois Law Review* 16 (1922): 645; Grover C. Grismore, "Book Review," *Michigan Law Review* 20 (1922): 373.
24. Julian S. Waterman, "Book Review," *Texas Law Review* 13 (1934): 152.

25. See Gary Neustadter, "Rethinking Electronic Casebooks," *Jurist* (1998), available on line at http://jurist.law.pitt.edu/lessons/lesjun98.htm#archive.

26. Klare, "Contracts Jurisprudence.

27. Case selection and relation could even be used to expose deeper challenges in the course, at levels of doctrine and theory. The famous example is how Friedrich Kessler and Malcolm Sharp presented cases as paired opposites, both challenging reconciliation and showing some nagging irreconcilability and thus incoherence in the common law. Kaplan, "Book Review," 1039. Similarly, Charles Knapp's selections were credited as "distinctive" in teasing out the emergence of new trends and themes in the case law through the mid-1970s, especially the roles of reliance and good faith. Klare, "Contracts Jurisprudence."

28. Kaplan, "Contracts Jurisprudence,"

29. E. Allan Farnsworth and W. F. Young, "A Casebook for All Seasons?: Another Casebook Review," *Seattle University Law Review* 21 (1998): 725.

30. Delong, "An Agnostic's Bible," 295.

31. Farnsworth and Young, "A Casebook for All Seasons?: Another Casebook Review," 725.

32. Ledwon, "Storytelling and Contracts," 117.

33. Clarke B. Whittier, "Book Review," *Yale Law Journal* 31 (1921): 220.

34. Harold Shepherd, "Book Review," *Journal of Legal Education* 1 (1948): 151; Sharp, "Book Review," 795.

35. John P. Dawson, "Book Review," *Journal of Legal Education* 6 (1954): 405.

36. Geoffrey R. Watson, "A Casebook for All Seasons?" *Seattle University Law Review* 20 (1997): 277.

37. Douglas L. Leslie, "How Not to Teach Contracts," *St. Louis University Law Journal* 44 (2000): 1300.

38. Dawson, "Book Review," 405 (noting how Havighurst and Mueller "concentrated their recent books on function or economic context," respectively).

39. Kellye Y. Testy, "Intention in Tension," *Seattle University Law Review* 20 (1997): 319; Delong, "An Agnostic's Bible," 295.

40. Klare, "Contracts Jurisprudence," 885 (noting how, with Kessler and Sharp: "historical and theoretical issues are posed as the very organizing principle of the field, superseding doctrinal categories.").

41. Watson, "A Casebook for All Seasons?" 278–7.

42. Kelly, "Reflection on Barnett's Contracts, Cases and Doctrine," 343.

43. Ledwon, "Storytelling and Contracts," 117.

44. Amram, "Book Review," 373; Whittier, "Book Review," 220; Henry W. Ballantine, "Book Review," *Yale Law Journal* 31 (1922): 569.

45. Grismore, "Book Review," 373.

46. D. W. Woodbridge, "Book Review," *Virginia Law Review* 24 (1938): 824 ("While the book is called Cases and Materials on Contracts I, about 95 per cent of the book (exclusive of notes and references) consists of cases."); T. A. Smedley, "Book Review," *Texas Law Review* 18 (1939): 118 (notes and other commentary "constitute a text discussion of some" 125 pages in a 1,200-page book); J. Denson Smith, "Book Review," *Texas Law Review* 16 (1938): 294.

47. Smedley, "Book Review," 118 ("Shepherd has made available a Contracts case book according with the case-text trend.").

48. Shepherd, "Book Review," 151.

49. Shepherd, "Book Review," 151. ("The first year is not too soon to learn that the whole story may not appear in the reported opinion.")

50. Delong, "An Agnostic's Bible," 295; "A Casebook for All Seasons?" 285.

51. Shepherd, "Book Review," 151.

52. E.g., Michael Hunter Schwartz and Denise Riebe, *Contracts: A Context and Practice Casebook* (Durham, NC: Carolina Academic Press, 2009) (innovative casebook loaded with specific tutorials to students about technique, including how to read a case, marginal annotations highlighting important points in a case, tips on preparing for class, formulas for writing legal analysis, and graphical maps of the doctrinal structure of contract law and the book).

53. M. L. Ferson, "Book Review," *Yale Law Journal* 43 (1933): 165.

54. Ferson, "Book Review," 165.

55. Crane, "Book Review," 512 (quoting from Edwin Patterson's 1935 Contracts casebook).

56. Watson, "A Casebook for All Seasons?"; see Anthony D'Amato, "The Decline and Fall of Law Teaching in the Age of Student Consumerism," *Journal of Legal Education*, 37 (1987): 485.

57. Leslie, "How Not to Teach Contracts," 1300.

58. See Kevin D. Ashley, "Designing Electronic Casebooks That Talk Back: The CATO Method," *Jurimetrics* 40 (2000): 275.

59. E.g., Whittier, "Book Review," 220.

60. E.g., Frederic P. Storke, "Book Review," *Stanford Law Review* 6 (1954): 745 (addressing the issue in the context of property security, where jurisdictional variation could be significant).

61. George W. Goble, *University of Illinois Law Review* 27 (1933): 592; Crane, "Book Review," 512.

62. Woodbridge, "Book Review," 24.

63. Smith, "Book Review" 294.

64. "Books Received," *Stanford Law Review* 23 (1971): 386.

65. Klare, "Contracts Jurisprudence," 896.

66. Kelly, "Reflection on Barnett's Contracts, Cases and Doctrine," 343.

67. See Edward Rubin, "What's Wrong with Langdell's Method and What to Do about It," *Vanderbilt Law Review* 62 (2007): 609.

68. C. Steven Bradford and Mark Hautzinger, *Digital Statutory Supplements for Legal Education: A Cheaper, Better Way* (2009).

69. I encountered these costly and burdensome copyright limitations when preparing a course book, *Law and Accounting: Cases and Materials* (St. Paul, MN: West, 2005). It featured extensive authoritative accounting regulations, legally binding on public companies and their auditors, yet protected by copyright of the organizations that produce them. See Lawrence A. Cunningham, "Private Standards in Public Law: Copyright, Lawmaking, and the Case of Accounting," *Michigan Law Review* 104 (2005): 291.

70. Whittier, "Book Review," 220.

71. Whittier, "Book Review," 220.

72. Oliphant, "Book Review," 645; Grismore, "Book Review," 373

73. Amram, "Book Review," 373.

74. Ferson, "Book Review," 175; "Reflection on Barnett's Contracts, Cases and Doctrine," 343; Havighurst, "Book Review," 661; George K. Gardner, "Book Review," *Harvard Law Review* 51 (1937): 188.

75. Kelly, "Reflection on Barnett's Contracts, Cases and Doctrine," 346 ("The case selection emphasizes the classics, though modern developments are thoroughly represented.").

76. Crane, "Book Review," 512.

77. Woodbridge, "Book Review," 24; I. Maurice Wormser, *Journal of Legal Education* 3 (1950): 145 ("students are always clamoring for the most recent cases.").

78. Woodbridge, "Book Review," 24 (lamenting that *Foakes v. Beer* was demoted from a principal case).

79. I do the former regularly with material in my book *Introductory Accounting, Finance and Auditing for Lawyers* (St. Paul, MN: West, 5th ed., 2010). Professor Knapp and his colleagues did it with an introductory case when transitioning from the fourth to the fifth edition of their Contracts book.

80. The referenced cases are *Laidlaw v. Organ*, 15 U.S. 178 (1817) (tobacco); *Raffles v. Wichelhaus*, 2 Hurl. & C. 906, 159 Eng. Rep. 375 (Eng. Excheq. 1864) (shipping); *Britton v. Turner*, 6 N.H. 481(1834) (itinerant farm labor); *Ayyad v. Sprint Spectrum, L.P.*, 2009 WL 4048035 (Cal. App. Nov. 23, 2009) (cell phone early termination fees); *New England Patriots v. StubHub*, 2009 WL 995483 (Mass. Super. Jan. 26, 2009) (internet tickets); *Leonard v. Pepsico, Inc.*, 88 F.Supp.2d 116, *aff'd*, 210 F.3d 88 (2nd Cir. 2000) (Harrier jet).

81. Ballantine, "Book Review," 569 ("more problem material should be included in our case-books").

82. Ballantine, "Book Review," 569.

83. Sharp, "Book Review," 795.

84. Sharp, "Book Review," 795.

85. Klare, "Contracts Jurisprudence," 898.

86. Klare, "Contracts Jurisprudence," 898.

87. Not all contemporary books contain problems, and there is nothing mandatory about them. As long as materials provide the springboard, teachers can add problems, even using old exams. Kelly, "Reflection on Barnett's Contracts, Cases and Doctrine," 349–50.

88. Edward Rubin, "Why Law Schools Do Not Teach Contracts and What Socioeconomics Can Do about It," *San Diego Law Review* 41 (2004): 55.

89. Sheppard, "Casebooks, Commentaries, and Curmudgeons," 626.

90. Delong, "An Agnostic's Bible," 295.

91. See Paul L. "Caron, Back to the Future: Teaching Law through Stories," *University of Cinncinatti Law Review* 71 (2002): 405.

92. Shepherd, "Casebooks, Commentaries, and Curmudgeons," 547 ("The first year is not too soon to learn that the whole story may not appear in the reported opinion.").

93. Ledwon, "Storytelling and Contracts," 117.

94. Ledwon, "Storytelling and Contracts," 117.

95. Ledwon, "Storytelling and Contracts," 117.

96. See Eric E. Johnson, Torts Compendium, vol. 2 (2011), available online at www.papers. ssrn.com/abstract_id=1753786.

97. A different version is offered in a single volume.

98. Amram, "Book Review," 373.

99. Crane, "Book Review," 512.

100. Woodbridge, "Book Review," 824.

101. Oliphant, "Book Review," 645.

102. Grismore, "Book Review," 373.
103. Ballantine, "Book Review," 569 ("The almost entire omission of section headings for fear of giving too much aid to the student seems a mistake. If there is an orderly development of topics in the various chapters it is easy for the student to overlook it, even with the aid of section headings.").
104. Grismore, "Book Review," 373; Woodbridge, "Book Review," 824; Wormser, *Journal of Legal Education*, 145.
105. Ballantine, "Book Review," 569.
106. Wormser, *Journal of Legal Education*, 145.
107. Waterman, "Book Review," 145 (addressing lack of parallel citations from local courts to national reporting system and using tentative rather than final section numbers for the Restatement).
108. Ledwon, "Storytelling and Contracts," 117.
109. Ballantine, "Book Review," 569 (Costigan's 1922 book is "clearly printed on excellent paper").
110. Smedley, "Book Review," 118 ("The type remains as clearly readable as in the previous editions.").
111. Dawson, "Book Review," 405 ("somewhat smaller type and a fuller page give about 20 per cent more reading matter page than most of the standard books.").
112. Woodbridge, "Book Review," 824.
113. E.g., Watson, "A Casebook for All Seasons?" 277.
114. Debra Moss Curtis and Judith R. Karp, "In a Case, on the Screen, Do They Remember What They've Seen? Critical Electronic Reading in the Law Classroom," *Hamline Law Review* 30 (2007): 247.
115. Woodbridge, "Book Review," 824 (applauding a 1.5-inch spine); Watson, "A Casebook for All Seasons?" 277 ("Even the compact size of the book is a plus: never has a one thousand-page tome seemed so slim and easy to carry.").
116. Woodbridge, "Book Review," 824.
117. Ballantine, "Book Review," 569.
118. I recently wrote a book on Contracts using this pedagogy. It tells stories of contract issues from current events and then introduces venerable principles and classic cases to analyze and resolve them. Lawrence A. Cunningham, Contracts in the Real World: Stories of Popular Contracts and Why They Matter (Cambridge University Press 2012). It will be useful for required or recommended first-year reading. It provides an example of the sort of book that could be prepared for torts and other first-year law courses, as well as upper level courses. A series is envisioned.

5

Smarter Law School Casebooks

John Palfrey

A. A WALK THROUGH THE LAW LIBRARY IN 2011

If one were to walk through the main reading room in the library at Harvard Law School on more or less any day during the school year, one would find most of the seats occupied by students. These students are arrayed, elbow to elbow, at long tables beneath a high, vaulted ceiling and the steady gaze of legal luminaries from the past (mostly white men, some in wigs). Though they are from many walks of life and are of varying ages, the students often have the very same objects in front of them. Some of these objects are what one would expect of young people of their generation, immersed in study. Coffee is ordinarily close at hand, primarily in school-approved, oversized mugs with tight lids to protect the library and its books from spillage; there is also a lap-top computer, connected to the wireless network as an on-ramp to the Internet.

But there is another common feature as well: an old-fashioned bound thick legal casebook. These casebooks look very much like what law books have looked like for more than a century. They are an enduring feature of the study of law – even in our increasingly digital age.

Beside the casebook, these law students have a few other, smaller objects in front of them: a ballpoint pen and a fat yellow highlighter. (An empirical review would almost certainly show that sales of yellow highlighters are higher at law school book-stores than at comparable stores on other parts of campus.) The most diligent of our law students, poring over the same cases again and again, saturate the pages of their casebooks with yellow ink as they underline the points they regard as essential; sometimes, they underline them twice, for double emphasis. And they use the ball-point pen to fill the margins of the book with notations about the holdings or dicta embedded in the opinions.[1] These casebooks have survived the advent of the digital era for a sound reason. They are an effective way to convey information to our students. They serve as useful canvases on which students can work and interact with the core material, the raw data, of legal information.

It is worth asking, though, whether we could do better in light of emerging youth practices, changes in the legal profession, and changes in the world of information and technology. As we consider what a casebook that reflects the current electronic revolution – a smarter casebook – might look like, we should do so in the context of our goals for legal education at large, as well as what we know about youth practice with respect to information and digital technologies.

B. THE ON-AGAIN, OFF-AGAIN RELATIONSHIP BETWEEN LEGAL EDUCATION AND INFORMATION TECHNOLOGIES

It is hardly a surprise that our students still use traditional textbooks to learn the law. After all, e-books have yet to take hold among youth in general, although the tide may well be turning in this area.[2] But the reasons run deeper, and they run toward those of us who teach in and lead law schools. In legal education, when it comes to technology, we tend to lurch a bit into the future, and then retreat, before – perhaps – advancing again.

In the late 1990s, we at the Harvard Law School invested millions of dollars to modernize some beautiful old classrooms. Among other things, those in charge of the renovations decided to install new chairs. The old ones were uncomfortable, harkening back to a harsher era of legal education. One gets the idea that students were expected to sit still and ramrod straight, responding to hard questions and taking notes as the professor enlightened them in legal doctrine and legal thinking. These new chairs, decidedly low-tech, were noncontroversial. The high-tech aspects of the renovation, though, presented a problem.

Along with new chairs, we decided it would make sense to install an Ethernet jack at each student's seat, along with an electric outlet for laptops, to enable students to go online during class. This renovation coincided with the dot-com era, in which students were jumping ship to start their own Internet companies. Even law firm associates and partners were leaving to join dot-coms. We decided that a modern classroom at Harvard Law School (HLS) ought to have Internet access at every seat. But we had not focused on what the effect of access to the Internet during class would be. Earlier attempts at building technology into the learning experience at HLS – like Project PERICLES and the Bridge Project – had involved experimentation in specific, limited contexts. In contrast, these Ethernet jacks at every seat represented a sea change, masked as a room renovation, in terms of how our students would relate to information.

Shortly after they were installed, we decided that the Ethernet jacks – the on-ramps to the Internet – should be turned off. Students could plug their laptops into the electrical sockets and take notes during class, if they must, but the notion of a classroom full of students surfing the Web during a Socratic teaching session was disconcerting. Other proposals included an intricate compromise plan whereby professors would be given access to a Frankenstein switch at the front of the room to make their own decisions on any given day as to whether or not the Ethernet jacks would be live. Most recently, we considered a proposal whereby students' schedules would be automatically tracked, and Internet access would be unavailable whenever the students were in class.

A decade later, no one uses the Ethernet jacks in our renovated classrooms. But the students consistently access the Internet during class when we permit them to bring their laptops. They do so through the wireless networks that blanket the Harvard campus (and much of the city of Cambridge, for that matter). During class, if we let them, our students go online.

Their online activities during class vary. Some are doing their e-mail, reading the news on CNN, or sending instant messages in an elaborate network of back-channel communication with their peers; others are accessing Wikipedia to learn (maybe) what happened in that case they did not quite finish reading in advance of class. There is no effective technological way to stop them from doing so, short of banning laptops in the classroom – a topic that comes up, more or less annually, in our information technology (IT) committee (and the IT committees of our peer schools, for that matter). Other kinds of regulation could plausibly work: tactics such as installing mirrors and situating teaching fellows at the back of the room to keep an eye on every screen might adjust student behavior, to a certain extent. Across legal academia, some faculty members seek to keep the technology out of the classroom; others seek to harness the Web for pedagogical purposes; and others are still scratching their heads about it all, wondering what happened, so quickly and with so little deliberation, to legal education. But all such measures and concerns miss the fundamental issues at work.

C. LAW STUDENTS AS DIGITAL NATIVES

Instead of asking how we can best keep technology out of legal education and the publication of teaching materials, we ought instead to work harder at solving the problem of how to use it to our advantage. A look into the data regarding youth practice is an instructive place to start.

Schools at every level of education have struggled with the onset of digital technologies, much as law schools have. Many schools have invested in the technological infrastructure before working out exactly what they want to do with that technology in teaching and the publication of teaching materials. Some schools have distributed a laptop or a tablet personal computer (PC) to all the students, often the result of a specifically directed subsidy, and then wondered what to have the students do with the computers (or regretted what they *did* do with them).[3] Others have spent tens of thousands of dollars to equip every classroom with a SmartBoard (a computerized chalkboard that sits at the front of the room) only to wonder, after the substantial checks were cashed, whether the SmartBoards belong there. Now that wireless Internet access, both commercial and academically provided, blankets many campuses and urban areas, schools are wondering whether to boost the signals or to find ways to try to block them from bleeding into the classrooms (almost certainly a futile task). Teachers and administrators at large are utterly confused about the potential impact of technology on learning.

Forward-looking schools know that technological infrastructure is likely to be a worthwhile investment over time. Information technology can enhance productivity, burnish the image of a school for the purpose of attracting new faculty and the strongest student applicants, and facilitate access to information in libraries and elsewhere. But very few schools have any idea about when to use these technologies to support their pedagogical missions – and, just as important, when *not* to use them. And very few schools have figured out the connection between their own missions and the way young people are learning, both formally and informally, in a digital age.

The way to approach this problem is not to start with the technology per se or the format of the casebook, for that matter. We should begin instead with a broad conceptual framework about the shifting nature of information, knowledge, and learning. We need to understand better the changing ways that young people relate to information, to one another, and to institutions. We need to examine how learning and information-processing behaviors – for better *and* for worse – are changing over time for the students who are entering law schools. We need to seek to understand the manner in which information in general, and new media in particular, are increasingly constitutive elements of what it means for young people to function as productive, well-adjusted social beings.[4] We need to understand the cognitive processes and constraints associated with the youth practices that we observe. And then, in turn, we need to apply this understanding to the project of legal education and scholarship. We need to be clear about our theories of teaching and learning and how technology can help us to accomplish our pedagogical goals, and then to work from there to think about the role that we would like technology to play in the way that our students learn the law.

Many adults, including law professors, are worried about how kids are learning. We worry, with reason, that kids are not reading books cover-to-cover the way they used to. Librarians worry that kids are only looking at a narrow range of sources to which they have been referred by a single monolithic corporation, such as Google; or, conversely, that they are looking at an infinite number of sources, making no distinction about their relative credibility. Senior faculty members worry that their students are failing to find highly relevant articles that online databases do not go far enough back to include. Slogans in headline format, they fear, dominate the information seeping into young people's brains, with kids developing too few analytical skills along the way. Our students, the worry goes, are channel-surfing through their education. Some neuroscientists argue that their brains are being rewired in the process; at a minimum, students are forming habits of interacting with information that may be hard to break over time.

Some, though not all, of the concerns we have about the way students are learning in a digital age have merit. We know that students entering law school spend a growing amount of time engaged in activities mediated by digital technologies.[5] For the young people I and others have studied, research is much more likely to mean a Google search than a trip to the library or the use of sophisticated databases.[6] They are more likely to check Wikipedia, or to turn to an online friend, than they are to ask a reference librarian for help unless we tell them they have to show up, physically, in the library. They rarely, if ever, buy the newspaper; instead, they graze through copious amounts of news and other information online. They multitask during class (to the detriment of what they are learning) and during dinner (to the detriment of family harmony). On the positive side of the ledger, our most talented students can be extremely creative and innovative using these new tools when given the opportunity to do so.

These attributes of these students' information-seeking behavior are relevant to our teaching and policy making. The Internet is changing the way that young people gather and process information in all aspects of their lives. Our challenge, as teachers and researchers, is to pry apart the challenges from the opportunities and find ways to use these insights to inform our academic practices, the way that we publish our teaching materials, and even the way that we disseminate our own scholarship.

D. HOW DIGITAL NATIVES BEHAVE

1. *Methodology of the Investigation*

While we know that the mode of learning for many young people is changing rapidly, understanding the precise dynamics of this change is a major challenge.[7] Too often, we make decisions – public and academic policy generally, and plans for new course materials specifically – without the benefit of any data about how young people are relating to information and to one another through digitally mediated technologies. The costs of doing so are most easily seen in the chaotic public policy related to child safety and privacy online, as well as in the futile and ill-advised attempt to strengthen intellectual property protections along nearly every dimension.[8]

In framing policy for legal education, this chapter draws upon multiple data sources, derived through a variety of methods. First, I rely upon large-scale quantitative and ethnographic studies of youth in the United States conducted by other researchers.[9] Second, along with colleagues in our law library, I surveyed enrolled Harvard Law School students in 2009, and again in 2011, through a short online survey and conducted a series of focus groups about their research interests and information use. Third, in 2007, along with colleagues at the Berkman Center, I conducted a series of three focus groups and interviews with young people that explored the way they relate to information and to one another.[10]

Focus groups suited our investigation, since we sought to gain access to youth discourse regarding their digital practices. This method of investigation enabled us to explore issues surrounding learning practices and information-seeking behaviors, because students seemed to be at ease in discussing their varying styles of behavior when in a group of their peers.[11]

The focus groups in the 2007 study consisted of students in three separate age categories: twelve to thirteen, fourteen to eighteen, and nineteen to twenty-two. A survey was administered to the participants to obtain background information about the technologies they owned and had access to, their usage patterns and practices, and the sorts of issues they were aware of with regard to digital technologies. Survey administration was followed by a ninety-minute semi-structured conversation with students about a range of issues surrounding technology use. We also contacted some students for sixty-minute one-on-one follow-up interviews.

The focus group sessions were structured using a protocol under which we asked students about their experiences with digital media: their behaviors, their opinions, the role information and technologies play in their lives, and the way they negotiate specific issues and situations. While the protocol provided the basic structure of the sessions, the moderator encouraged respondent-led explorations of the topics, including how young people conduct research, how they seek information in their daily lives, and the role that technology plays in their learning. These data have obvious limits in terms of how much we extrapolate on the basis of them, but I offer them as a starting point for thinking about a smarter casebook and how technology might fit better in legal education.

On the basis of these data, my colleagues and I define the subset of young people whose practices we examine and learn from as "Digital Natives." We embrace this awkward term because of its cultural resonance.[12] We define "Digital Natives" as a specific population of young people born after 1980, who have grown up in a networked world and have the skills to use digital technologies. They relate to information, to new technologies, and to one another in common ways. When they chat with each other online, broadcast their latest videos, post messages on their social network profiles (or, less frequently, on blogs), or share music over peer-to-peer networks, they do so across states, national boundaries, and continents. These digitally mediated habits are grounded in real-world customs, habits, and values that vary by region, race, age, socioeconomic status, and other factors.

2. *Youth Practices Regarding Information and Technology*

These studies, along with those that others have conducted, reveal a range of practices that characterize our Digital Natives. First, we know that they multitask. Our students do so in class and while doing their homework, as well as at other times (what we call "interstitial moments") throughout the day. Law teaching faculty do not need focus group or survey data to reveal this behavior. We see it with regularity in our classrooms: In courses where laptops are permitted, most students have a computer in front of them, connected to the Internet, at all times. As teachers at the front of the room, we can tell that students are using the Internet during a seminar to instant message (IM) one another, read news online, and otherwise amuse themselves. They smirk, trying in vain to suppress a smile, when they receive a funny IM from a classmate while others in the class are working through a complex and utterly serious appellate opinion. We have legitimate concerns about students' not paying enough attention to the task at hand – learning about legal doctrine, how to think like lawyers, and so forth. With a world of information and connections to friends at their fingertips at all times, the temptation to stray from the course is great – often, too great.

Multitasking is almost always bad when a student is trying to learn new things or is doing something that requires a lot of attention.[13] One of the reasons that we did not want access to the Internet in the classroom was to prevent students from being distracted by playing solitaire (or, thanks to Internet connectivity, playing hearts, as my colleague Jonathan Zittrain notes) on their computers during class. With good reason, we might sometimes wish to return to the day when the students were still sitting up ramrod straight in those uncomfortable chairs and (maybe) paying more attention during class.

Second, there is reason to worry about shorter attention spans of Digital Natives. There are real issues brewing here. Many kids do demonstrate a preference for reading shorter works rather than longer ones. They migrate from things like extended format magazines and books to the Web.[14] On the Web, shorter formats ordinarily work better, whether in text, audio, or video. The same is true for text messaging, instant messaging, and even e-mailing. In ways both of their own making and of mass media generally, our students are living in a sound-bite culture.

Some of the young people we interviewed stressed their preference for instant messaging and texting, as a mode of communication with others, as compared to voice communications (by phone or face to face). This is true of many of us, not just of our youth. All news seekers are rewarded for flitting about with tighter and tighter sound bites from more and more sources. For Digital Natives, the phenomenon is the same, only amplified.[15]

Third, the extensive use of technology can lead to a "copy-and-paste" culture. This practice is a source of concern because it is in tension with educational ethics. Digital Natives report consistently that technology-enabled cheating is on the rise on college campuses, especially in technical disciplines, where students increasingly work together on assignments while they are required to submit their "own" answers.[16]

Fourth, and most important, Digital Natives gather information through a multistep process that involves grazing, a deep-dive, and a feedback loop. They graze through the huge amount of information that comes their way on a daily basis.[17] While grazing, they absorb a headline or a bit more – perhaps a paragraph's worth – about any given story. The information is valuable insofar as it is timely, relevant, and easy to process. The fact that it can be accessed from anywhere – that Facebook newsfeed is channeled through a cell phone that is constantly attached to a Digital Native's body – is equally important. And the interface through which Digital Natives get this information is more useful and attractive to them the more that it can enable them to sort through the vast rivers of information flowing around them all the time.

With some of those stories a Digital Native sees, he or she decides to go beyond the headline, to learn more about a topic or event – to take what we call a "deep dive." In this way, she is searching for what is behind the headline, what the facts are, what they could mean for her, what the people involved looked like, and so forth. It might involve clicking on a hypertext link, loading up a video, or downloading a podcast to listen to on the train. The deep dive helps her to make sense of the news, to put it into a frame or context. This stage in the news-gathering process for Digital Natives is when they interact with traditional media, especially the most powerful and wealthy institutions – those firms and other organizations able to afford bureaus and extensive online presences in addition to local newsrooms. The key factors for salience of information online, beyond timeliness, are accuracy, trustworthiness, insight, analysis, new angles, and relationships.

Some Digital Natives will go further by creating a feedback loop. This means that they actively engage with the information, sometimes in new ways.[18] The form of a Digital Native's feedback loops varies. She is most likely to post a link to a news story on her Facebook page. She might write a post to her blog to critique a story she saw on CNN. She might comment on someone else's blog, or on a wiki or bulletin board. It is possible that she would "tweet" it to her "followers" (as of December 2010, eighteen- to twenty-nine-year-olds were the most likely to be using Twitter of all the demographic groups studied by the Pew Internet and American Life Researchers).[19]

Or perhaps she will send an e-mail to a listserv or to a network news program. If she is especially creative she might create her own podcast or video-blog (some call it, unfortunately, a "vlog"). In short, she may react publicly to the story or to remake and retell it in some fashion.

The feedback loop might also involve passing the information around to friends and family. Digital information has a social life in the hands of Digital Natives. They share it with one another, post stories to their profiles in social network sites, and talk about it on instant messaging or on blogs. It is not every young person who engages with information in this interactive way, but it is more than most parents and teachers think. The same instinct that leads a new Web user to circulate so many e-mail jokes (and scams) animates the news- and information-sharing behavior of Digital Natives. The difference between a Digital Native and one's aunt with the new e-mail account in this regard is that the Digital Native is likely more sophisticated about what she shares and how. Digital tools enable her to have an impact on the way the story is told. This feedback loop can be a powerful aspect of learning; it is one that is largely untapped in formal education.

Digital Natives' familiarity with technology, however, can make them overconfident about their ability to perform research. Despite high comfort levels with searching for information in the digital realm, students require more research instruction, not less, as they need to unlearn behaviors such as trying to adapt simple keyword searches learned through Google searching to the more complex research engines we rely on in legal scholarship and practice, including Westlaw, Lexis, and the new Bloomberg Law service.

These behaviors are obvious to anyone who teaches Digital Natives or manages them in a workplace. And the generational divide is not as crisp as some perceive it to be. Many adults who have migrated to the Web do just the same things as young people. Obvious though they may be, the concerns they raise are serious ones.

E. DESIGN PRINCIPLES FOR A SMARTER CASEBOOK

The fact that Digital Natives do not learn things in the same way that their grandparents did does not mean that the way that they are learning is worse. The evidence that we have so far does not indicate that they learn things less effectively than their grandparents did, or even more superficially.[20] The people to be worried about are those who are growing up in a digital age but who are not learning these sophisticated information-gathering, -processing, and -creation skills. A key part of our job as teachers of future lawyers is to ensure that all of our students gain the best skills they can to navigate this increasingly complex information environment.

Learning will always have certain enduring qualities that have little or nothing to do with technology. We should not overhaul legal education, nor the format of the casebook on which we rely so heavily today as a teaching tool, in an attempt merely to conform to the ways that our students are using digital media. But we should explore the means to unlock new ways to teach our students to thrive as lawyers in the information-rich environment in which they will be practicing.

Given what we know about how students are learning in a digital age, there are many ways we can harness what is great about the way Digital Natives relate to and use information. At the same time, we need to address the legitimate problems that are cropping up in their learning processes.

A central part of this effort should be for law schools to participate, with publishers and others, in the design of a smarter casebook. The idea of a smarter casebook should be, at a general level, to harness what is great and possible about the digital era and how young people are using new technologies and relating to information as they learn. At the same time, these smarter casebooks should be geared toward scaffolding the student learning experience in a way that will help them to avoid some of the mistakes that we know they are making as they learn. The idea would be to engage students more actively in the material, connect their learning to the work of their peers, and tie the teaching materials into the broader context of primary and secondary legal materials increasingly found in reliable formats on the open Internet.

As part of the process of designing smarter casebooks, law schools should also work to develop new kinds of cases. Law schools might disseminate our learning and teaching innovations by becoming publishers of specially designed teaching cases. Examples from Harvard Law School might be those prepared for the new Problem Solving Workshop and our Executive Education program, designed for integration into a smarter casebook framework. The stronger form of this argument might call for us to gravitate toward a combination of broad, centralized delivery of core information (such as case materials) and decentralized discussion and reflection. The reach of our work beyond the law school classroom, facilitated by new technologies, could serve the broader legal community as well as each law school's own students and faculty.

The following five principles ought to guide our own design of a smarter casebook and how they might be integrated into our evolving approach to law teaching with technology.

1. **We should use technology in our teaching and casebook development *only* where it serves an express, stated pedagogical purpose.** We need to determine what our goals are, as teachers of law students entering practice and scholarship in the early twenty-first century, and then figure out how technology can help us, and our students, reach those goals.[21] We should not use advanced technologies for their own sake. We should ask hard questions to

ensure that our use of technology is doing more good than harm. We ought to experiment with ways in which technology can become part of the law school curriculum – but only where it belongs and where it can help to meet an articulated purpose as determined by us as teachers.

The things that schools and teachers do best should not be scrapped in the rush to use technologies in the classroom. In every field, there are aspects of the curriculum that should be taught with screens and net connections nowhere in sight. The computer has no place in the classroom where a wonderful teacher is firing questions at a first-year student. This approach yields positive externalities: When students are not on their laptops, class gets better (and more worth paying attention to, in a virtuous cycle) for everyone. Some of our students agree. Surveys of young people consistently indicate that they prefer only a moderate use of technology in the classroom.[22]

One way to avoid banning laptops in the classroom, but use them instead to our advantage, would by developing smarter casebooks that drew upon the information-gathering styles of Digital Natives. A casebook that worked, for instance, on a tablet PC might include digital versions of the case material, as a first step toward a more interactive learning experience. Links from the core cases being discussed to the cases that the court is citing constitute an obvious next step, allowing students to perform a "deep dive" into the material. In the context of a course on administrative law, or a first-year class on Legislation and Regulation, it might be useful to have an interactive statute in front of students during the in-room discussion. But these changes are little more than an incremental improvement on having a pile of books open in front of students in class.

These smarter casebooks might do more. One problem in legal education is the tendency of students, especially in the fall semester of the first year, to take steno-graphic notes, meant to capture every word the professor says. A smarter casebook might draw upon the Digital Native's feedback loop to integrate the functionality of shared note taking and annotation, either for a study group of four or five students or for a first-year section of, say, eighty students. Through collaboration, a designated student could be the primary note taker for the day, rotating to another person the next day. These notes could be stored in the cloud in a manner that is tied to the smarter casebook itself, with links and references to the texts. This approach could allow the students who are not on note-taking duty to pay greater attention to the flow of discussion in the class without the fear of losing the ability to review the material in written form. If a student wished to take notes locally and individually, rather than in the cloud and collaboratively, he would still retain that option, but he would be freed from the necessity of doing so. Students might also comment on one another's notes, as they do in the feedback loop stage of their news- and information-gathering processes in the social media context.

There are many variations on this theme. It might be applied to annotation during the process of studying: Instead of taking notes via yellow highlighter on one's own, students in a study group could use an improved, networked interface to share notations and to accept or reject the notations of a fellow student after the fact. The basic idea would be to use the smarter casebook as one vehicle to take advantage of the networked classroom and library, rather than having students use it only for distraction and multitasking that detract from the learning experience.

2. **We should promote innovative uses of information and technology where they can best support the preparation of our students for the practice of law.** Lawyers in practice are increasingly dependent on the use of advanced technology tools for information retrieval and processing to do their work. The use of information is having profound effects on the way the law is practiced and the way the marketplace for legal practice is changing.[23] Our efforts to apply the use of technology in teaching should be coordinated not just with our research on how our students' information-related behaviors are changing, but also how the profession in which we work is changing and the role of information in driving some of these trends.

Programs in which students are doing problem solving, applied work, research and writing, or collaborative work are obvious places to experiment with new technologies in learning.[24] Examples include the Problem Solving Workshop offered to first-year students at Harvard Law School; legal research courses, including both the first-year Legal Research and Writing and advanced courses; many, if not most, of our clinical offerings; courses in Evidence, where the discovery process has already been transformed by information technology; and courses in which the substantive topic involves this technology, such as Internet law and certain intellectual property courses.

Consider the means by which we might use technology to help students work more effectively in teams, a pedagogical goal employed in certain courses and tied to the way that lawyers work in practice. In each of our winter terms since 2010, seven of us at Harvard Law School have taught a new Problem Solving Workshop to the current first-year class. In that course, we assign students to teams of four or five for the purpose of completing more or less daily assignments. Teams use collaborative software – such as Google Docs, EtherPad, and MindManager – to work together in and out of class.

Digitally supported environments, including smarter casebooks, can help students working in teams perform their tasks more effectively and improve their output by enabling them to give feedback to one another. In addition to the idea of group note taking, simple technologies such as wikis, blogs, and podcasts – all of which are supported by our course-management platform – can help team-based learning in other contexts. These technologies could easily be integrated with the teaching materials in a smarter casebook.

Research indicates that interaction and a strong sense of community are among the most common requests of those born digital when it comes to online learning.[25] As students research, write, and create collaboratively through online environments, they will be learning skills that will serve them well over time, even as digital economies evolve. For any class that involves writing, digital technologies can be put to work as a feedback loop for students to comment on the material they are studying or on the ideas of their peers.[26] This feedback loop could be much better developed and facilitated through a smarter casebook than as a standalone application. It will not only improve legal learning, but also redound to the benefit of society at large over time. But this will not happen unless we pay attention to fostering the positive behavior that it involves.[27]

A smarter casebook could also help to prompt integrated, effective forms of legal research training. Hiring partners in law firms complain that our students are not entering practice with the technological skills that they ought to have.[28] We can use information technologies as a means of improving the way we teach research, both through sophisticated databases like Westlaw and Lexis and through empirical data sets and other nonlaw sources of information that are increasingly relevant to legal practice and scholarship. One area where technology will play a role of this sort is through "Prepare to Practice"–type short programs for students in the spring semester before they enter their summer employment. The premise of these programs, in large part, is to ensure that students *unlearn* some of the research assumptions they took with them to law school and replace them with the legal research skills that they will need to succeed in their first forays into practice. A smarter casebook could also serve as the platform through which such programs can be taught.

3. **We should promote targeted, creative uses of technology by students and experimentation by faculty; establish mechanisms to assess outcomes of these experiments; and disseminate best practices for information- and technology-related projects.** We have not set out to promote innovation in the use of information and technology in legal education as an institutional priority in the past. We have not yet established means of engaging students through active learning in classrooms or in our library in ways that build upon emerging youth media practices.[29]

This third principle is plainly in tension with the first principle. I have argued that we should only use technology in our teaching where it can serve a pedagogical purpose; here, I argue that we should experiment, take risks, and even fail periodically. These conflicting principles can be reconciled in two ways. First, there is no chance that every member of any law school faculty would agree to a single mode of teaching. As a result, what may sound like a crazy idea to one faculty member may serve an articulated pedagogical goal for another. Given that students have different learning styles, this diversity is generally a good thing. Second, in some classes, experimentation with the technology per se – tinkering, coding, remixing material – may itself be a pedagogical goal.

Smarter casebooks can help to support this experimentation and can enable comparisons between various innovative approaches and more traditional modes of teaching. Creative teachers and their students will come up with exciting ideas if we provide them with the support and the institutional structure to experiment, to fail, and to build on successes. Faculty members and students might look to important aspects of youth practice and find ways to leverage them in the teaching enterprise. Schools that can discover ways to tap into young people's love of gaming have an opportunity to capture an area of substantial creativity and engagement, most easily seen in younger learners, for whom games help to teach mathematics, science, and languages.[30] Likewise, we know from research that students are extremely creative when it comes to making videos and can convey a great deal of information through graphical and audio representation.

These practices hold promise in terms of engaging students in active forms of learning. But both are puzzling in terms of how we might integrate them into our law school curriculum.

Smarter casebooks are an obvious way to experiment with active learning approaches. The best application of these ideas in legal education, via smarter casebooks or otherwise, is not obvious. But the payoff could be substantial, for student and teacher alike.[31]

We ought to support, incentivize, and reward experimentation by faculty who wish to use technology in new ways in their teaching and their publication of teaching materials. We should strive to make it easy for faculty to experiment – especially those who do not have the ability to write code themselves – by thinking of smarter casebooks as highly configurable by those without technical ability. Teachers know best which problems they need to solve and which opportunities they want to seize. We need to provide enough support for experimentation so that we can try out new approaches, assess critically their effectiveness, and enable the most successful forms of creativity to take hold and to flourish, in step with and in support of, curricular reform.[32] We should invest in a series of experiments designed to accomplish specific pedagogical goals and then offer support to others who wish to adopt the successful innovations.[33]

In addition to promoting innovation, we will need to invest in modes of sharing successes with one another to enable their easy adoption by others. Where one faculty member, for instance, has successfully developed and integrated technological tools that support a particular course, we should find ways for him or her to share those practices with teachers whose classes might benefit from the innovation. From a collection of successful experiments, we should build a system of teaching one another to adopt best practices for the integration of technology in teaching where it can help. Institutions like the Center for Computer-Assisted Instruction (CALI), which has experimented with the eLangdell platform for smarter casebooks, could be the cross-law-school means of sharing best practices of this sort.

4. **We should look to librarians as partners in teaching our students in a digital era in ways that build on our respective strengths.** This chapter has focused primarily on the way we as classroom teachers and authors of smarter casebooks ought to adjust to the changing relationship between our students and information. But law librarians also have a major role to play as our partners in this work.

To the extent that we frame the issue as being about "information" and how we interact with it, rather than about "technology" as such, the connection between the institution of the library – especially the library of the future – and the teaching of law students becomes clearer.[34] Librarians can, and should, serve as key partners to faculty and academic administrators in accomplishing the school's mission, especially during this period of transition with respect to information and how our students interact with it.[35]

There has never been a greater need for librarians than there is today, given the new skills that our students need and the depth and breadth of materials available to them.[36] Libraries will be staffed increasingly by those who can serve as guides to students who need to navigate an increasingly complicated information environment – and who do not all have the "native" skills to do so. This is a teaching role that must complement the teaching that is going on in the classroom and in our clinics. The point is not to give in to every whim of every user; after all, much of the Google-search practice of Digital Natives often translates poorly into searching in Westlaw and Lexis. Rather, librarians need to figure out which information-seeking practices to reinforce and which to correct during a period of rapid change in user behavior. The job of the librarian of the future should in part be to help to create a self-service information environment that allows students and faculty members to navigate the increasingly complex array of choices for getting the information that they need.

There are many specific examples of how librarians can partner with faculty to help improve our teaching through technology. First, they can develop forms databases, which include many commonly used legal documents as forms to be filled out with specific details, akin to what students will encounter in legal practice, and teach students to use them as they learn legal research and writing. Second, in addition to traditional pools of knowledge (such as books, journals, and case studies), librarians can help our students figure out how to manage the rivers of digital information that they encounter every day. Right now, libraries are focused on the pools; librarians needs to redirect them to focus on the rivers. A third way in which librarians can help is to codevelop specialized course materials using software such as MindMaps, as one librarian has with a Harvard Law School professor, Terry Fisher, for advanced courses on Intellectual Property. Each of these approaches could be integrated into a smarter casebook framework to improve the way our students learn the law.

5. **We should use technology to help break down the barriers between law schools and those communities with whom we seek greater interaction in the service of our core mission, such as scholars in other disciplines and legal practitioners.** Technology can help us to engage practicing lawyers in teaching specialized classes where their expertise can enrich the learning experience of our students. This engagement might take the form of an appearance by video conference in a course, a recorded video session shared with students as a supplement to course materials, or interactive sessions using digital media that enable students to connect to experts who are not physically present in the classroom. These approaches might well complement our outreach to international communities as well as to those in other, related academic disciplines.

F. LOOKING FORWARD

Law school casebook publishers have yet to offer students a compelling digital alternative to the traditional printed casebook. The reasons for this slow development may appear obvious. For starters, the traditional casebook remains an effective way to convey legal information for a traditional doctrinal course in law. Also, the casebook market remains profitable for law professors, publishers, and campus booksellers alike. Law students still appear willing to spend as much as one hundred dollars or more for a mass-produced book that contains mostly state-generated, public domain texts in the form of cases, along with commentary and questions from faculty members. Last, there are barriers associated with copyright concerns, initial investment costs, and general inertia in the publishing world that have stood in the way of developing a smarter casebook.

An additional, possibly even more important reason for the slow development of smarter casebooks is that law school faculty have not yet led the way. We as law faculty can, and should, work on the design of smarter casebooks. Smarter casebooks need to be more than just lighter and cheaper in order to gain mass adoption; they need to be better at conveying legal information and at supporting the kind of legal education that we strive to provide to our students in the twenty-first century. We should work from sound data and first principles, related to pedagogical goals, and from there design and build platforms on which these smarter casebooks might emerge.

In addition to our own research, we should incorporate learning from other academic disciplines into the process of smarter casebook design. From a research perspective, many hard questions remain to be asked and answered about how our students are learning in a digital environment as compared to a predominantly analog world. How does extensive reading of Web sites, instead of books and broadsheet-style newspapers, change the way that law students process information in the short and long terms? Do law students remember the information that they gather online more or less effectively than material they read on a printed page? Is the way that law students read these days a cause or an effect of diminishing attention spans (or both)? Are law students learning anything of value while playing all those video games that consume so much of their free time – or, put another way, could they be learning something? How will these changes in learning and thinking patterns affect performance of our students in law school and in the practice of law? Psychologists, neuroscientists, and educational theorists, among others, are working on these and many other questions about how new technologies are affecting the ways that our law students absorb and retain information. Their findings can help us to translate observable behavior in our law students into better teaching, learning, and publishing practices, using technology and otherwise. We should commit to finding ways to draw upon the work of the best of these researchers to inform our own academic practice and policy making.

At many law schools around the United States, we as legal educators are in the midst of implementing the most radical reform of law school curricula in more than a century. At the same time, we also seek to expand our international and interdisciplinary reach, as well as to connect more effectively to those in the legal profession. The use of technology in learning, research, and publication – grounded in empirical data about how our students relate to information – can play a key supporting role in this curricular reform. During this transition, we need to focus on discerning what we want to preserve about traditional legal education and information-related practices and what to replace with new, digitally mediated processes. Sometimes, this will mean teaching our students how to use technologies better; sometimes computers will have no place in the room. We need to get much better at telling the two apart. We need to avoid the trap of fetishizing youth technology practice, on the one side, and of fearing youth media practice and learning styles, on the other. We should devote ourselves to setting academic policies and experimenting with new teaching, research, and publication practices that exploit what we know about how students are learning in this increasingly digital era to prepare them for careers in the law. Smarter casebooks are not an end in themselves, but a means of helping us to achieve our broader goals. A smarter casebook, if thoughtfully designed to take advantage of what is great about youth practice in the digital era, while mitigating its downsides, can play a major role in this reform process.

G. CONCLUSION

We should design smarter new law school casebooks that will help us to prepare our students for a life in practice or in legal scholarship in the twenty-first century. The process of designing these smarter new casebooks should be grounded in two sets of data. First, we ought to build from data external to the law school environment, including what we know about youth practices and about the exciting interactive possibilities of information technologies. These social scientific and technical data can help to inform this process of remaking law teaching materials. Second, the design of smarter casebooks should be grounded in a clear understanding of our own pedagogical goals and should be integrated fully into the ongoing process of redesigning law school curricula for the twenty-first-century practice of law. The design of smarter casebooks ought to be situated alongside other experimentation with the role of digital technology and information in the classroom, in research, in the law school library's collections, and in clinical practice. Taken together, these are investments that can pay substantial dividends over the long term for our students and for the profession of law as a whole.

NOTES

1. Notations in the margins of law school casebooks are not new to this generation of law students. Rather, this tradition goes back for hundreds of years. In its Historical and Special Collections, the Harvard Law School, among others, has developed a collection of early casebooks from the nineteenth century, in which marginal comments appear regularly.
2. In summer 2010, Amazon.com reported that the sales of e-books for its Kindle device surpassed sales of hard covers for the first time. Claire Cain Miller, "Amazon Says E-Books Now Top Hardcover Sales," *New York Times*, 19 July 2010, at http://www.nytimes.com/2010/07/20/technology/20kindle.html.
3. For instance, the former governor of the state of Maine, Angus King, initiated a laptop program statewide, in which all public school children are provided laptops. The program is still rolling out, several years later, and the conversations about what to do with the technology in the schools continue to be fierce. Private schools are frequently described as "lap-top schools" or "tablet schools." *See*, e.g., Dwight-Englewood School in Englewood, NJ, at http://www.d-e.org.
4. *See* Mizuko Ito, et al., *Hanging Out, Messing Around, and Geeking Out: Kids Living and Learning with New Media* (Cambridge, MA: MIT Press, 2010), 18.
5. This fact is sufficiently well established as to be something of which one could take judicial notice. One study that shows change of this sort over time in a peer-reviewed journal is Steve Jones, Camille Johnson-Yale, Sarah Millermaier, and Francisco Seoane

Perez, "Everyday Life, Online: U.S. College Students' Use of the Internet," *First Monday* [Online], 14 (10) (September 25, 2009).

6. This concept has been established in a series of national studies of U.S. college students, as well as in our smaller studies, in the form of focus groups and interviews, of students in the Northeast of the United States. *See* Alison J. Head and Michael H. Eisenberg, "Lessons Learned: How College Students Seek Information in a Digital Age," Project Information Literacy Final Report, December 2009, at http://projectinfolit.org/pdfs/PIL_ Fall2009_Year1Report_12_2009.pdf. *See also* Head and Eisenberg, "Finding Context: What Today's College Students Say about Conducting Research in the Digital Age," PIL Progress Report, 2009, at http://projectinfolit.org/pdfs/PIL_ProgressReport_2_2009. pdf (last accessed February 2010).

7. It is not the case that all young people are Digital Natives. Nor is it the case that young people are the only ones who happen to relate to information in the ways that I describe in this chapter. One of the most important public policy issues to emerge from this research is the participation gap between those students who have great facility with digital technologies and those who do not.

8. *See*, e.g., John Palfrey, Urs Gasser, Miriam Simun, and Rosalie Fay Barnes, "Youth, Creativity, and Copyright in the Digital Age," *International Journal of Learning and Media* 1(2) (2009): 79 (for discussion of ways to address intellectual property concerns raised by youth media practices).

9. Many of the best large-scale quantitative research studies have been conducted by the Pew Internet and American Life project, led by Amanda Lenhart and her colleagues. Eszter Hargittai of Northwestern University has conducted excellent studies of college-age learners. The Kaiser Family Foundation has performed important work in this respect. Qualitative studies and ethnographies by researchers such as Mizuko Ito and Danah Boyd are equally important sources of understanding youth practices with respect to information and technology. As one example of a source on which I rely heavily for background as to the practices of today's youth, *see* Ito et al., *Hanging Out* (which describes the findings of a multiyear, multimethod ethnographic study of youth media practices, supported by a $3.3 million grant from the MacArthur Foundation).

10. We recruited respondents via educators and administrators at the middle school, high school, after school, and university levels. We expended particular effort to obtain a diverse group of respondents with regard to socioeconomic status, as well as inclination toward participating in creative activity online.

11. It is important to address at the beginning the limitations of our study: We explored youth discourse surrounding their use of digital technologies within a particular and limited population, one not representative of any larger group. We do not aim to make generalizable statements about youth perceptions of those issues at a larger scale.

12. *See*, e.g., Marc Prensky, "Digital Natives, Digital Immigrants," *On the Horizon* 9(5) (2001): 1–6.

13. The topic of mutlitasking and whether it is good or bad is much more complex than I have let on in these few paragraphs. There is a great deal of work being done by neuroscientists to try to understand this phenomenon. One question is whether "multitasking" is in fact possible. Most research suggests that it is not: that the proper term is "switchtasking," whereby people (young or older) are not holding two thoughts in their heads but rather switching quickly from one idea to another. There are instances in which switchtasking may be beneficial for productivity, and it may be that young learners are becoming

effective at switching quickly between tasks in ways that will make them more productive learners. But, as a matter of shorthand, we know with certainty that doing e-mail during class time does not enhance the learning experience. *See* Urs Gasser and John Palfrey, "Mastering Multitasking," *Educational Leadership*, March 2009, at 15.

14. *See* "Young People and News," at http://www.ksg.harvard.edu/presspol/carnegie_knight/ young_news_web.pdf. Also, see anecdotal reports, such as http://www.newyorker.com/ online/blogs/hendrikhertzberg/2007/08/omen.html (not just Digital Natives, but others, too, are turning away from printed newspapers in favor of online news sources).

15. William Zinsser, in his book on writing, described his reader as someone "assailed on every side by forces competing for his time: by newspapers and magazines, by television and radio, by his stereo and videocassettes, by his wife and children and pets, by his house and his yard and all the gadgets that he has bought to keep them spruce, and by that most potent of competitors, sleep." William Zinsser, *On Writing Well* (New York: Harper, 1998), 9.

16. *See* Ben McNeely, "Using Technology as a Learning Tool, Not Just the Cool New Thing," in *Educating the Net Generation*, eds. Diana G. Oblinger and James L. Oblinger (Washington, DC: Educause, 2005), 4.6 et seq.

17. Another way of describing the grazing practice is "fortuitous searching." *See* Ito et al., *Hanging Out*, 54–7.

18. This dynamic – whereby young people have gone from consumers to creators of information – lies at the heart of some of the most exciting developments in the digital era. This transition is chronicled and theorized by Yochai Benkler in his seminal work, *The Wealth of Networks: How Social Production Transforms Markets and Freedom* (New Haven: Yale University Press, 2007); Lawrence Lessig, in multiple works including *Code and Other Laws of Cyberspace, Version 2.0* (New York: Basic Books, 2006), *Free Culture: The Nature and Future of Creativity* (New York: Penguin, 2004), and *Remix: Making Art and Commerce Thrive in the Hybrid Economy* (New York: Penguin, 2008); and William W. Fisher III in *Promises to Keep: Technology, Law and the Future of Entertainment* (Stanford, CA: Stanford University Press, 2004). *See also* the community of news producers at Global Voices, at http://www.globalvoicesonline.org/.

19. *See* "Overview: The People Who Use Twitter," at http://www.pewinternet.org/Reports/2010/ Twitter-Update-2010/Findings/Overview.aspx.

20. Others disagree with me on this point. *See* Mark Bauerlein, *The Dumbest Generation: How the Digital Age Stupefies Young Americans and Jeopardizes Our Future (Or, Don't Trust Anyone under 30)* (New York: Jeremy P. Tarcher/Penguin, 2008).

21. Howard Gardner, professor at the Harvard Graduate School of Education, has given a lot of thought to how technology can play a part in teaching. He and his research team have, for decades, been paying close attention to how children learn and what role ethics play in their lives, online and in real space. Through a project called Good Play (a derivative of his long-running Good Work project), he and his team are interviewing educators and young people about how they use technologies in learning and development. In a short essay he wrote about teaching and technology, Gardner starts by stating two educational goals, and then asks how the technologies can help us to get there with our students. "First," Gardner writes, "we should help students become certain kinds of adults." This goal makes particular sense in the context of our broader frame for learning. We should think in terms of both what we as educators should strive to accomplish and how we need to think about our role vis-à-vis Digital Natives. We want to encourage Digital Natives

to become responsible citizens. Here we are faced with a particular challenge. Digital Natives often (though not always) think that they are more anonymous than they really are when they act online. That challenge can also be an opportunity: to turn the experiences when this anonymity proves to be an illusion into ways to teach about accountability, about taking responsibility and acting ethically, whether online or off. Second, Gardner says, we should use technology to help students understand how thinking within certain disciplines works. The goal of these applications of new technologies would be to help them to improve their own analytical skills by, say, experiencing how scientists think about conducting an experiment or how a composer goes about writing a sonata. This, too, seems just right. This approach allows teachers to tap into two of the great promises that new technologies hold out. One is offering greater access to more people to more primary information at little or no cost. Think of the data sets that can be made available to young scientists or the copies of original documents to young historians. Another great promise is the ability to experiment with those primary materials oneself, to create in a nearly costless way in the manner that professionals do. *See* Howard Gardner (2000). "Can Technology Exploit Our Many Ways of Knowing?" In D. T. Gordon (Ed.), *The Digital Classroom: How Technology Is Changing the Way We Teach and Learn* (Cambridge, MA: President and Fellows of Harvard College, 2000), pp. 32–35.

22. According to one survey, roughly 30 percent of students preferred taking courses that use extensive levels of technology, while about 25 percent preferred limited or nonuse of technology in the classroom; not surprisingly, engineering students were the ones with highest preference for its use. *See* Robert B. Kvavik, "Convenience, Communications, and Control: How Students Use Technology," in Oblinger and Oblinger, *Educating the Net Generation*, 7.8–7.10.

23. Milton C. Regan, Jr., and Palmer T. Heenan, "Supply Chains and Porous Boundaries: The Disaggregation of Legal Services." *Fordham Law Review*, 78 (December 2010): 2137–2191; Georgetown Law and Economics Research Paper No. 11-04.

24. *See*, e.g., Alma R. Clayton-Pedersen with Nancy O'Neill, "Curricula Designed to Meet 21st-Century Expectations," in Oblinger and Oblinger, *Educating the Net Generation*, 9.1–9.16.

25. Joel Hartman, Patsy Moskal, and Chuck Dziuban, "Preparing the Academy of Today for the Learner of Tomorrow," in Oblinger and Oblinger, *Educating the Net Generation*, 6.7–6.10.

26. Jonathan Zittrain and his team at the Berkman Center have developed custom software, called the H2o Rotisserie, to facilitate this process. It can be accessed on the Web and used for free at http://h2o.law.harvard.edu.

27. While the effects of this mode of learning – both in gathering and in recreating information – pose real problems for print and other content-owning industries, those with strong brands should be able to thrive. There is no evidence that Digital Natives have less interest in news and information than those who are older. But studies do show clearly that Digital Natives are not engaging with news and information in the same way as it has historically been offered by these industries. Studies of the user-generated content environment show that the news items that spur the most conversation on blogs and similar sites are often first published by mainstream news providers such as the *New York Times*. The *Times* is an example of a company that has invested heavily in an accessible, effective online format for its world-class news. Their senior leadership has a strong vision for how the news will be provided and engaged with in the future. Good things in new

formats will enable strong brands to lead in a digital era. The work of many researchers shows graphically the importance of strong brands and mainstream voices in setting the agenda for the user-generated content world in many instances. John Kelly, chief scientist at Morningside Analytics and an affiliate of the Berkman Center, has shown this effect in the U.S. blogosphere, as well as in others around the world. The findings of Clay Shirky, in his famous works on the power law distribution, similarly suggest that strong brands set agendas and drive discourse. See http://www.shirky.com/writings/powerlaw_weblog. html.

28. *See* Gene Koo, "New Skills, New Learning: Legal Education and the Promise of New Technology," Berkman Center Publication Series, No. 2007–04, 26 March 2007, at http://papers.ssrn.com/sol3/papers.cfm?abstract_id=976646.

29. *See* Paul Caron and Rafael Gely, "Taking Back the Law School Classroom: Using Technology to Foster Active Student Learning," *Journal of Legal Education*, 54, (2004): 551.

30. Experimentation by faculty might include creative use of gaming in the classroom, for instance. Many parents and teachers complain about the short attention spans of their kids; those same kids seem to have very long attention spans for gaming. The technologies themselves can be used to address the problems to which their use contributes, such as short attention spans. *See*, e.g., Marc Prensky, "Engage Me or Enrage Me," *Educause*, September/October 2005, at http://www.educause.edu/ir/library/pdf/erm0553.pdf.

31. Zephyr Teachout, one of our most creative colleagues (an associate professor of law at Fordham Law School), wrote about an idea of this sort in an op-ed in the *New York Times*. She said we should use the changing nature of presidential debates in the United States to make available online much more primary material of presidential candidates speaking to one another. The idea would be to make the results of minidebates available for any-one, Digital Natives or not, to remake these files themselves and to repost them. A high school world history class might splice together the most revealing interactions on foreign policy with one another, perhaps with added commentary built in by the remaker of the film. Zephyr Teachout, "Time of Their Lives," *New York Times*, 17 August 2007, Op-Ed page (A23).

32. A group of pioneers in the field of education have developed great curricular materials that are a good place for schools to start. Experimental curricula for many subject areas, at many levels of teacher, are under development across the world. Many of these tools are available for free reuse. The BBC launched a multiyear effort, BBC Jam, to develop interactive teaching materials for school-age children over several years. Howard Gardner is developing curricula along with Henry Jenkins and the New Media Literacies program at MIT. The MIT OpenCourseWare project offers free access to the teaching materials related to nearly all MIT courses. More and more free teaching materials are posted to the Web each year. See also http://teachdigital.pbwiki.com/curriculum.

33. A great example of a faculty development program is the Virginia Tech's Faculty Development Institute, which helps faculty members to use teaching strategies that lever-age instructional technologies to improve learning (http://www.fdi.vt.edu/). *See* Anne H. Moore, John F. Moore, and Shelli B. Fowler, "Faculty Development for the Net Generation," in Oblinger and Oblinger, *Educating the Net Generation*, 11.1–11.16.

34. We are headed into an era that is neither purely analog nor purely digital, but rather "digital-plus." Legal information is born digital, as in the case of a Word document that becomes a book or law review article, but we may choose to render it in both digital

(i.e., the Kindle edition) and analog (i.e., the paperback) formats. Digitization has meant that books and printed journals – in their classic, bound format – are not the only way to convey information. Patrons have more options than they used to. Just as iTunes offered customers an à la carte approach to obtaining music that transformed the recording industry's revenue model, publishers are signing on to allow people to buy one chapter at a time. Google lets customers sample books before buying them and offers full-text search access to scholarly material in Google Scholar and the Google Books project. More profoundly, we can access materials from around the world, in law and in related disciplines, at no cost for our patrons and deliver them electronically to their desks. Legal information itself is much more accessible. Librarians have a key role to play in working with faculty members to redefine access to legal information and to rethink the legal casebook to take advantage of digital technologies and different modes of learning. For all the wonder and excitement of the digital era, it is important to stress that books are not dead. Far from it, in fact. Books for many people remain a very good technology. Hard copies of books are important on many levels. Many people, including young people we have studied, prefer to read hard copies of books to digital forms of books. (Kids often describe their preference for books roughly in the same terms as adults: They prefer books for the "three Bs": the bed, the bath, and the beach. Annotation in the margins of books is another important factor for users who prefer books in hard-copy formats.) Despite massive investments in technologies like the eInk at the MIT Media Lab and other user-interface improvements, the experience of reading books on a screen cannot yet compete with the experience of reading a book printed on rich paper. Books do not run out of batteries on airplanes, as an Amazon Kindle does all too quickly in the middle of a gripping novel. Some people, including our students, still collect books on bookshelves as signals of knowledge (or for easy access). Books represent a stable format, unlike the constantly changing digital formats that imperil digital record-keeping processes over the long term. Books are the cornerstone, for now at least, of the large and important publishing industry, whose leaders play an important role in democracies and cultures around the world. Books have the advantage, under U.S. and European law at least, of being covered by the first sale doctrine and the principle of exhaustion, respectively (you can give them away, or lend them, or sell them in a secondary market). But books have downsides, too – the slow fire phenomenon (whereby books of a certain vintage are deteriorating quickly), the high cost of production (compared to their digital counterparts), and the high cost of storage and distribution (though that cost may in fact prove lower, over long periods, than that of virtual materials, counterintuitively). We continue to acquire monographs primarily in hard-copy format. In contrast, we are now acquiring many serials in electronic format through online databases.

35. There is an important tangent that starts here – about the future of libraries broadly – but falls outside the scope of this paper. Changes for libraries are, in the near term, more radical than the changes in the classroom. Libraries are the facet of education that is today changing the most substantially as a result of changes in digital technology and usage patterns. Librarians at every level, and certainly in law schools, are asking hard questions about every aspect of their role. As our students situate themselves differently with respect to information, so too must librarians. In nearly every aspect of their job, librarians face harder and more important tasks than ever before. The conversation about the future of libraries ordinarily centers initially on the question of collections. Librarians face hard questions in terms of selecting materials to acquire, especially given the increasing

importance of digital resources, as well as those in hard copy, to the library's core users. The problem is that both digital works and traditional print materials cost more money than they used to, and far more in the way of material is published every year around the world in fields such as law. The ideal scenario – in which a collection includes a hard copy of every book or serial and a digital copy as well, for searching, cataloging, borrowing, and citation – is implausible. The cost of acquiring an increasing number of works in two formats and maintaining dual systems (analog and digital) is prohibitive. For the first time, we at the Harvard Law School have written and published a collection development policy to describe our mode of maintaining and growing our collection of materials, including books but also datasets and digital materials of many sorts. Librarians face a perfect storm of changes, including major transformations (and threats) in the publishing world. The combination of print-on-demand and digitization of new works is the largest growth story in publishing and in libraries. Law school libraries are devoting less and less room on campus to books and printed serials; nearly half of our library's materials are now more than twenty-five miles away, in remote storage in Southborough. Concurrently, libraries are teaming up with one another to acquire books that can be delivered just in time to patrons, but not collected at each physical library. And librarians can also serve as partners with faculty members in developing new course materials, such as helping to develop MindMaps for, say, courses on intellectual property.

36. Libraries will play many different roles in the future. For instance, libraries in law schools and elsewhere have a role to play in preserving knowledge over time as well as providing access to our patrons of today. The correspondence of our current faculty members (not to mention Digital Natives) and of everyone living in the digital age may well be less likely to be preserved than the writings of ninth-century monks on sturdy parchment. Libraries should also think in terms of collections that will amount to the digital heritage of the Digital Natives and their peers. The collection of digital resources by every library, historical society, museum, and other collecting institution will become an essential part of what it means to gather resources for the public. In a world where our children are born digital, these collections can be freely online and available to anyone, anywhere in the world – not just those within walking or driving distance of each library. This heritage needs to be preserved. It should take the form of a digital commons without the constraints of physical (as in, via atoms) distribution, from the start, as Digital Natives create many of the artifacts that successive generations will wish to study. Consider, for instance, the Canadian digital heritage initiative: http://www.alouettecanada.ca/home-e.php.

6

Law Games: The Importance of Virtual Worlds and Serious Video Games for the Future of Legal Education

Gregory Silverman

Indeed, what is a "career" or a "vocation" except a role-playing game extended over an adult lifetime?

  – Merlin Donald, Professor of Cognitive Science, Case Western Reserve University

I never try to teach my students anything. I only try to create an environment in which they can learn.

  – Albert Einstein

PROLOGUE

Arno stood before the large glass windows of his corner office looking out over the smooth lowland plains of Powell. The subsurface water-ice just below the cold and lifeless plains glistened eerily under the two moons of the Martian night sky. His eyes tensed as he tried to make out the distant furrows formed by civilian prospectors when the planet was first settled a century ago. The early settlers had thought that the plains would contain rich deposits of a rare mineral needed for interstellar travel found elsewhere on the planet. Only after they had burrowed their warrens into the planet's surface at the edge of the plains did they discover their error, and when these miners manqué moved on to more lucrative land claims, Starfleet had moved in and turned this early settlement into its primary Martian base, housing, among other bureaucratic departments and offices, the legal division, in which Arno was the Judge Advocate responsible for matters involving mineral rights and land transactions. As Arno gazed out into the Martian night, he reflected on the curious path that his life had taken. Who would have thought five years ago when he had begun his studies at Starfleet Academy that he would end up an off-world lawyer negotiating mineral rights for the Federation and drafting deeds on Mars. Yet here he was, after a busy day of negotiations and drafting, standing in his office, looking out over the plains of Powell.

But Arno's thoughts are not his own. Arno is Michael's avatar and Arno's thoughts, Michael's projections. Michael is a first-year law student and, through Arno, is participating in a massively multiplayer online role-playing game designed to teach him and his fellow students the law of property. The game takes place in a virtual world, an imaginative depiction of Mars in the second half of the twenty-third century. Within this game, Mars is a member of the United Federation of Planets, and the relevant Martian land law is curiously similar to early twenty-first-century property law in the United States. Michael is just completing the latest challenge that the game has presented to him. Through his avatar Arno, Michael has been tasked with the challenge of negotiating the mineral rights to a large deposit of dilithium crystals, a mineral used to regulate the matter-antimatter reaction in the gravimetric field displacement manifold of a warp engine enabling faster-than-light travel by Federation starships. The settlers, who at the start of the challenge had held the rights to the dilithium deposit, were represented by Veronica, another student in his property class, through an avatar named Niki. Niki had turned out to be a tough negotiator, and Michael had been unable to secure an unconditional fee interest in the deposit within the budget that the game had given him. Instead, he had to settle for a defeasible fee – one that would revert to the settlers if the Federation stopped using dilithium crystals in the warp engines of its starships. As they negotiated the form of the grant, however, it soon became apparent to Michael that Veronica had not yet completed the game's learning path on defeasible fee simple estates. She had allowed Michael to draft the grant as a fee simple determinable, rather than as a fee simple subject to condition subsequent. While not exactly an overwhelming victory, it did at least preserve the possibility that the Federation could quietly acquire a fee simple absolute interest in the deposit by adverse possession, should it ever stop using dilithium crystals in its warp engines. This little nuance had earned Michael enough bonus points that he was now sure he would be able to level up after the next challenge.

Professor Silverman, an unrepentant Trekker (not Trekkie) since his youth, imagines for the briefest moment that he is seated in the captain's chair on the bridge of the Starship *Enterprise* as he swivels before several large monitors. The monitor on his right contains a window into the game world through which he is watching in real time the avatars of two of his students negotiating over Martian mineral rights. A few clicks of the mouse and Silverman can see below each avatar the learning paths within the game that each student has completed. If he so desires, Silverman can enter the game himself as the fabled law wizard Lex Rechtigkeit to assist, advise, and instruct his students at any time during their game play. Silverman has also created and strategically positioned a series of in-game videos of the law wizard to provide just-in-time instruction to the students automatically as they reach various points in the game. On the center monitor,

Silverman is running a data mining algorithm, the results of which are used to generate a series of reports on the progress of his ninety property students. Some reports highlight individual students at risk of not adequately mastering the course subject matter. Others provide a statistical analysis of those course topics giving the class the most difficulty – Silverman often uses these reports to design lesson plans for their face-to-face class sessions. Still other reports document the progress and status of each student along the myriad learning paths embedded within the game. At any time, Silverman can also call up a complete learning profile of any of his students, including a detailed history of his or her play within the game. The monitor on the left provides a view of the game's discussion forum, Facebook page, and Twitter feed. These communication technologies support a robust community around the game, and using them, Professor Silverman can jump in and out of student online conversations about the individual challenges with which they are struggling within the game and the property topics that they have to master in order to meet those challenges.

Professor Silverman's property class has been virtualized – it has become a liminal hybrid existing half in this world and half in another. At present, this property class is but a virtual virtuality, subsisting as mere idea. Nonetheless, the concept and eventual development of such a class are of the utmost importance for the future of legal education, but to appreciate its significance, we must first focus on the here and now and confront the current crisis in American law schools.

A. THE CURRENT CRISIS IN AMERICAN LEGAL EDUCATION

American law schools and legal education are in crisis. Our students tell us that they are bored and unhappy. Judges and lawyers tell us that our students are not adequately prepared to practice law. Our colleagues from other parts of the university tell us that our teaching methods are antiquated and ineffective. The federal government tells us that the education that we are providing to our students is not worth the price that we are charging – implying that its continuing existence in its present form must be due to some type of unlawful collusive activity. As if to lend credence to this charge, the American Bar Association tells us that it is reforming its accreditation standards for law schools – presumably to prevent prosecutions for collusive activity under the antitrust laws. Most recently, a spate of articles in the national media report that a growing number of our students are demanding their money back – arguing that we somehow fraudulently induced them to enter law school.

Yet, ostrichlike, resisting the obvious conclusion to be drawn from these critiques, comments, and charges emanating from the myriad constituencies American law schools serve, more than a few law professors defensively intone that American legal education is the finest in the world. Lamentably, even if these colleagues of ours are correct, it proves only that the crisis in legal education is a global one – an unfortunate and unsettling conclusion.

No doubt, an American legal education was once indeed the finest in the world, but since those glory days the world has changed. We now live in a high-tech, digital, postindustrial world of global competition that is evolving as quickly as the information technologies on which it relies. As part of this societal transformation and evolution, pedagogical practices have changed, the practice of law has changed and, most importantly, our students have changed. The problem is that American law schools have not kept pace with these changes, and it will take more than occasional curriculum reforms to realign American legal education with the needs of our students in the twenty-first-century digital society in which we live.

I do not pretend to have the needed blueprint for comprehensively reforming legal education to address the many problems it faces, but I do have one suggestion for reforming, in part, our present pedagogical practices and activities in response to the current crisis: We should start playing video games: games with our students, serious games.

Serious games are games used for a purpose other than mere entertainment, usually to train and educate. Serious video games were pioneered by the Department of Defense. In 1995, together with the National Science Foundation, it sponsored a conference on the way that recent advances in computer games and entertainment might impact military strategic planning. This conference included not only members of the military and computer scientists, but also TV and movie directors, studio executives, and other professionals from the Hollywood creative community. After this conference, the Defense Modeling and Simulation Office, the Army Research Center, and the Defense Advanced Research Projects Agency (the government agency that brought us the Internet, originally conceived as a military communications network that would survive a nuclear attack), intrigued with the possibility of using story-based simulations to improve military training in skills crucial to leadership, strategic analysis, and tactical decision making under stress, initiated a series of projects in collaboration with Paramount Digital Entertainment and the University of Southern California. Over the next nine years, this collaboration of Hollywood, the academy, and the military yielded a series of training systems of increasing sophistication, culminating in *Leaders*, a system using a 3-D virtual world inhabited by virtual characters – one of the first serious video games of the twenty-first century.[1]

During this same period, the significance of gaming technologies for education did not go unnoticed outside the defense establishment and Hollywood. In 2001, the corporate trainer and consultant Marc Prensky wrote his groundbreaking manifesto, *Digital Game-Based Learning*,[2] and in 2003, the literacy scholar Professor James

Paul Gee published his immensely influential book, *What Video Games Have to Teach Us about Learning and Literacy*.[3] These two works founded today's serious games movement, a movement that has grown tremendously over the last seven years.

In light of these developments, my suggestion is a simple and obvious one: Law schools should take serious games seriously. In this article, I briefly sketch the reasons why serious video games should be incorporated into the law school curriculum. Part B explores the close connections among play, games, and learning and explains why serious games are superior to both free play and simulations in education. Part C sets out several reasons why playing video games in particular is being heralded as an essential element in the reform of our schools for the twenty-first century. Finally, Part D considers how incorporating serious video games into the law school curriculum would address many of the concerns voiced by the myriad critics of American legal education.

B. THE THEORY OF SERIOUS GAMES

1. *Playing and Learning*

In the popular imagination, playing games and school have very little to do with one another. Every elementary school pupil has had the experience of glancing up at the classroom clock and watching the second hand move ever more slowly as the big hand approaches the minute when class is scheduled to end and recess begins. "Playing games happens on the playground, not in the classroom" is a precept held with certitude by generations of teachers and well understood and accepted by students. Recent work in neuroscience, cognitive psychology, and evolutionary biology, however, suggests that the disjunction between school and playing games is misplaced. Researchers from across the disciplines now realize that there is a close, fundamental, and indeed primal connection between playing and learning.

The significance of play to learning is demonstrated, at the most primal level, by the ubiquity of play throughout the animal kingdom and down the evolutionary ladder. The evolutionary biologist Robert Fagen has documented play behavior in many species of social mammals and smart birds, including aardvarks, apes, bears, bats, chimpanzees, leopards, lions, wolves, hyenas, ravens, rats, sparrows, squirrels, deer, pigs, bison, and hippopotamuses – not to mention dogs and cats.[4] For example, Stuart Brown remarks, ravens will slide down snowy slopes on their backs, only to fly back to the top of the hill and do it again; hippos will do backflips in the water over and over again; and bison will "repeatedly run onto a frozen lake and slide on all fours while trumpeting exultantly."[5] Beyond social mammals and smart birds, play behavior is also found in the lower orders of the animal kingdom, including octopuses, certain territorial fish, and ants.

The pervasiveness of play behavior throughout the animal kingdom and down the evolutionary ladder suggests that play, far from being purposeless, is favored by natural selection. Fagen points outs that given the significant costs of play (expenditure of energy, increased vulnerability to predators, increased risk of injury, etc.), the "play instinct" must serve an important purpose to have survived in so many species of animals.[6] Fagen's own research with bears has demonstrated that "the bears that played the most were the ones who survived best."[7] On the basis of this and a growing body of research on play, the emerging consensus of the scientific community holds that play is favored by natural selection because it provides a safe environment, inter alia, to learn about one's environment, practice the skills one will need to survive in the future, and successfully socialize – all tasks that a developing lawyer must accomplish!

Proceeding from animals to people, the preeminent neuroscientist on play, Jaak Panksepp, notes that "[a] leaflet in a box of Lego® toys says it all." The leaflet, quoted in his leading textbook on affective neuroscience, reads as follows:

> When children play, they exercise their senses, their intellect, their emotions, their imaginations – keenly and energetically.... To play is to explore, to discover and to experiment. Playing helps children develop ideas and gain experience. It gives them a wealth of knowledge and information about the world in which they live – and about themselves. So *to play is to learn*. Play is fun for children. But it's much more than that – it's good for them, and it's necessary. ... Play gives children the opportunity to develop and use the many talents they were born with.[8]

Nor does the importance of play to learning end with childhood: Panksepp observes that Albert Einstein "remained mentally young and playful throughout his life" and reminds us that Einstein was being playful "when he imagined what it would be like to ride a beam of light" – the playful *Gedankenexperiment* that led to his greatest discovery.[9] Indeed, there is now a consensus among researchers that an adult's capacity for creativity and innovation in all areas of human endeavor is a direct result of the neotenous extension of such juvenile characteristics as playfulness into adulthood, an extension facilitated by the fact that humans have the longest childhood of any creatures on the planet.

Recent work in neuroscience further establishes the close connection between play and learning. Indirectly, play promotes neurogenesis and brain development. Panksepp, for instance, has shown that "active play selectively stimulates brain-derived neurotrophic factor (which stimulates nerve growth) in the amygdala (where emotions get processed) and the dorsolateral prefrontal cortex (where executive decisions are processed)."[10] More directly, play "promotes the creation of new connections ... between neurons and between disparate brain centers."[11] In other words, play "seems to be a driving force helping to sculpt how the brain continues to grow and develop."[12] It creates and strengthens the dendritic connections among neurons and regions of the brain that form the neural network and brain circuitry constituting the physical substrate of an individual's knowledge and skills.

The foregoing makes clear that psychologists, evolutionary biologists, ethologists, and neuroscientists agree that play is very important to learning. All this is to say that the idea of playing games in school should not be rejected out of hand as somehow not sufficiently serious. The crowning achievements of the arts and sciences – for the sake of which schools exist in the first place – are likely no more than the inevitable result of the mature neocortex's channeling our primitive, playful, ludic urges in different, more symbolic directions. While many educators have written on the importance of play, many schools, and most law schools, have yet to embrace play as a pedagogical method and harness the power of these ludic urges in the service of education.[13] It is time to do so: The question is how.

2. *Games versus Free Play*

The human brain's ability to recognize and match patterns is unrivaled in nature. Our development of the knowledge and skills necessary to our survival in the world ultimately rests on this ability to see patterns and formulate generalizations based upon them. Nonetheless, our ability to recognize subtle and nuanced patterns does not guarantee that we will always arrive at fruitful and important generalizations concerning the world around us. "Humans don't learn well when they are just left entirely on their own devices to operate within complex contexts about which they know very little."[14] Students, for example, "left to discover Galileo's laws of the pendulum on their own by mucking around with bobs, string, and pendulums are likely only to be frustrated."[15] As Professor James Gee observes, "the real world is not in and of itself well designed for learning," and "[l]eaving children to the mercies of the real world by just letting them loose to think and explore is not education."[16]

If a student is to master a discipline through play, both the play and the environment in which it occurs must be initially designed and structured in a manner that will facilitate the student's grasp of the basic and fundamental patterns and generalizations of that discipline and provide the student with opportunities to learn and practice that discipline's core skills. Moreover, as the student masters these basic and fundamental patterns and skills, the play environment must facilitate the student's progress by confronting her with situations from which she can discern more advanced patterns and generalizations of that discipline as well as learn and practice more advanced skills.

How is this to be done? How are we to structure a student's play so that it will result in mastery of a specific subject? The answer is with games. To promote the mastery of specific subjects through play, play must be structured in the form of a game.

Philosophers, linguists, anthropologists, economists, mathematicians, cognitive psychologists, and computer scientists have long reflected on the nature of games to gain insight into various topics within their own disciplines.[17] Curiously, however, it is only relatively recently that scholars have begun to study games for their own sake. While the emergence of game studies as an academic discipline may be dated to the writings of Johan Huizinga and Roger Caillois in the 1950s,[18] the growth in excitement and energy surrounding the study of games closely tracks the increasing commercial and cultural importance of video games. At the turn of the new millennium, this work gave birth to a new subdiscipline, now known as video game studies. Throughout this entire period, game scholars have attempted to develop a general account of games and the manner in which video games differ from classic nonelectronic games. While not all game scholars have endorsed the endeavor, much ink has been spilled trying to define what a game is.

Recently, the video games scholar Jesper Juul has surveyed these various definitions and distilled their common elements into what he calls the Classic Game Model. Under the Classic Game Model, "a game is

1. a rule-based formal system;
2. with variable and quantifiable outcomes;
3. where different outcomes are assigned different values;
4. where the player exerts effort in order to influence the outcome;
5. the player feels emotionally attached to the outcome; and
6. the consequences of the activity are optional and negotiable."[19]

According to Juul, the Classic Game Model characterizes the necessary and sufficient conditions for something to be a game.[20]

Of the various features composing the Classic Game Model, the one most relevant to the learning process is the rule set. The formal system of rules at the core of every game has two key functions. First, it limits the actions that a player may take within the game. "Rules are 'sets of instructions,' and following those instructions means doing what the rules require and not doing something else instead."[21] In a race around a track, for example, one must remain on the track; one may not cross through the center to reach the finish line. Second, rules create the possibility of meaningful actions that are not available outside the game. Only within the game of chess can one (literally) checkmate one's opponent. A team's quarterback cannot make the winning touchdown, or the losing fumble, outside the game of football. Rules provide these two functions for the modern video game just as they do for more traditional games: "the video game needs rules that let the characters move as well as that prevent the character from reaching the goal immediately."[22] It is worth emphasizing that an essential potential action set up by the rules of a game is, of course, achieving the goal and meeting the challenge required to win the game. The rules direct the play of the game by setting the goal; without this, the activity would be aimless "free play."

By both limiting and creating potential player actions, "rules give games structure,"[23] and it is through this structure that game designers can shape and control the patterns presented within a game – the patterns that the game teaches. These patterns may arise in two different ways. First, an individual rule may represent a pattern. For example, the en passant rule in chess represents a pattern involving pawns from both players,[24] while the castling rule represents a pattern involving a player's king and rook. The ability of rules to represent patterns is not unique to rules of games. The legal rule of battery, for example, represents a pattern of liability in the law of torts. Second, patterns emerge from the interaction of different rules. The rules of chess, for example, generate such patterns as forks, discovered checks, pins, skewers, and many other tactical formations – none of which is represented by individual rules.[25] In a game, the emergent patterns are simply those patterns "that players cannot immediately deduce from the rules of the game."[26] A game's rules represent and generate the patterns that the game contains. The player discerns and learns these patterns through gameplay. Unless she learns these patterns, she will not be able to develop the strategies that she needs to achieve the goal and meet the challenges presented by the game. Effective strategies are developed with knowledge of the regularities and structures immanent in the patterns contained in the game. In other words, learning is essential to success in a game – if you want to win, you have to learn. Hence, the power of playing games for learning.

It should now be clear why play must be structured as a game in order to facilitate learning a specific subject such as law. Free, unstructured play does not have any rules, and rules are necessary to represent and generate the patterns from which a student can discern and learn the regularities and generalizations that form the content of the subject to be learned.

3. *Games versus Simulations*

The final feature of games under Juul's Classic Game Model is that the consequences of playing a game be optional and negotiable. While players can choose to impose real world consequences on a game's outcome as in gambling, they need not do so. Games do not necessarily have consequences in the real world. As the French philosopher and sociologist Roger Callois emphasized, "the game's domain is a restricted, closed, protected universe: a pure space."[27] In this space, "[t]he confused and intricate laws of ordinary life are replaced ... by precise, arbitrary, unexceptionable rules that must be accepted as such and that govern the correct playing of the game."[28] Games are "separate: circumscribed within limits of space and time, defined and fixed in advance."[29] The historian Johan Huizinga called this space in which games are played "the magic circle," explaining that "[i]nside the circle of the game the laws and customs of ordinary life no longer count."[30] But what exactly fills this "pure space" and "magic circle" of the game? The game designers Ernest Adams and Andrew Rollings provide a hint when they define gameplay as "one or more causally linked series of challenges in a simulated environment."[31] This definition implies that the magic circle or space of a game contains a simulation. The educational theorist David Shaffer makes this explicit when he writes that "any game has, at its core, a simulation."[32] As he notes, "most of the things that we call computer or video games – educational titles like *Math Blaster*, casual games like *Tetris*, sports games like *Madden Football*, and even controversial games like *Grand Theft Auto* – are actually simulations."[33]

While recognizing that all games have simulations at their core, it is equally important to recognize that games cannot be reduced to the simulations that they contain. There are at least three reasons for this, which are elaborated in the sections that follow. First, as Shaffer notes, the game must provide "the framework in which we make sense of what happens when we interact with the simulation"[34] (Provision of the Framework). Second, the game must embed fun and engaging goals and challenges in the simulation to keep the player motivated and direct her behavior (Motivation and Direction). Third, the game must abstract and simplify the reality being simulated by modeling only those aspects of a situation that are necessary to the gameplay and – in the case of serious games – achieving the learning objectives around which the game is designed (Abstraction and Simplification).

a. Provision of the Framework

The significance of the framework added by a game becomes clear once we appreciate that "wandering around in a rich computer environment without guidance is a bad way to learn. Learners are novices, and letting them work in a simulation without support leads to a very real human tendency to look for patterns and to develop creative but spurious generalizations."[35] For this reason, "[a]ny simulation for learning needs to be set in context if you want someone using it to develop professional vision about what is being simulated."[36] In this regard, a simulation is like the real world: "not in and of itself well designed for learning." Accordingly, for the same reason that play should be structured as a game when intended to promote education, any simulation for learning should be set within a game.

The lesson for law schools considering the use of simulated environments in legal education is easily stated: simulations for learning law should be set in games that will guide law students to develop the professional vision of a lawyer, while helping them to discern and learn the genuine patterns and generalizations that must be acquired by every law student before he or she can be admitted to the practice of law.

b. Motivation and Direction

Many simulations outside games quickly become boring. When, for example, was the last time you got excited about a fire drill? If your experience is similar to mine, you were still in grade school. To quote the corporate trainer and game designer Marc Prensky, "[S]imulated tasks, which many praise as learning by doing, can easily lack any motivating factors and turn into merely a succession of boring things to do."[37] Consider, for example, flight simulators. Their invention revolutionized training in both the military and the private sector. Flight simulators provide a safe environment for pilots, flight students, and interested hobbyists to learn and practice how to fly everything from 747s to F-14s and Apache helicopters. Yet, "simulated flight can become boring in the same sense that driving your car to work is boring or doing any move over and over is boring."[38]

To prevent simulations from becoming boring, you have to make the simulated experience fun and engaging. As Prensky notes, "making them into games is a great way of doing this."[39] This transformation is accomplished by adding game elements such as goals, rules, and challenges. In the case of a flight simulator, the goal could be take off and land ten times, deal with wind shear, land safely even though the port engines have just flamed out, shoot down as many enemies as you can and return to base safely, or determine the best way to attack a target. The point is that once you make the simulation into a game, "suddenly there is more engagement, whether or not there is actually a 'score.'"[40]

c. Abstraction and Simplification

If a simulation mimics the activity being simulated too closely, it can also become tedious and boring – paradoxically, a simulation can be too good! Imagine a cooking simulation in which you were forced to wait until a pot of water boils in real time or while a roast cooks in the oven for two hours. It would not take long before you were hitting the "escape" key. Of course, some simulations must maintain a high level of fidelity to the activity being simulated even if tedium is the inevitable result. But apart from situations like this where high-fidelity simulations are required to develop the necessary competencies, learning is generally better served by low-fidelity simulations. As Prensky notes, "having a high fidelity simulation that exactly imitates life can sometimes take the fun out of it."[41]

Every video game with a fictional world, whether designed for leisure or learning, can be seen as embodying a simulation of a real or fantasized reality and, as such, must ensure that the simulated environment embedded within it does not immure its players in an enervating verisimilitude. For this reason, "[s]implification and stylization can be found in most games with fictional worlds."[42] As Juul observes, "[g]ame fictions and rules are not perfect and complete simulations of the real world; they are flickering and provisional by nature."[43] "By removing detail from the source domain," he continues, "the game focuses on a specific *idea* of what the game is about such as capoeira, soccer, tennis, driving cars."[44] In this fashion, "[a] game does not as much attempt to implement the real world activity as it attempts to implement a specific stylized *concept* of a real world activity. ...The simulation is oriented toward the perceived interesting aspects of soccer, tennis, or being a criminal in a contemporary city."[45] Beyond minimizing the tedium and boredom of the real world, there are sound pedagogical reasons why the simulated environment embedded in a serious game should present only an abstracted, simplified, and stylized version of reality. By abstracting from and ignoring those aspects of a situation that are unrelated to the learning objectives of the game, an imperfect simulation foregrounds and emphasizes those aspects of the situation that are important and prevents the student from being overwhelmed and confused by unnecessary facts. Moreover, to ensure that students will discern, focus upon, and grasp the particular patterns that are targeted by a "lesson" embedded within a serious game, the game's simulated environment must present situations and circumstances conforming to those patterns with a frequency greater than that found in the real world. To do this, however, it must deviate from the reality that it appears to simulate. Although it may sound counterintuitive, to promote learning better, a simulation must fail as a simulation: Failing to represent certain aspects of the source domain is as important as accurately imitating others.

C. WHY VIDEO GAMES?

Part B of this chapter argues that play is an essential form of learning and that such learning will best occur when play is structured as a game. I now want to focus on one particular type of game that offers the greatest potential for learning in the setting of modern law school. I believe that schools should develop and use serious *video games*. The principal reasons for using video games are their fit with our students and their use of cutting-edge technology. First, I will explain why video games are the best match for the learning styles, abilities, and expectations of our present and future students, then I will highlight why video games provide the most powerful and advanced platform for developing serious games.

1. *Learning Styles of the Games Generation*

Our present students, and those for the foreseeable future, are members of what Marc Prensky has dubbed the Games Generation, the first generation to grow up playing video games embedded in a digital lattice of virtual worlds, social networking, game boys, mobile telephony, texting, instant messaging, chat rooms, discussion boards, skyping, online gaming, MP3 players, and myriad other digital technologies of the late twentieth and early twenty-first centuries. The 21st Century Fluency Project reports that by the time an average member of the Games Generation reaches the age of twenty-one, *at a minimum* he or she "will have played more than 10,000 hours of video games, sent and received 250,000 emails and text/instant messages, spent 10,000 hours talking on phones, and watched more than 20,000 hours of television and 500,000 commercials."[46] Other researchers have estimated that "one-half of all 4-to 6-year old children and three-fourths of teenagers play video games on handheld devices, computers, or consoles several hours a day, several times a week."[47] By the time these same children reach twenty-one, they will have spent "only about 4,300 hours reading."[48] Should it really be a surprise that the Games Generation is not composed of text-based learners?

Recognizing the great and growing prevalence of video games, social scientists began to investigate the impact that these games were having on the minds of children. In her 1984 book *Mind and Media*, the UCLA psychologist Patricia Greenfield observed that "[v]ideo games are the first example of a computer technology that is having a socializing effect on the next generation on a mass scale, and even on a worldwide basis."[49] "The video game and computer," she continued, "in adding an interactive dimension to television, may also be creating people with special skills in discovering rules and patterns by an active and interactive process of trial and error."[50] Her insight that video games would produce a generation of active learners was prescient, but we now know that the impact of video games on the developing minds of a generation has wrought changes even more profound.

Throughout the history of the West, philosophers and scientists have assumed that although people around the world might think about different things, they all think in basically the same way. Recent work by social psychologists, however, suggests that this assumption of universality is in fact wrong. According to Nisbett, Choi, Peng, and Norenzayan, "it is not possible to make a sharp distinction between cognitive process and cognitive content."[51] In outwardly similar situations, individuals from different cultures may process information differently as a result of differences in the naïve metaphysical systems, tacit epistemologies, and social organization of each culture. As a result, "the cognitive processes triggered by a given situation may not be so universal as generally supposed, or so divorced from content."[52]

This connection between cognitive processes and content is confirmed by contemporary neuroscience. "In the late 1960s and early 1970s," neuroscientists "made a series of unexpected discoveries," which demonstrated that "the brain changed its very structure with each different activity it performed, perfecting its circuits so it was better suited to the task at hand."[53] This property of the human brain became known as neuroplasticity. In light of these findings, the brain "can no longer be considered a definite, fixed organization of neuronal networks whose connections are definitively established at the end of the period of early development, setting up a kind of rigidity in the treatment of information."[54] Instead, "plasticity shows that the neuronal network remains open to change, to contingency, that it can be modified by events and the potentialities of experience, which can always alter what has come before."[55] As Paula Tallal puts it, "you create your brain from the input you get."[56] "Reading," notes the neuroscientist Michael S. Gazzaniga, "is an invention that is going to have a different neurology to it than the things that are built into our brain, like spoken language."[57] Similarly, we might add, playing video games and living on the net will have a different neurology yet.

The content and input being encountered and absorbed by the Games Generation are significantly different from the content encountered by Baby Boomers and most Gen Xers. In light of the findings about neuroplasticity, it should come as no surprise to us that members of the Games Generation may have developed different cognitive processes and employ different learning styles than their parents. This is exactly what a number of recent studies and reports have concluded.[58] As Prensky summarizes the matter, the "cognitive changes caused by the new digital technologies and media have led to a variety of new needs and preferences on the part of the younger generation, particularly – although by no means exclusively – in the area of learning."[59]

So what are these new needs and preferences in the area of learning, and why do serious video games fit them better than traditional pedagogical methods? While I recognize that many educators and researchers have compiled long lists of the ways that the present generation differs from previous generations, for present purposes we will focus on just seven:

1. *The ability to process information quickly, especially through a computer interface.* "Growing up on twitch-speed video games, MTV (more than 100 images a minute)," scrolling rapidly through Web pages, discussion forums, Twitter feeds, Facebook statuses, and "the ultrafast speed of action films, the Games Generation's minds have been programmed to adapt to greater speed and to thrive on it."[60] It is no wonder that when faced with traditional classroom

methods taught at a speed with which a Baby Boomer would be comfortable, they become restless and bored and surf the net to prevent themselves from screaming. Incorporating serious video games into the curriculum would meet the Games Generation's need for speed because students would control for themselves how quickly they moved through the game world.

2. A *preference for parallel processing over linear processing.* This preference explains the well-known trait of the Games Generation to multitask – their tendency to attend to many things simultaneously. "Having all the information needed to do their job at their fingertips – numbers, video feeds, links, simultaneous meetings, and the ability to move seamlessly between them – is the Games Generation worker's nirvana."[61] Professor Greenfield writes that parallel processing is a "cognitive requirement of skillful video game playing."[62] Hence, serious video games in the curriculum would fit today's students' preference for parallel processing.

3. A *preference for random versus serial access to relevant information.* Members of the Games Generation have grown up clicking around the Web. They are used to exploring information ecologies on their own, pulling in information from multiple sources, and combining them in nonsequential ways. Mash-ups are natural to them. They resist being force fed a linear stream of information, viewing such linearity as rigid intrusions on their autonomy. Marshall McLuhan presciently anticipated this trait of the Games Generation when he wrote that "[w]e can no longer build serially, block-by-block, step-by-step, because instant communication insures that all factors of the environment and of experience coexist in a state of active interplay."[63] It is just such an environment of active interplay that the Games Generation has been raised in, living online and inhabiting game worlds that vibrate in a constant state of interplay, teeming with multiple sources of information to help players learn what they need to know to complete their mission or quest, both inside the game world (information kiosks, maps, nonplayer characters, quest logs, spell books, pop-ups, etc.) and out (tutorials, online manuals, discussion forums, and myriad Web sites created and run by the gamer community for a particular game). Serious video games in the curriculum would have and would motivate the creation of these same kinds of resources, catering to the Games Generation's preference for random rather than serial access to information.

4. A *preference for graphics, animation, and full-motion video over text.* For the Games Generation, the image trumps the word. From their perspective, text is derivative and supplementary. Prensky captures this change from Baby Boomer to Gamer nicely when he writes that "[i]n previous generations, graphics were generally illustrations, accompanying the text and providing some kind of elucidation. For today's Games Generation, the relationship is

almost completely reversed. The role of text is to elucidate something that was first experienced as an image."[64] Needless to say, serious video games with animated 3-D worlds and cut-scenes give pride of place to the image, providing a learning environment conforming to the Games Generation's learning style and preference for graphics over text.

5. *A preference for active, experiential, participatory learning.* Baby Boomers are happy to sit passively on the couch and watch TV. Members of the Games Generation prefer the interactivity of video games and the Internet. The Games Generation's preference for interactivity expresses itself in their preferred learning style as well. As Professor Greenfield first observed, growing up has led members of the Games Generation to be active learners. Their preference for active, experiential learning can be seen in how the Games Generation typically approaches learning a new software program. Unlike Baby Boomers, who want to read the manual first, members of the Games Generation "rarely even *think* of reading a manual. They'll just play with the software, hitting every key if necessary, until they figure it out. If they can't, they assume the problem is with the software, not with them – software is *supposed* to teach you how to use it."[65] Given that the learning style of the Games Generation was shaped by playing video games, it seems only logical to use serious video games to teach them.

6. *A preference for being constantly connected to their peers.* As teenagers, Baby Boomers often called up one friend and talked for hours on the telephone, or at least until their parents told them to get off the phone. More affluent families may have dealt with this "problem" by installing a second (land) line. Today, members of the Games Generation are connected to all their friends all the time. Enmeshed in a web of digital communication technologies, they are constantly receiving or sending texts, instant messages, Facebook status updates, tweets, e-mails, voicemails, and discussion board posts. They are speaking with others in an online multiplayer game via Skype, using a webcam and videoconferencing software on a cell phone, or watching a movie together (virtually) through the Microsoft Xbox 360 connected to Netflix. This connectedness has influenced how the Games Generation seeks and shares information as well as solves problems. While a Baby Boomer who needs information or advice is likely to telephone a specific person with known expertise, a member of the Games Generation is much more likely to post a question on a discussion forum related to the problem with which he or she is grappling or put out a request for help on his or her Facebook feed. In other words, the Games Generation broadcasts their concerns to the entire community and then sifts through and compares the many responses returned.

In addition, the members of the Games Generation have become adept at working in virtual teams to win battles, accomplish missions, and complete quests, as well as in teaching each other what they need to know in order to level up in their favorite online games. Educators call this sort of behavior peer-to-peer learning. The challenge for educators is "to become more adept at managing these connected capabilities and directing the acquisition, enhancement, and appropriate development of information, knowledge, and intellectual capital."[66] Given that the Games Generation is already engaged in this kind of learning when they are playing their favorite online multiplayer video game, does it not make sense simply to incorporate into this kind of online virtual world the content that we would like our students to learn – that is, to have our students play serious video games?

7. *A preference for known payoffs and immediate feedback.* As Prensky points out, "[o]ne of the biggest lessons the Games Generation learned from growing up with video games is that if you put in the hours and master the game, you will be rewarded – with the next level, with a win, with a place on the high scorers' list."[67] The Games Generation carries this mind-set from games over to other activities. Before they put serious effort into some project or activity, they want to know what the payoff will be so that they can determine whether it is worth the time and effort required to achieve it. In school, members of the Games Generation want to know what they have to do to get an A, not because they necessarily want an A, but so they can determine whether it is even worth the effort to try.

At the same time, once a member of the Games Generation decides a particular undertaking is worthwhile, he or she can be incredibly patient and diligent in pursuing it. "Contrary to what many adults believe, many digital games require players to work hard at frustratingly difficult tasks that can take a considerable amount of time to complete. Young people today will spend hours, days, weeks, or even months trying to master computer games."[68] Indeed, members of the Games Generation insist on knowing the payoff of a task precisely because they have learned from experience that the effort to complete a task can be so great. The Games Generation is careful to determine whether the contemplated task or undertaking is in fact worth the effort.

The payoff, however, best not be deferred. The Games Generation is not particularly interested in deferred gratification and rewards. They are unlikely to be motivated by a teacher who tells them that if they study, stay focused, and behave, then they will receive good grades, get into a good college, or get a good job. The Games Generation wants immediate gratification and reward. The origin of this preference can also be traced to playing video games. Video games "are organized so that the player has to make a decision every one-half to one second, and ... are rewarded for those efforts every seven to ten seconds."[69] In other words, the Games Generation expects and requires constant positive feedback to sustain them as they work toward longer-term goals.

2. *The Virtues of Video Games for the Games Generation*

The sad truth is that "[t]o a huge, underappreciated extent in our training and education, we offer the Games Generation very little worth paying attention to from their perspective, and then we blame them for not paying attention."[70] Members of the Games Generation, "accustomed to the twitch-speed, multitasking, random-access, graphics-first, active, connected, fun, fantasy and quick payoff world of their video games, MTV, and Internet, feel bored by most of today's approaches to training and learning, well-meaning as it may be."[71] Accordingly, if we are to reach and motivate our present students, it is imperative that we conform our pedagogical practices to their learning styles. Serious video games "provide one of the few structures we currently have that is capable of meeting many of the Games Generation's changing learning needs and requirements."[72] The need to conform our teaching methods to the dominant learning style and preferences of our present and future students is an important and compelling reason to incorporate serious video games into the curriculum.

In addition to meeting the changing learning needs and requirements of our students, another compelling reason for using video games to harness the power of play for learning is their consistent use of the most advanced and cutting-edge technologies. Running on a computer with a recent graphics card, video games can contain richly detailed three-dimensional virtual worlds. This is a far cry from embedding a simulated battlefield in a game of chess with a chess board. Moreover, unlike with a classic game, the players do not need to know the rules of the game before the play begins. The rules are programmed into and enforced by the video game itself. As a consequence, the gameplay of a video game can involve the players' discerning and learning the rules as the game unfolds. The game rules become just another pattern to be recognized and learned, creating a much richer set of possible game mechanics for the development of law games in particular. In addition, since the computer is implementing and enforcing the rules, the game rules can be much more complex and detailed than is possible with a classic game where the rules cannot be beyond a person's ability to apply them.

The outcome of a video game can also depend on many more variables than in a classic game. Again, since the computer running the video game has the computational power and storage to keep track of every move each player makes over the course of the game, the conditions for winning and other challenges presented by the game can be much more flexible, detailed, and sophisticated. The storage capacities of current server technologies that can host a virtual world embedded in a video game also create the possibility of persistent virtual worlds, in which a player can temporarily leave the game world without interrupting the gameplay for others and with the ability to return to the game at a later time and pick up the gameplay in light of events that occurred while the player was absent.

With these advanced technical features and capabilities, video games transcend the limits of the Classic Game Model and allow for the design and development of serious games not possible with classic games. In particular, video games can provide a much more immersive experience than a traditional game: Because the game implements and enforces the rules as well as tracks the behavior of the players, each player is freed up to focus on the appearance of the fictional world and lose herself in its exploration. The player can forget that the simulated world is embedded in a game and can identify more completely with the fantasy role assumed by her and represented by her avatar. In a law game, one can more readily and completely become the lawyer in the game. In these ways, a massively multiplayer online role-playing video game provides a powerful platform for situated, experiential, and collaborative learning and an obvious choice for the development of serious games.

D. ADDRESSING THE CRITICISMS OF LEGAL EDUCATION WITH SERIOUS VIDEO GAMES

In Parts B and C of this chapter, I have attempted to sketch my reasons for believing that law schools should incorporate video games into their curriculum. I have explained how games provide an invaluable space for learning and why video games are likely to be the most effective type of games for the present generation of law students. In this part, I want to suggest briefly how the adoption of such games would respond to the prevailing and extensive concerns about the effectiveness of legal education in its present form.

As I mentioned at the start of this chapter, laws schools have been severely and repeatedly criticized by a number of groups that one would expect to be their natural allies: our students, the bench and bar, fellow educators, and the federal government. These criticisms may be roughly expressed in four separate claims: First, the methods of teaching and assessment used by law schools are outdated and ineffective; second, law schools are failing to train and prepare their students adequately for the practice of law; third, the principal pedagogical methods employed by law schools lead to student boredom and unhappiness; and fourth, a legal education is too expensive. I believe that incorporating serious video games into the law school curriculum should be part of the comprehensive reform of legal education needed to address these criticisms.

Critics of teaching methods have focused particular attention on the failure of law schools to provide sufficiently active, experiential, and participatory forms of learning. As we have seen, virtual game worlds are ideal learning spaces for active, experiential learners. They would enable situated learning from experience in practical contexts typical of the legal profession that would anchor the textual knowledge and learning that law students receive from more traditional methods of instruction. Moreover, the use of serious video games in legal education would carry over into American law schools the culture and norms of the online gaming community for cooperative and collaborative learning.

Law schools have also been criticized for their use of assessment methods that fail to provide immediate feedback to students and sever any predictable connection between effort and result. Regarding the failure to provide immediate feedback to students, the Carnegie Foundation for the Advancement of Teaching has noted that law schools rely almost exclusively on summative assessment.[73] "Summative assessment is concerned with gathering information about learning after the learning should have occurred, usually for the purpose of assigning grades to students."[74] As the Carnegie Report correctly emphasizes, "heavy reliance on summative assessment" by law schools "forecloses the possibility of giving meaningful feedback to the student about [his or her] progress in learning" and precludes useful feedback to the professor that would provide "a basis for midcourse correction in teaching."[75] The principal form of summative assessment on which law schools heavily rely is, of course, the final exam at the end of the semester. The Carnegie Report recommends that law schools employ more formative assessment.[76] "Formative assessments provide students and teachers with information about how students are progressing toward a stated goal."[77] This allows "the teacher and student to close the gap between the instructional objectives and the understandings and performances that the student has demonstrated."[78] Myriad studies "have shown that formative assessment information increases achievement for all students, with the largest gains for lower-achieving students and students with learning disabilities."[79] One of the great strengths of serious video games is their ability to provide nearly constant formative assessment in real time. Every move and decision that a player makes in an online game provides her with feedback that contributes to her mastery of the knowledge and skills that she needs to complete the quests and challenges posed by the game successfully.

Traditional modes of law school assessment, such as grading on a curve, also sever any predictable relationship between a student's effort and final grade. As Dr. Michael E. Carney, a New York psychoanalyst who has treated quite a number of law students from an elite New York law school over the past two decades, notes, "when notification finally arrives, ... the delay between performance and feedback ... weakens students' confidence in their legal knowledge."[80] "In some cases," Dr. Carney continues, "the grades received evoke considerable confusion and questioning, because students often perceive an incongruity between their subjective sense of performance and the grade awarded. Inevitably, students view this grade as a global evaluation of their abilities, not as a grade accorded on the basis of one exam."[81]

Incorporating serious video games into the law school curriculum would mitigate these shortcomings. As noted earlier, serious video games give today's students the immediate feedback and known payoffs that are needed to keep them motivated. Serious law games will give students immediate feedback on whether they have mastered the skills and knowledge that the game is designed to convey: If they fail to meet a particular challenge or to complete a specific quest successfully, they must redo it. Accordingly, the student will know immediately that she has not yet acquired the skills and knowledge required to succeed at this segment of the game. Conversely, a student who has met the challenge or successfully completed the designated quest will know immediately that she has mastered the required skills and knowledge because she is presented with the next challenge and may proceed to the next segment of the game. In addition to immediate feedback, success at a law game can be tied to known payoffs. In the real world, the student could receive a higher grade in the course using the game. In the game world, the student could receive some virtual coin for successfully completing a given challenge or quest – coin that could then be used to purchase virtual furniture for one's virtual office or virtual clothes for one's avatar, all of which could confer status and signal success within the game. Finally, serious video games give the professor an opportunity to monitor the students' thought processes and mastery and intervene where he or she deems beneficial, either in real time or from an electronic record – recall the enormous amount of information that Professor Silverman had available as he sat in his swivel chair watching his students negotiate a land transaction on twenty-third-century Mars.

In addition to the criticisms of their pedagogical methods, law schools have been criticized by the bench and bar for their pedagogical results – for graduating students who are not adequately trained and prepared for the practice of law. This criticism is articulated in the 2007 report *Best Practices for Legal Education, a Vision and a Roadmap*, commissioned by the Clinical Legal Education Association: "[i]t may not be possible to prepare students fully for the practice of law in three years, but law schools can come much closer than they are doing today."[82] Recognizing that to improve this situation law students must better understand what it is like to be a lawyer, the report wisely notes that "[t]here is no more effective way to help students understand what it is like to be a lawyer than to have them perform the tasks that lawyers perform.... One cannot become skilled simply by reading about skills or watching others perform lawyering tasks. One must perform the skills repeatedly."[83]

The report concludes, however, that "[t]he truth of the matter is that few, if any law schools, have programs or resources to develop the full range of the skills needed for law practice to the degree of proficiency expected of practicing lawyers."[84] This lack of resources is especially dispiriting because "law students will not develop adequate entry level lawyering skills as long as professional skills instruction for most law students is relegated to one course in the second or third year of law school."[85]

But the situation is not as hopeless as the report suggests. Even though most law schools lack the financial resources to provide multiple clinical opportunities to every single student, proficiency in the required lawyering skills could be achieved by every student using well-designed serious video games. Serious video games have been successfully used to train, inter alia, doctors, engineers, military commanders, troops, firefighters, first responders, police, policy analysts, airline pilots, fighter pilots, restaurant wait staff, and business managers. There simply is no reason to think that serious video games could not be used as well to develop lawyering skills. In fact, such a game already exists. Professor Ashley Lipson has created a serious two-dimensional (2-D) game to develop a lawyer's skill at making evidentiary objections at trial. The game, appropriately enough, is called "Objection!"[86] Also, while not technically a game, the University of Glasgow Graduate School of Law has developed a multiuser virtual environment for teaching various kinds of legal transactions, including a land conveyance, drafting the initial writ in a civil court action, and probating a will.[87] Like good clinical education, serious video games can be used to help students to "adjust to their roles as professionals, become better legal problem solvers, develop interpersonal and professional skills, and learn how to learn from experience."[88]

A third criticism of American legal education is that it leaves students bored and unhappy. While this is not the place to attempt a full diagnosis of law student boredom, it is not unreasonable to speculate that the use of the case method through all three years of law school is a significant factor. The case method involves reading and briefing appellate cases from a casebook in order to prepare for Socratic questioning by the professor in class. Professor Alan Watson calls the casebook method of teaching law "an exercise in futility" and likens learning law from a casebook to studying "the status of a grain of sand by walking around inside the grain and without reference to the rest of the beach, the surf and the sky."[89] A similar view of casebooks is voiced by Professor Philip Kissam, who writes that "[c]asebooks present complex information in highly fragmented and relatively isolated forms, and many students initially at least are overwhelmed and bewildered."[90] According to Professor Watson, during the first year, the students may be confused and frustrated by being forced to use casebooks, but they are too scared to be bored. After "[t]he students have overcome the terror of the first-year, and have had the summer vacation," however, "boredom with law school is what awaits them."[91] With resignation, he writes that "most courses, are, indeed, Same old, same old, but without the terror. In most classes, I insist, the boredom is palpable."[92]

Since I doubt that the legal academy is going to give up the use of the case method any time soon, the only alternative strategy to combat student boredom is to counterbalance this bulwark of traditional law school pedagogy with some alternative method of learning that the students will find fun and engaging. For my money, as the perspicacious reader will no doubt anticipate, the preferred course of action is to incorporate serious video games into the law school curriculum.

No doubt bored students are destined to become unhappy students, but in law school student unhappiness is likely overdetermined. Traditional law school pedagogy can be very damaging to a student's confidence and self-worth. Here, again, Dr. Carney's observations are quite helpful: The potential for injuries to a student's self-esteem "thrives within the law school environment. The sheer volume of the material to be assimilated would tax the capacities of the most brilliant scholar" and "[t]he Socratic method often intimidates the best-prepared students, reducing them to faltering, uncertain neophytes."[93] In addition, "students can experience a sense of helplessness in their efforts to master the nuances and complexities of the law."[94] "Accustomed to academic successes, ... they often find it impossible to match those achievements," becoming "disillusioned and embittered."[95] Moreover, the lack of formative assessment creates a vacuum in which "self-doubt spirals and confidence falters, resulting in the unspoken but incessant comparisons with other students that lead to self-devaluation and depression."[96]

Serious video games can provide a positive and enriching educational experience that will bolster a student's self-worth in an attempt, if not to neutralize, at least to lessen the impact of all the destructive influences unleashed by simply matriculating to law school. A well-designed serious video game will help students build confidence in their developing legal knowledge and skills. The problems, missions, and challenges within a game can be presented to the student in a manner that gently increases in difficulty, allowing them to learn and master the knowledge and skills they need to succeed with later, more difficult problems and challenges. At each stage, as they meet a challenge, level up, complete a mission, and finally win the game, well-designed serious video games will allow students to feel good about themselves, empowering them and increasing their sense of worth. Thus, in addition to providing students with a safe environment to learn substantive legal doctrine and develop important lawyering skills, well-designed serious video games will also protect and support a student's sense of well-being, confidence, and worth.

The fourth criticism leveled at law schools has been the cost of a legal education. As in other parts of the university, law school tuition has risen faster than inflation. The increased revenue has allowed law schools, among other things, to increase faculty size and reduce the faculty-student ratio, to expand clinical offerings, and to finance research centers that contribute to the intellectual life of the school. Nonetheless, the federal government, the ABA, our own students, and many law professors themselves now agree that law school tuition is fast becoming prohibitive. If a legal education is to remain accessible to all students who have the ability and desire to become lawyers, the cost of attending law school must be held to its present levels or reduced. How is this to be done?

Clearly any meaningful answer to this question will be multifaceted and complex. Nonetheless, one part of the answer will surely be to harness the power of digital technologies and the economies that they offer by using serious video games and the virtual worlds that are embedded within them in order to deliver a part of a student's legal education online. To be sure, the initial development costs to create appropriate and well-designed virtual game worlds will be great, and various strategies to share or defray these costs must be explored, but once such games are created, they may be duplicated at a marginal cost approaching zero and used to educate our students through positive and challenging virtual experiences. It is only one cost-reducing measure but serves nonetheless as an additional reason for incorporating serious video games into the law school curriculum.

E. CONCLUSION

The overarching problem with American legal education is that its principal pedagogical practices do not fit the learning styles and preferences of the current generation of law students. Serious video games do. In addition, using serious video games in legal education can help address the myriad criticisms leveled against law schools by groups that should be our natural allies: our students, the bench and bar, fellow educators, and the federal government. To conform our pedagogical practices and activities to the learning needs and requirements of the present generation of law students and to begin the process of placing legal education on a firm foundation for the future, we should begin to develop and use serious video games and the virtual worlds embedded within them to educate the next generation of lawyers. In short, law schools should start taking serious video games very seriously indeed.

NOTES

1. Nicholas Iuppa and Terry Borst, *Story and Simulations for Serious Games: Tales from the Trenches* (Oxford: Focal Press, 2007).
2. Marc Prensky, *Digital Game-Based Learning* (New York: McGraw Hill, 2001).
3. James Paul Gee, *What Video Games Have to Teach Us about Learning and Literacy* (New York: Palgrave Macmillan, 2003).
4. A much more extensive list may be found in Edward O. Wilson, *Sociobiology, the New Synthesis* (Cambridge, MA: Belknap Press, 2000), 165–6.

5. Stuart Brown, *Play, How It Shapes the Brain, Opens the Imagination, and Invigorates the Soul* (New York: Penguin Group, 2009), 29–30.
6. Letter to Edward O. Wilson, quoted in Wilson, *Sociobiology*, 165.
7. Brown, *Play*, 30.
8. Jaak Panksepp, *Affective Neuroscience: The Foundations of Human and Animal Emotions* (New York: Oxford University Press, 1998), 280 (emphasis added).
9. Panksepp, *Affective Neuroscience*, 281.
10. Brown, *Play*, 33.
11. Brown, *Play*, 40.
12. Brown, *Play*, 41.
13. The only article of which I am aware that discusses the potential significance of play for legal education is Lisa Brodoff, Marilyn Berger, Anne Enquist, Paula Lustbader, and John Mitchell, "Can the Professor Come Out and Play?: Scholarship, Teaching, and Theories of Play," *Journal of Education* 58 (2008): 481. These authors focus on free play. For the reasons detailed later, I believe that to unleash the true potential of play for legal education, we must focus on structured play in the form of games.
14. Gee, *What Video Games Have to Teach Us*, 113.
15. Gee, *What Video Games Have to Teach Us*, 113.
16. Gee, *What Video Games Have to Teach Us*, 141.
17. Ludwig Wittgenstein and Ferdinand de Saussure garnered important insights into the nature of language through reflection on games. Ludwig Wittgenstein, *Philosophical Investigations* (Oxford: Blackwell, [1953] 2001); Ferdinand de Saussure, *Cours de linguistique générale* (Paris: Payot & Rivages, [1916] 1995). The relationship within games between rules and representations led Vladimir Propp and Claude Lévi-Strauss to a structuralist understanding of meaning and narrative. Vladímir Propp, *Morphology of the Folktale* (Austin: University of Texas Press, 2nd ed., 1968); Claude Lévi-Strauss, "The Structural Study of Myth," in *Structural Anthropology* (New York: Basic Books, 1963). The investigations of Oskar Morgenstern and John von Neumann into games and game strategies yielded the economic theory of games, now viewed as forming the conceptual foundations of microeconomics. John von Neumann and Oskar Morgenstern, *Theory of Games and Economic Behavior* (Princeton, NJ: Princeton University Press, 1953). The central focus on chess by Claude Shannon and Adriaan De Groot has shaped the development of artificial intelligence. Claude Shannon, "Programming a Computer for Playing Chess," *Philosophical Magazine* 41 (1950): 256–75; Adriaan D. De Groot, *Thought and Choice in Chess* (Hague: Mouton Publishers, 1965). And Leonhard Euler's work on the Königsberg Bridge Problem led to an entirely new branch of mathematics, now known as graph theory. Leonhard Euler, "Solutio problematis ad geometriam situs pertinentis," *Commentarii academiae scientiarum Petropolitanae* 8 (1741): 128–40, translated in Norman L. Biggs, E. Keith Lloyd, and Robin J. Wilson, *Graph Theory 1736–1936* (New York: Oxford University Press, 1986).
18. Johan Huizinga, *Homo Ludens* (Boston: Beacon Press, 1950), and Roger Caillois, *Man, Play, and Games* (New York: Simon & Schuster, [1961] 2001), translation of *Les Jeux et les Hommes* (Paris: Gallimard, [1958] 1985).
19. Jesper Juul, *Half-real, Video Games between Real Rules and Fictional Worlds* (Cambridge, MA: MIT Press, 2005), 6–7.
20. Juul, *Half-real*, 7.

21. Katie Salen and Eric Zimmerman, *Rules of Play: Game Design Fundamentals* (Cambridge, MA: MIT Press, 2004), 122.

22. Juul, *Half-real*, 58.

23. Juul, *Half-real*.

24. The en passant rule states that a pawn, having advanced exactly three squares from its original square, "attacking a square by-passed by an opponent's pawn, the latter having advanced two squares in one move from its original square, may capture the opponent's pawn as though the latter had moved only one square." U.S. Chess Federation, *Official Rules of Chess* (New York: David McKay Co., 4th ed., 1993), 15.

25. The notion of emergence employed here is taken from complexity theory, which studies how relatively simple entities or rules at one level can interact to create much more complex entities and patterns at a higher level of organization. M. Mitchell Waldrop, *Complexity: The Emerging Science at the Edge of Order and Chaos* (New York: Simon & Schuster, 1992). Biology affords many examples of complex systems such as simple neurons simultaneously interacting to generate such mental entities and events as thought, emotion, and consciousness. Stuart Kaufman, *At Home in the Universe: The Search for the Laws of Self-Organization and Complexity* (New York: Oxford, 1995). Economics does so as well, describing how complex market economies emerge from simple exchanges. Waldrop, *Complexity*, 1–51.

26. Juul, *Half-real*, 80.

27. Callois, *Man, Play and Games*, 7.

28. Callois, *Man, Play and Games*, 7.

29. Callois, *Man, Play and Games*, 9.

30. Huizinga, *Homo Ludens*, 12.

31. Ernest Adams and Andrew Rollings, *Andrew Rollings and Ernest Adams on Game Design* (New York: New Riders Publishing, 2003), 201.

32. David Williamson Shaffer, *How Computer Games Help Children Learn* (New York: Palgrave Macmillan, [2006] 2008), 69.

33. Shaffer, *How Computer Games Help Children Learn*, 69.

34. Shaffer, *How Computer Games Help Children Learn*, 69.

35. Shaffer, *How Computer Games Help Children Learn*, 68.

36. Shaffer, *How Computer Games Help Children Learn*, 68.

37. Marc Prensky, *Digital Game-Based Learning* (St. Paul, MN: Paragon House, 2001), 212.

38. Prensky, *Digital Game-Based Learning*, 213.

39. Prensky, *Digital Game-Based Learning*, 212.

40. Prensky, *Digital Game-Based Learning*, 213.

41. Prensky, *Digital Game-Based Learning*, 216.

42. Juul, *Half-real*, 170.

43. Juul, *Half-real*, 170.

44. Juul, *Half-real*, 170, 170–172.

45. Juul, *Half-real*, 170, 172.

46. Ian Jukes, Ted McCain, and Lee Crockett, *Understanding the Digital Generation, Teaching and Learning in the New Digital Landscape* (Kelowna, BC: 21st Century Fluency Project & Corwin, 2010), 28.

47. Jukes, McCain, and Crockett, *Understanding the Digital Generation*, 25.

48. Jukes, McCain, and Crockett, *Understanding the Digital Generation*, 28.

49. Patricia Marks Greenfield, *Mind and Media: The Effects of Television, Video Games and Computers* (Cambridge, MA: Harvard University Press, 1984), cited in Prensky, *Digital Game-Based Learning*, 44.
50. Greenfield, *Mind and Media*, 44.
51. Richard Nisbett, Incheol Choi, Kaiping Peng, and Ara Norenzayan, "Culture and Systems of Thought: Holistic versus Analytic Cognition," *Psychological Review* 108 (2001): 306.
52. Nisbett, Choi, Peng, and Norenzayan, "Culture and Systems of Thought," 307.
53. Norman Doidge, *The Brain That Changes Itself* (New York: Viking Penguin, 2007), xviii–ix.
54. François Ansermet and Pierre Magistretti, *Biology of Freedom, Neural Plasticity, Experience, and the Unconscious* (New York: Other Press, 2007), 6.
55. Ansermet and Magistretti, *Biology of Freedom*, 6.
56. Sharon Begley, "Rewiring Your Gray Matter," *Newsweek*, 1 January 2000, at http://www.newsweek.com/1999/12/31/rewiring-your-gray-matter.html.
57. Robert Lee Hotz, "In Art of Language, the Brain Matters," *Los Angeles Times*, 18 October 1998, A1.
58. Diana G. Oblinger and James L. Oblinger, eds., *Educating the Net Generation* (Washington, DC: Educause, 2005), at http://www.educause.edu/educatingthenetgen. Jukes et al., *Understanding the Digital Generation* (Kelowna BC, Canada: 21st Century Fluency Project, 2010), 19–44. Larry Rosen, *Rewired: Understanding the iGeneration and the Way They Learn* (New York: Palgrave Macmillan, 2010), 1–49.
59. Prensky, *Digital Game-Based Learning*, 39.
60. Prensky, *Digital Game-Based Learning*, 51–2.
61. Prensky, *Digital Game-Based Learning*, 54.
62. Greenfield, *Mind and Media*, 112.
63. Marshall McLuhan and Quentin Fiore, *The Medium Is the Message, An Inventory of Effects* (New York: Bantam Books, 1967), 63.
64. Prensky, *Digital Game-Based Learning*, 55.
65. Prensky, *Digital Game-Based Learning*, 59.
66. Prensky, *Digital Game-Based Learning*, 58.
67. Prensky, *Digital Game-Based Learning*, 61.
68. Jukes, et al., *Understanding the Digital Generation*, 40.
69. Jukes, et al., *Understanding the Digital Generation*, 40.
70. Prensky, *Digital Game-Based Learning*, 64.
71. Prensky, *Digital Game-Based Learning*, 64.
72. Prensky, *Digital Game-Based Learning*, 65.
73. William M. Sullivan et al., *Educating Lawyers, Preparation for the Profession of Law* (San Francisco: Jossey-Bass, 2007) (frequently referred to as the Carnegie Report as it was written under the auspices of the Carnegie Foundation for the Advancement of Teaching), 164–5.
74. Lorin W. Anderson et al., eds., *A Taxonomy for Learning, Teaching, and Assessing: A Revision of Boom's Taxonomy of Educational Objectives*, abridged ed. (New York: Addison Wesley Longman, 2001), 102.
75. Sullivan, *Educating Lawyers*, 164.
76. Sullivan, *Educating Lawyers*, 171.
77. Mary Alice Gunter et al., *Instruction: A Models Approach* (Boston, MA: Allyn and Bacon, 5th ed., 2007): 12.

78. Gunter, et al., *Instruction*, 58.
79. Gunter, et al., *Instruction*, 58.
80. Michael E. Carney, "Narcissistic Concerns in the Educational Experience of Law Students," *Journal of Psychiatry & Law* 18 (1990): 16–17.
81. Carney, "Narcissistic Concerns," 16–17.
82. Roy Stuckey and Others, *Best Practices for Legal Education: A Vision and A Road Map* (Columbia, SC: Clinical Legal Education Association, 2007), 7.
83. Stuckey and Others, *Best Practices*, 170–1.
84. Stuckey and Others, *Best Practices*, 171.
85. Stuckey and Others, *Best Practices*, 181.
86. A demo of the games is available at http://www.objection.com. The game, developed in the 1990s, uses a simple 2-D virtual courtroom, rather than an immersive, 3-D virtual environment.
87. Paul Maharg, *Transforming Legal Education: Learning and Teaching the Law in the Early Twenty-first Century* (Burlington, VT: Ashgate Publishing Co., 2007), 171–203.
88. Stuckey, *Best Practices*, 169.
89. Alan Watson, *The Shame of American Legal Education* (Lake Mary, Fl: Vandeplas Publishing, 2006), 9–10.
90. Philip C. Kissam, *The Discipline of Law Schools: The Making of Modern Lawyers* (Durham, NC: Carolina Academic Press, 2003), 32.
91. Watson, *The Shame of American Legal Education*, 137.
92. Watson, *The Shame of American Legal Education*, 137.
93. Carney, "Narcissistic Concerns," 16.
94. Carney, "Narcissistic Concerns," 16.
95. Carney, "Narcissistic Concerns," 16.
96. Carney, "Narcissistic Concerns," 16, 16–17.

7

Law Students and the New Law Library

An Old Paradigm

Penny A. Hazelton

"... the Library is a direct expression of a comprehensive ideal about professional education."[1]

Will electronic textbooks really change the relationship that law students have with their traditional law libraries? Why would a law student want to go to or use a law library in an all-digital world? Is there a reason to have a library in an academic institution at all? And even if law libraries continued to exist, would law students use them? "Everything is on the Internet" is the common refrain. "Why would I go to a library?" "Bound books are so old-fashioned – I haven't used one in years." "Everything I need for my research is online." If these statements are actually or mostly true today, imagine how much truer they will be in the future.[2]

This chapter explores these questions in an effort to discover whether the digital information world of tomorrow still permits a law school to have any kind of a library at its core. In particular, I will look at digital information's impact on law students and their relationship with a law library. I will begin (Part A) by discussing the law library as a physical space. How do law students use law libraries' physical space, what is its meaning for them, and how will that meaning change in the digital future? Next (Part B), I will consider the assistance provided by the law library staff. Do students go to libraries to consult library staff? Is the library's virtual presence a place law students visit in any meaningful way? Finally (Part C), I will look closely at the library's physical collections since this is likely to be the area of the most dramatic change.

A. LAW STUDENTS AND THE LIBRARY AS PLACE

First, it must be observed that many law students move through three or four years of law school and never darken the physical door of the law library for any reason. It is less clear whether these same law students also do not use the law library's virtual presence, the web page, for any reason during their law school experience. Perhaps even the law library's web page can be ignored in schools with no upper-class analytical writing requirement or with research courses that exclude electronic legal resources completely. But while it is clear that some law students eschew the law library in any of its guises, this fact does not diminish the library's role in the life of most law students.[3]

Today use of the law library takes two different forms – physical and virtual. Use of the physical library involves the space, collections, or staff services in the library – or some combination of these three. Use of the virtual library can be accomplished by going to the physical library or accessing that library off-site through the Internet.

To begin with the question of physical space, why do students use or go to the physical law library? There are probably as many answers to this question as there are law students. But one of the main reasons has to be the convenience of the law library in relation to the classrooms students regularly use. Other reasons include:

- Comfortable seating with a variety of options, including tables, carrels, group study rooms, computer workstations, and casual seating
- Quiet, uninterrupted space
- Wireless Internet
- Access to printers and photocopy machines
- Help from library staff
- Access to print materials on course reserve or for course assignments
- Access to library-licensed electronic resources
- Access to student study aids not part of the student's own collection

We can articulate the reasons that students use law libraries, but what is it they actually want to accomplish on their visit? Again, the reasons will vary, but they at least include the following:

- Prepare or study for class
- Research course papers
- Carry out research for an employer
- Work for a student journal
- Complete class assignments
- Check e-mail
- Create outlines and study for exams
- Review trial/moot court/conferences/class recordings
- Find a friend/colleague
- Ask a question of library staff

The specific reasons most law students go to the library are obvious, but what activities are they actually engaged in while in the law library? What functions do they perform? Students are:

- Reading printed books, paper copies, or online documents
- Writing notes by hand or using their computer or other mobile device
- Watching a podcast of class, a performance such as trial advocacy or moot court practice, a speaker presentation
- Listening to music, a class recording, and other audio media
- Thinking, processing complex information, on a path to self-discovery or applying information to create knowledge[4]
- Asking questions of themselves, other students, and library staff
- Searching for library books or information from online sources
- Taking breaks from law study – checking e-mail, facebook, news; shopping online; planning a vacation; looking at photos, text, blogs, and tweets; playing video games; napping or relaxing[5]

What are some of the behaviors law students engage in when they are in our physical library space? Perhaps an understanding of these behaviors can help inform the current relationship law libraries have with their law student users.

- They take frequent breaks from any one task – not necessarily moving from their physical space
- They may collaborate with others; they may work solo, even if they arrived in a group
- Most have two or three electronic devices – laptop plus smart phone/cell phone/tablet Pc/mp3 player
- Most use ear buds to signal "Do not disturb!"; to block out noise; to listen to music or other audio media; to aid concentration on another task
- Most still have paper around them – textbooks, notebooks, copies of research or study materials, library books, notes, outlines
- Virtually all have drinks and food snacks
- They may stay for the time between two classes or for hours
- Even if they have lockers, students may have coats, umbrellas, and backpacks

"Students constantly juggle complex social, personal, and academic responsibilities; if we want to communicate with them, then we have to recognize how the library fits within their lifestyle."[6]

Law student use of their law libraries varies depending on the time of day, the day of the week, the progression of the semester or quarter, and whether the student is a first-year student or a third-year student. What kind of assignments are given in class? Does the student have a family? Where does the student live relative to the law school? How much is the student working while in school and at what kind of job? What types of courses are being taken – doctrinal, clinical, experiential, or externship? All of these factors will be relevant when looking at law student use of the physical law library.[7] Thus, individual needs will vary considerably from one student to another.

Note that few of the student motivations, tasks, or behaviors involve the use of the library's physical collections. There is an assumption that law students in the past regularly went to the law library to use law library collections. This myth must be put to rest. The reality is that most students have never had a need to consult library collections for the work demanded as part of their legal education. Law library print collections were used for special tasks that most law students were never required to perform. For decades law schools taught law students from casebooks that included the edited versions of important cases the students read and study. Class preparation for doctrinal courses rarely required students to use law library collections.[8]

Can all of the activities students perform in the law library be done in other spaces in the law school, in other nearby buildings, or at home? The simple answer is, of course. Many of these functions can be and are carried out in nonlibrary spaces. Law students use cafes, lounges, computer labs, corridors, classrooms, student offices, and outdoor patios, to name a few on-campus spaces. And just as many different places are possible once students are off campus.

So what makes the law library unique and different from all these other places? For one thing, the law library has a decidedly academic purpose that none of the other spaces have. "The library building is a powerful symbol in our culture. For many the library stands as the metaphor for knowledge and wisdom."[9] Law libraries have been described as the intellectual commons of an academic enterprise[10] and "a place of intellectual stimulation and a center for self- or group-directed learning."[11] Langdell, the founder of our current system of legal education, described the library as the law students' laboratory; despite its much-disparaged analogy to natural science, the metaphor indicates his perception of the library's importance.

Libraries are seen as neutral places – that is, spaces in which a student can feel safe and secure. They are accessible while providing spaces for interaction, solitude, relaxation, and reflection – a leveling environment for human contact and conversation. Libraries are not judgmental. Their very purpose as a place of learning has none of the possible negative connotation of the classroom, for example. "And the very space facilitates a sense of belonging to a community."[12] These types of spaces are often called the third place.[13]

These somewhat intangible factors figure prominently in law student choice about the use of law library space over other spaces. And the nicer and more comfortable the environment, the more law students will choose the law library. As long as there are residency-based law schools, law libraries of tomorrow will be used by law students for the physical spaces they offer. In fact, it is easy to imagine that the physical library space will become more desirable in the future and that library services designed to help students in the study of law and to prepare them for "effective and responsible participation in the legal profession"[14] will increase.

A word of caution, however: if law libraries ever forget their law student users – that is, they fail to take into account student needs in the academic environment[15] – law students will not even darken the law library door. Law library space will be completely converted to other law school purposes, or our libraries will be the cold, empty spaces the naysayers foresee in a future without books. Success in the current paradigm in serving the needs of law students with flexible facilities and enhanced services available anytime, anywhere does not guarantee our future success.

B. LAW STUDENTS AND LIBRARY STAFF SERVICES

Aside from the more subtle reasons law students chose to be in the physical law library, there are two unique law library resources to consider – its staff and its physical collections. Both required the law student of the past to visit the law library in person. Is this still true today?

Before the Internet, ubiquitous mobile phones, and e-mail, library staff[16] could only be contacted if students went into the library to find them. Some students would call the library staff, but since service to law students is normally based on the we-will-help-you-find-the-answer-for-yourself model rather than the we-will-give-you-the-answer model, virtually all library staff services to law students were provided face-to-face. This is not to claim that all law students used library staff services, only that law students did have to go to the library in person if they chose to ask library staff a question. Similarly, the library's print collection had to be used on-site in the law library.

What has been the impact of the Internet and digitization of legal information on the use of the law library by law students for staff services and use/access to physical collections? Looking first at student access to library staff, it is clear that law students no longer have to go to the law library to get help. The students *can* go to the library, but they do not have to go. Library staff services are available via e-mail, phone, and the Web as well as through an in-person visit. Perhaps more important, staff expertise is shared through robust, content-rich Web sites created by most academic law libraries. Legal research guides, the library's public catalog, tutorials, policies, and procedures all help answer questions that law students may have – without the need for the student to be in personal contact with any library staff at all. Adding mobile applications for fast access to the heavily used Web content of the law library opens even more points of contact.

This strong virtual presence of the law library continues, and for some, simply extends the reach of library staff services by providing a great deal of specialized information for law students that they can access from the convenience of their computer. It enriches the law students' experience by providing choices about when and how they retrieve the information they need.

Virtualizing access to library services will not, however, eliminate the need for library staff.[17] In fact, even if in-person library staff services were eliminated, library staff are even more essential in this potentially all-digital environment, for they create the tools that will help students in the learning process. They are the guides who add value to information so students can create knowledge. They help law students learn the lawyer skill of legal research. Through their extensive understanding of legal information sources, law student needs, and the practice of law, they maintain their historical role of human intermediation[18] whether they have face-to-face contact with law students or not.

And while many of these services can and will be offered virtually, law libraries have not yet been able to create guides or frequently asked questions (FAQs) that answer every question a law student might have. Furthermore, some law students prefer face-to-face contact in order to get more responsive answers to their specific information needs – needs that may extend well beyond the general information found in the law library's virtual place. Or perhaps the information students seek virtually is not easy to locate or does not seem to apply to their situation. In fact, Stephen Abram reminds us that "[l]ibrarians aren't just about search; we're about improving the question." He argues that to improve the quality of the question the library must put its staff and programs at the "center of the question space, spending more time on finding and understanding than searching."[19]

Law libraries could conceivably follow the path taken by so many businesses, using complex telephone trees to make it difficult to talk with a real person or employing an e-mail contact from a Web site from which you never receive a helpful reply. But neither of these models satisfactorily responds to the law student whose information needs are not quickly met by virtual means. As a result of high tuition, heavy student debt, and the competition in the legal education market, law schools are even more customer driven than they were in the past.[20] The best law schools will be known for the exceptional service given to law students by the faculty, the placement office, the registrar, and the law library – both virtually and in person. In this service environment, the law library can play an essential role in creating the sense of community so crucial to the success and future of any law school.

The new paradigm for law library services involves being where students are. Robust Web pages accessible anywhere with an Internet connection, blogs, support for technologies that push content to students, creation of information tools in small as well as complex pieces to meet different levels of information need, remote access to library staff experts, and fast access to any information students need whether the library owns it or not are ways law libraries now interact with students in the virtual plane. Libraries must better market their virtual offerings, making library information more discoverable for all of their users. As Stephen Abram contends, we want users to trip over libraries in the virtual world.[21]

But the face-to-face features of the current paradigm remain very important. Libraries must still offer the human touch.[22] In many law schools, library staff are the only staff in law school buildings after regular business hours, and they competently handle a surprising array of questions and issues that have nothing to do with legal information.[23] And with respect to legal information, law library services depend on building relationships with the research-dependent partners in law schools (student journals, clinics, moot court teams), integrating legal research skills into the entire law school curriculum, locating difficult to find materials, and offering individual appointments with students who need a start or help with a research strategy. These and other in-person library services recognize that law students are able to handle the easy questions, often by using nonlibrary resources. But the complex questions and law and law-related research needs of law students are where library staff services are essential. Using their expertise to help students sort through the overload of information is just one way that library staff can offer value to the law student as information consumer.[24]

In sum, in this fast-paced legal information environment, law students need and will use the law library for the expertise library staff offer – virtually and in person. The most valuable commodity of any organization is not what it owns, but what and whom it knows. The role of law libraries in the future is to infuse library staff expertise and their knowledge base into the academic work of law students. "This is the post-Information Age where the competitive advantage moves from information access to knowledge creation, from physical access to intellectual access."[25] Just as the library's physical space may well become more desirable in the future, it is beyond argument that library services designed to help students in the study of law and to prepare them for the "effective and responsible participation in the legal profession"[26] will increase.

C. LAW STUDENTS AND LIBRARY COLLECTIONS

Our exploration of law student use of law libraries has examined two distinct elements. The use of the law library as place has many dimensions. But there is no arguing with the fact that law students do use and will continue to use *library space*, especially if it meets their needs as students in the academic enterprise.[27] My analysis of law student use of *library staff expertise* has a similar outcome. That is, many law students take advantage of the myriad ways library staff provide essential services to students by helping them build their knowledge and skills base. Law students do not have to go to the physical library to take advantage of these services, but many do and will continue to do so. So, in these two elements – library space and library staff services – most law students currently have a relationship with their law library. What about the role of the *library collection* in the law student's life in law school?

1. *The Role of the Collection*

Do law students need access to legal collections? Is there still a reason that a law student today needs to go to the law library to use its physical (print and microform) collections? Currently all law libraries have a collection of print materials that are only accessible in the physical library space.[28] I know of no academic law library whose print collection is completely duplicated and accessible electronically.[29] These print collections relate to the mission of the law school and are housed for free and easy access by students, faculty, and staff.[30] There is simply no question that today's students use these physical research tools far less than their predecessors did. Take away the print collections, and, voila, no need for a law student to go to a law library for any collections.

To be sure, the current and proposed ABA accreditation standards (ABA Standard 606 and Interpretation 606-2 as well as the most recent April 2011 draft revisions) are clear that law libraries with only one format of legal information (print or electronic) may not meet the accreditation standards.[31] Even in recent years no law school has received ABA accreditation unless the law library had both physical and digital collections. For the moment, then, law libraries must have physical collections on site. And it is unlikely that a law school that moved all of its physical collections to off-site storage or eliminated them completely would meet the ABA standards today.[32] But will this be true tomorrow? Even now the current and draft standard language could be interpreted to permit a law library collection in just one format. What will tip that interpretation or force totally new standards language toward an all-digital law library is not clear. Certainly changes in patterns of usage of legal materials and changes in the publication format of materials will be influential.

I happen to agree with John Palfrey that the future of law libraries will be represented by a digital-plus paradigm. Despite what law students might think, the law library of the future will not be entirely digital. "Our future will be a hybrid of yesterday's predominantly print-based world and tomorrow's primarily digital world," says Palfrey. New works will continue to be created, stored, and accessed in digital formats while print and other analog formats are unlikely to disappear, even if a digital form is created to improve access.[33] This vision of the future will make the advocates of books smile.[34] However, these analog or physical materials may well disappear from the shelves in some law libraries.[35] But whether they do or not, the vast majority of law students are unlikely to notice the difference since they have demonstrated a high preference for the convenience and ease of electronic resources.[36]

As noted in Section A, most of the tasks and behaviors that students perform in law libraries do not involve using the physical collection. The only law students using law library print collections are: (1) students using materials outside the assigned reading, including student study aids and the full text of edited materials from class; (2) students taking a legal research course that requires physical use of the library's print collection; (3) students working on a research project or paper that requires use of the print collection; (4) students reading assigned print materials on course reserve; (5) students doing research for their employer; or (6) students cite checking an article using print sources for a student journal.

Thus, even today, the use of law library collections is not the main reason law students use law libraries. While certain tasks require the use of a print collection – and will continue to do so for the foreseeable future – tangible collections are a small part of the reason law students venture into a law library.

2. *Law Libraries and Digital Collections*

Although I am thus inclined to agree with John Palfrey that we are unlikely ever to be in an all-digital legal information world,[37] I want to test today's paradigm against a future of the all-digital kind.

Once law school text and casebooks are published in electronic form only, and all of the important legal work of humankind is found digitally, would there be any role for the traditional (primarily print) law library collection in the educational life of a law student? There would be no print course reserves because everything would be digital. There would be no need to train students to use print legal materials because everything would be online. No research projects would require that students use print materials. Anything students needed to read outside their textbooks, which would be digitally published, would be online. But since most law students do not use print legal collections much today, whether the library collection is in print or exclusively digital form should make very little difference to this part of the complex law library/law student relationship.[38]

This inquiry about student use of library collections leads naturally to a much more important question for libraries and law schools: Is there a reason for libraries to collect or license anything at all in the digital world? Everything old and new is available digitally. An inquiry using any Internet search engine will pull up dozens of documents, many of which will be free. Perhaps, just as with music,[39] anyone will be able to put content on the Internet at no cost, as a public good. As search engines become more robust, the best, most relevant content is easily located.

It is easier and easier for researchers to locate legal documents, especially when they are searching for a known item. For example, think about a search for the *New York Times v. Sullivan*[40] defamation case. Even without the citation, a simple Google search will turn up dozens of Web sites with reliable, but not authenticated copies of this important U.S. Supreme Court opinion. Because I know what I am looking for, it is easy to know when I have found the correct document. This easy access to most of the primary legal information has led to a de facto change in the role played historically by print tools as the authenticated version of the work. Westlaw and Lexis versions of primary legal materials are assumed to have great authority, for example, even though their versions are not usually official or authenticated. Is the Google Scholar version of these court opinions similarly reliable? And when locating a Supreme Court opinion, does the expertise of the user come into play? Will the lawyer have the same conviction about the authority or authenticity as a layperson would have? And why should we care?

But a number of questions remain. First, will all legal information be free? Right now, governments are loading huge quantities of primary legal information onto their agency Web pages. All of this "law" is available free of charge, as Tony Reese's contribution to this volume points out. Most of this content is current, but little is authenticated[41] as the official, reliable source of the law. As long as the law, statute, regulation, court opinion, or administration action occurred in the past fifteen years or so, the legal authority can probably be located for free. But what if the material needed was published in 1930 or 1803? Where does the researcher go then?

Second, obtaining the relevant information may be more difficult if researchers do not know exactly which cases or statutes or regulations will help answer their question. How sophisticated are the search engines on these free government sites? How precise is the search algorithm? How quickly will relevant results be retrieved? Must different types of legal information (cases and statutes, for example) on different Web sites be searched? What if the researcher needs persuasive authority from any jurisdiction? Can searching the law of multiple jurisdictions in one search be accomplished on free sites? Is all the information (especially codes) updated immediately? And finally, most legal material on the Internet is current, but little is authenticated as the official, reliable source of the law.

Even if all primary, government legal information is digital, free, historically comprehensive, completely current, and authenticated as the official, reliable version, entrepreneurs will create packages of legal information either required or preferred by lawyers.[42] They will create multijurisdictional databases, software tools that analyze court opinions for strategic purposes or sort and analyze discovery documents, databases that transform complex legal theory into visual elements, highly specialized subject materials, analytical/synthesized scholarly works, and other products we cannot even imagine. And these business people and scholars will want an incentive to create and distribute their sophisticated information tools. Some will use a nonprofit model, and some of these ventures will have a profit motive.

So it is clear that not all primary legal information will be free. Reliable secondary sources are especially unlikely to be free. Specialized research tools with value-added content will command a premium in the marketplace. Digital resources that collect, synthesize, and organize topical content will be fast and efficient and, perhaps, expensive.

In this digital world, then, libraries still have an important service to perform relating to digital collections. Since all information will not be free, libraries can license digital content relevant to law as they do now,[43] and libraries can curate[44] the content that is free. Such a plan guarantees full access to appropriate materials that will be available at no cost to the law student. Imagine that a law student needs to read Professor Bob Berring's article on deconstructing a law library. A free finding tool such as Google or OCLC locates the article readily in the first page of results with a link to the full text of the article on a service called HeinOnline. The article is not on the Web in full text for free, however. But a law student who is an authenticated user of a law library that has licensed the *Minnesota Law Review* as part of an HeinOnline subscription will have authorized access and can link directly into the entire article. A blogger, Joshua Kim, said it best: "Academic libraries have an opportunity to do what they did for paper books. Take an expensive, scarce commodity and through the library model of cost sharing make these items available to everyone in their communities."[45]

3. *Threats to Law Libraries and Digital Collections*

However, libraries' ability to purchase or license collections of digital content for users does not have a clear path in the competitive digital world. This role for libraries is threatened[46] by several developments, any one of which will make it impossible for libraries to implement a meaningful and continued role of selecting and providing content for library users.

First, the *pricing models* for library purchase of digital content today have several flaws. There has been tremendous consolidation in the legal publisher market in the past fifteen years.[47] This consolidation has eliminated competition and given the few publishers left large market shares. Most publishers who license digital works aggregate lots of content for a hefty flat-rate price. And libraries that want to negotiate for content title by title find the charges for those à la carte items are disproportionately high, making it impractical to select only the content that the library's users need.[48] Complicating these license agreements for many law libraries are the print/digital bundles offered. Normally based on the continuation of a library's past print subscriptions, the practices vary so widely from library to library that understanding retail pricing structures is virtually hopeless.

The price of legal materials is one of the factors most law libraries consider when deciding what to license for their users. The inability to know the real price of an electronic legal resource complicates the decision-making process. This selection task is exacerbated when budgets have been cut or remain flat. It should be noted that this problem of retail pricing exists in the print publishing world as well. And trying to bridge the world from print to digital is especially expensive when both print and electronic versions of the same materials are needed because of user demand or the significant differences in the products available. Nondisclosure agreements are commonplace in vendor license agreements, making it impossible for libraries to know whether they are paying a fair price for the licensed content. Some states prohibit the nondisclosure provision, and it must be removed from contracts before they can be signed. In some state institutions, these licensing contracts are a public record and subject to a public records request. But even in these latter situations, law libraries most often do not make public the price they pay under license agreements for electronic content.

As e-books have become more popular, similar pricing problems arise, together with some distinctive ones. The à la carte problem can still exist, though some publishers, such as Cambridge University Press, permit a library to create a custom-built online collection.[49] Whether such a collection would be affordable is another matter. Vendors can license simultaneous, unlimited use or license only one user at a time. For example, HarperCollins had a license agreement for libraries that allowed one checkout at a time, with an unlimited number of checkouts. Recently, the company changed the terms of its license agreement so that libraries will now be required to buy additional license units once the e-book has been checked out twenty-six times.[50]

While a pay-per-use pricing model might be fine for those reading for pleasure, this model fails to take into account the way researchers use information from books in any format. Researchers search for relevant information without always knowing where that information might be located. They might look at a table of contents or index before rejecting the work as irrelevant. On many e-book platforms, this type of searching can be done at no charge. But often, a quick look at the actual content of various sections or chapters is needed. Would this count as one of the HarperCollins twenty-six uses?[51]

Law libraries and law students are thrilled to have as much digital content as possible. But buying the same content in digital form again and again, especially when libraries already have the print version, will never be cost-effective for law libraries. Typically, researchers do not want to buy all of the books they need or use for their scholarly work. Nor should they have to. Libraries need to continue to provide access to these books in their digital form and press vendors to find pricing models that work for their businesses and for libraries, just as they did with print. Or perhaps new legislation is in order.[52]

Second, library acquisition (really, licensing) of digital content is hampered by the *lack of standardization* in the digital industry. The proprietary nature of everything from platforms to search capabilities, software, license agreements, and readers makes the job of the library in providing licensed content to its users very difficult. In plain fact, these digital products are aimed directly at the consumer. The idea that a library might want to buy or license content for its users simply does not fit with this end-user driven model. Lack of standardization presents a serious challenge for libraries as they seek to provide free content to library users based on their patrons' needs.[53]

Third, issues concerning the *reliability of the information* abound in an all-digital world. Scanning without verifying the text can result in words or paragraphs that have unreadable characters. This may be worse with old type fonts and language, but it remains a problem even with current technology. Furthermore, inaccurate bibliographic information (metadata), such as in the Google Books Project, caused by scanning errors and mechanical extraction of metadata will be a disaster for scholars, claims Geoffrey Nunberg, an information professor at the University of California at Berkeley.[54] Failure to adhere to a fixed format for legal information, one that can be read on any number of different devices, with enhanced font size to accommodate the user, means the researcher's ability to cite to a specific page (the pinpoint citation) is compromised.[55] But how can we balance this need for stability and trustworthiness (authenticity) in our legal documents with the convenience and flexibility of the digital version, including the interactivity of the hypertext link that takes us directly to a referenced or cited source, greatly expanding the reader's access to potentially relevant information?[56]

Concerns about the authentication of official digital legal information are particularly serious for law librarians.[57] Currently, many state government Web sites with legal content include a disclaimer that refers the user to a print version or in any case stops short of authenticating the digital-only product.[58] Failure to use technology to verify the authority and official status of primary legal information will inhibit law libraries and law students from using more digital content and will force continued reliance on the printed forms. This whole question of what is the real language or content of a legal opinion, statute, constitution, or regulation goes to the heart of our democracy. If we cannot know which version to rely on, the rule of law fails. The law cannot be known – and will not be used and applied to solve legal conflicts.

Fourth, many law student library users still like *print for reading*. And this preference is likely to continue into the future, even with the perfection of e-book readers. This preference may be especially true in law schools, for deep reading and comprehension of text is a stock in trade for lawyers. As Nicolas Carr put it:

The kind of deep reading that a sequence of printed pages promotes is valuable not just for the knowledge we acquire from the author's words but for the intellectual vibrations those words set off within our own minds. In the quiet spaces opened up by the sustained, undistracted reading of a book, or by any other act of contemplation, for that matter, we make our own associations, draw our own inferences and analogies, foster our own ideas. Deep reading, as Maryanne Wolf argues, is indistinguishable from deep thinking.[59]

Communication, in all of its forms, is at the heart of the practice of law.[60] Any law library of the future must include cost-efficient ways for law students to have their "reading" material in the format of their choice.[61] The use of one library book by ten law students is more cost effective for society and for the students themselves (not to mention more green) than ten students' purchasing their own individual copies of that one book.

Fifth, the lack of *best practices for the preservation of and access to* our legacy print collections as well as to the born-digital legal information is a threat to the decision making of law libraries. Information needed by lawyers and law students disappears from the Internet every day. Who will find it and be sure it is preserved? How will it be preserved forever and made accessible over time? Print materials are disappearing as well, particularly as libraries weed legal materials or store them in substandard facilities. This may result in information's being lost before it can be digitized. Google Books is rapidly digitizing the content of some of the world's largest libraries, and most publishers make their works available in electronic, print, video, and audio versions. But how long will it really take to digitize all of the world's knowledge? And who will own it, once this is done?

And finally, digital-only access threatens and may change the *way we think about and use legal information*. The hypertext linking that allows horizontal access to information across separate packages of information instead of the vertical use most prominent in a book format has the potential result of separating information from its context. Without context, a lack of coherence in the theory and application of the law is possible. Can knowledge creation really move forward in this setting?[62]

In this hypothetically all-digital world, these and other threats could easily create a future in which law libraries no longer have adequate or useful collections in electronic form. Law libraries would no longer be able to collect, select, or license resources specifically for their users because the information would be too expensive, too inaccessible, too unreliable, too inconvenient, or too incomplete. So even though it is clear that law students will use the law library's physical space and library services in this future, students may well be driven to other sources for the content of the law. This time of transition to the new future requires caution *and* risk taking. An unsettled future means law libraries may be particularly vulnerable to the bondage of the past – the bondage of the law library print collection.

4. *Opportunities for Law Libraries and Digital Collections*

Outside threats to any enterprise often provide organizations with opportunities to create and implement better strategies for future success.[63] What opportunities do we see for law libraries in the future all-digital world?

The first threat has to do with the *pricing models* for access to digital legal information. Can law libraries find ways to negate these practices? One obvious opportunity here is to hire and train librarians to become expert negotiators. In the print world, a librarian selected a title and paid the retail price for it. Today, licensing for access (not ownership) of legal information is much more common. Developing best practices for librarians who negotiate with vendors can improve the kinds of pricing structures available from vendors.

Commentators also find many opportunities here. The open source movement that Matthew T. Bodie discusses in his contribution to this volume has been championed in law libraries by the Durham Statement and is one direct salvo at the enemy.[64] One issue raised by that statement – the cost to law libraries of buying back faculty scholarship – is a mere pittance for faculty works published in law reviews. This is because, of course, law journal publication is almost completely subsidized by law schools. However, faculty scholarship published and distributed by for-profit publishers is another matter. The 10 percent or greater annual price increases for legal materials (when the inflation rate in the United States has been below 3 percent for years) leaves no doubt that publisher profit is high, especially since they sell the same content in multiple formats.[65]

This cycle of paying exorbitant prices to buy back faculty scholarship can be broken. Law libraries can partner with faculty to create teaching materials to enhance student learning.[66] There is also an important role for law libraries in working with faculty to create the imaginative course textbooks of the future that several other contributors to this volume, including Ronald Collins and David Skover describe.[67] These works do not have to be published by a for-profit publisher but could use the model similar to the one forged by a collaboration between the University of California Libraries and the University of California Press.[68] Student textbooks and other scholarly works by faculty could also be published and distributed by the library itself at cost, as the law library reinvents its functions.[69] Or platforms such as eLangdell from CALI (free for CALI members) can serve as digital repositories for faculty work.[70] Digital and print on-demand access would be feasible in this model, driving down costs to law students and libraries. Any such initiatives must include the incentives needed for faculty authors to produce high-quality works. Robert Darnton describes a fascinating future in which he imagines librarians collaborating extensively with faculty authors to create a pyramid of information as e-books, with the concise account at the top followed by levels of deepening complexity.[71]

Law libraries can also press for the information needed to make good licensing decisions for digital content in their institutions. Cornell University Library recently announced its refusal to sign licensing contracts with nondisclosure agreements. It condemned these confidentiality agreements as anticompetitive and detrimental to the library and its users.[72]

Working collaboratively with consortia of all kinds to get a better price for digital content is an important action law libraries can take. These license agreements must take into account the use habits of researchers. Education of vendors about how lawyers and law student researchers actually do research would be a good place to start.

Lack of standardization in the e-book industry threatens law library licensing of digital collections. Creating best practices for publishers may force more vendors to move to standard, more ubiquitous platforms with less proprietary content. The power of the purse must be exploited here. Once law libraries understand what motivates vendors in the e-book industry, this information can be used to move toward the kind of standardization that will put e-books into the hands of law students through their law libraries. The American Association of Law Libraries is working on several fronts to empower law librarians to be effective advocates for users in their negotiations with legal information vendors.[73]

The *reliability of information* is threatened in the all-digital world. The failure of the current marketplace to provide for easy, cheap, and reliable authentication is a real barrier to the transition to the all-digital world. Many law libraries will retain their print collections until this barrier is lifted. Universal or vendor-neutral citation form may offer some solutions to the need to reference authority so prevalent in the legal profession. Other opportunities include forging active partnerships with governmental agencies that create and distribute primary legal information.[74] Sharing points of view by librarians and government officials through educational programming and one-on-one advocacy will help lift this barrier. The private law firm library has cared less about the authentication issue because most large firms use reputable (in terms of content), expensive databases. When law firms begin to use a wider array of resources, some of which may not have the historical provenance of Westlaw and LexisNexis, academic and public law libraries may be able to enlist private law firm libraries in advocating for authentication of digital legal materials.

How can we accommodate law students' desire to *read from print* in an all-digital law library?

First, law libraries can make the print in their collections as easy to find and use as possible. Online catalogs must be as user-friendly as Google.[75] Delivery of print books directly to law students may be a new service law libraries can offer. As one student told me, it is easier and more convenient to borrow a book from another library through the law library's interlibrary loan service than it is to find that same book in our own library's collection! Second, law libraries can make the tangible collections accessible 24/7, the same as the availability of electronic information. Third, law libraries could consider Robert Darnton's model that includes licensing content for searching and providing print on demand for reading.[76] Fourth, law libraries should join with their colleagues to support organizations that are struggling to find answers to these and many other questions. The Legal Information Preservation Alliance (LIPA) is one group grappling with issues relating to preservation of and access to the historical print legal record.[77]

The *lack of best practices for the preservation of and access to* legal information is another threat to library digital collection building. The sheer number of historical publications that need to find a digital format and home is staggering. Google Books has a head start on this project. Do we really want all of the world's knowledge in digital form to be owned by one giant for-profit company? The recent announcement of the Digital Public Library may provide a more affordable alternative.[78] In addition, the Hathi Trust has been established as a partnership of major research institutions and libraries working to ensure that the cultural record is preserved and accessible long into the future.[79] Essential to the preservation of large and small digital collections is the commitment to migrate the digital content into new media over time. Huge servers with pdf versions of millions of books will be useless to people in the future if the pdf format is no longer supported and is inaccessible to legal researchers.

I see many opportunities for law libraries to preserve and make accessible the library's own unique content through digitizing and creating imaginative databases of its institutional work product.[80] Collaboration with other institutions to create comprehensive digital collections in narrow areas of interest provides another model. Preservation of historical and digital materials must not take a back seat. Concerns about the stability and preservation of the copies of record and bibliographic reliability will require a new set of social and institutional arrangements for print repositories and digital collections.[81] Law libraries may be particularly well suited to thinking about solutions as they rely on the great record of human legal history every day to solve legal problems. We cannot afford to allow this legacy to disappear.

And finally, in the digital-only world, what are the opportunities presented by a different *way of thinking about and using legal information* – a disassembling of the context of legal information? One obvious opportunity would be to increase teaching by law librarians so that law students would understand the sources and forms of legal information in a holistic way, helping them to discern the differences in pattern and structure of primary and secondary legal materials.[82] Integration of legal information literacy into all law courses in the future will help reinforce these and other skills essential for the practice of law. Another opportunity would be to exploit the power of this breakdown of formal structure in order to encourage creative and imaginative problem solving by law students. Perhaps new ways of thinking about the law will emerge. Law libraries that can add value to these new ways of accessing information will be most successful in the future.

D. CONCLUSION: BACK TO LAW STUDENTS AND THE NEW LAW LIBRARY

The law libraries of the future will be different. As places, law libraries will emphasize flexible and friendly academically oriented uses by law students. Law libraries will provide in-person services designed to maximize student inquiry and learning. And these services will extend well beyond the physical library proper. Embedded librarians[83] will be where our student users are – working on group scholarship and individual discovery. Our Web sites will continue to be current and relevant to law students, providing quick, free access to myriad legal information resources.

But will law libraries have collections in the future? Yes, provided we can transform the threats to library acquisition into opportunities. Law students will still need electronic and print collections. At the moment, most academic law libraries still own physical print and microform collections. We obviously cannot ignore the demand for electronic legal materials by our law students. Moving from a model of owning the content needed by our law student users to merely providing licensed access to what law students need has many ramifications. Assessing the consequences of the many decisions law libraries make today is an important part of the equation.

Finally, with respect to the general theme of this volume, will electronic textbooks really change the relationship that law students have with their traditional law libraries? The answer to this question is that digital content has already changed the kind of collections available in academic law libraries. More digital content will not drive law students from libraries. In fact, I am confident that law libraries of the future will remain an important part of the life of every law student. Law students will use the new law libraries of the future for space, services, and, collections.

But there will be no new law library in the future without constant attention to what our law student users are doing and want to do.[84]

NOTES

1. Kenneth L. Penegar, "The Academic Leadership of Earl Borgeson," 54 *Journal of Air Law and Commerce*. xiii (1988–89) (Professor Ken Penegar's tribute to Professor Earl Borgeson on Borgeson's retirement).
2. OCLC, "Perceptions of Libraries, 2010: Context and Community, A Report to the OCLC Membership" (2011) 2. This report summarizes the results of surveys aimed at understanding the ties among the library, the Internet, and information-seeking behavior. One of its important findings was that consumers are confident in their ability to find and evaluate information, and they rarely think to go to libraries first, even virtually. The report asks,

"what are the best strategies to support and improve, not discourage, this self-service, self-assessment model of information literacy?" *Id.* at 99.

3. The University of Washington School of Law participated for the first time in the *Law School Survey of Student Engagement* 2010. Law students are asked to rank "library assistance" (not defined) in these categories: not used, very unsatisfied, unsatisfied, satisfied, very satisfied. Of interest for the point of this chapter is the "not used" category. While 21 percent of the first-year class did not use library assistance, this percentage had dwindled to only 3 percent of the 3L class. The questionnaire is not clear about whether this "library assistance" is through use of the physical or virtual library, so it would be inappropriate to make too many assumptions from these data. However, it is clear that the vast majority of law students at the UW Law School (75 percent of the J.D. student body responded to this question) have contact with the library in some way over the course of their three-year education. *Law School Survey of Student Engagement* 2010, University of Washington School of Law, Gallagher Law Library, Library Assistance, on file with the author.

4. *See* Brian Mathews, *Marketing Today's Academic Library: A Bold New Approach to Communicating with Students* (Chicago: American Library Association, 2009). 96–7.

5. Mathews, *Marketing Today's Academic Library.*

6. Mathews, *Marketing Today's Academic Library,* 7.

7. Mathews, *Marketing Today's Academic Library,* 8–22. "[I]nstead of just trying to imagine ways to get more students to use the library, we flip the question around and ask, what do students need this week and how might the library help provide it?" *Id.* at 22.

8. Paul D. Callister, "Seeing the 'Whole Elephant': A New Model for Law School Libraries," in *The Changing Role of Academic Law Librarianship* 7, 9 (2008).

9. Robert C. Berring, "Deconstructing the Law Library: The Wisdom of Meredith Wilson," *Minnesota Law Review* 89 (2005): 1381, 1385.

10. Penny A. Hazelton, "Configuration of the Law Library of the Future," in *The Future of Law Libraries* 44, 46 (2005).

11. Callister, "Seeing the 'Whole Elephant,'" 10. For a discussion of redeveloping the library as an informal learning space, see David W. Lewis, "A Model for Academic Libraries 2005 to 2025," paper presented at Visions of Change, California State University, January 26, 2007, at http://hdl.handle.net/1805/665.

12. Stephen Young, "Looking beyond the Stack: The Law Library as Place," *AALL Spectrum* (July 2010): 16, 18.

13. Young, "Looking beyond the Stack," 17; see also Berring, "Deconstructing the Law Library," 1388–9.

14. See specifically ABA Standards Review Committee, Draft Standard 606a and Interpretation 606–2 (April 2011), which has added this new language to the library standards, at HYPERLINK "https://email.vanderbilt.edu/owa/redir.aspx?C=dc6695e0bd29481 baeef3eded7ef9263&URL=http%3a%2f%2fapps.americanbar.org%2flegaled%2fcommitte es%2fStandards%2520Review%2520documents%2f"http://apps.americanbar.org/legaled/committees/Standards%20Review%20documents/April%202011%20Meeting/Report%20 of%20Subcommittee%20on%20Library.pdf.

15. John Palfrey, "Cornerstones of Law Libraries for an Era of Digital-Plus," *Law Library Journal* 102 (2010–11): 171, 177; see also Mathews, *Marketing Today's Academic Library.*

16. Throughout this chapter, I use the phrase "library staff." This phrase should always be interpreted to include all people who work in the law library including librarians, professional staff, clerical, or technical staff by whatever title. While librarians are most often

referred to when thinking about library services, no law library could run competently without the people who catalog, process library materials, file looseleafs, shelve books, circulate library materials, pay bills, and the like. Most library users have no idea which staff are the librarians and which are not. And for all practical purposes it really does not matter. Users think of all people who work in libraries as librarians.

17. *See* R. David Lankes, "Turn Right at the Obelisk," keynote at AALL Annual Meeting, 12 July 2010. See http://quartz.syr.edu/rdlankes/Presentations/2010/AALL-Lankes.pdf for the slides and http://quartz.syr.edu/rdlankes/Pod/2010/AALL.mp3 for the audio.

18. *See* Callister, "Seeing the 'Whole Elephant,'" 18–19. For an interesting discussion of the law library as information facilitator, see Beatrice Tice, "The Academic Law Library in the 21st Century: Still the Heart of the Law School," *University of California Irvine Law Review* 1 (2011): 157, 169–71.

19. Stephen Abram, "Competing with Google," in *Out Front with Stephen Abram: A Guide for Information Leaders* (compiled by Judith A. Siess and Jonathan Lorig, Chicago: American Library Association, 2007), 93, 96.

20. *See* generally Taylor Fitchett et al., "Law Library Budgets in Hard Times," *Law Library Journal* 103 (2011): 91, 91–7.

21. *See* generally Abram, "Competing with Google," 98, and OCLC, "Perceptions of Libraries, 2010."

22. Abram, "Competing with Google," 93–8; Berring, "Deconstructing the Law Library," 1402. *See* also Femi Cadmus, "Things in Common: Challenges of the 19th and 21st Century Librarians," *Green Bag 2d*, 14 (2011): 193, 199.

23. Recently, in my own law library, an illustrative example occurred that comes to mind. It was the Friday before finals, in the very late afternoon. The law library was crammed with students frantically trying to turn information into knowledge. Suddenly, the library circulation supervisor heard a loud pounding on a door just outside the main library entrance. When she investigated, she discovered that the only door to the student journals' office would not open from the inside! Thus, students who wanted to go home for the evening or even to the restroom could not leave the space since they were locked in. Propping the door open emitted an unbearable, constant high-pitched sound. A call to university facilities resulted in a trip to the library, but no replacement part was available. So, the circulation supervisor had students call her when they wanted to leave, and she opened the door for them. Part of her job description? No. But a clever solution to a serious problem. Her solution allowed students to stay to study and complete journal work.

24. *See* Richard A. Danner, S. Blair Kauffman, and John G. Palfrey, "The Twenty-First Century Law Library," *Law Library Journal* 101 (2009): 143, 146. *See* also Tice, "The Academic Law Library in the 21st Century," 170–1.

25. Stephen Abram, "Shift Happens: Ten Key Trends in Our Profession and Ten Strategies for Success," 147, 154.

26. See ABA Standards Review Committee for information about the ABA revised standards and the source of this language at http://apps.americanbar.org/legaled/committees/Standards%20Review%20documents/April%202011%20Meeting/Report%20of%20Subcommittee%20on%20Library.pdf

27. Mathews, *Marketing Today's Academic Library.*

28. Many law libraries have portions of their collections in off-site storage, but all ABA-approved law schools in the United States still have a tangible collection of print and microform materials on-site in the law school's physical library. While the ABA Annual

Questionnaire now asks what percentage of the law library's tangible collection is available off-site, the takeoff statistics for 2010 do not include that comparative information.

29. Penny Hazelton, "How Much of Your Print Collection Is Really on WESTLAW or LEXIS-NEXIS?" *Legal Reference Services Quarterly,* 18(1) (1999): 3–22; Elizabeth Breakstone, "Now How Much of Your Print Collection Is Really Online? An Analysis of the Overlap of the Print and Digital Collections at the University of Oregon Law Library," *Legal Reference Services Quarterly* 29(4) (2010): 255–75.

30. For a short history of the economics of library collections, see Paul N. Courant, "The Future of the Library in the Research University," in *No Brief Candle: Reconceiving Research Libraries for the 21st Century* (Washington, DC: Council on Library and Information Resources, 2008) 21, 24–6; see also Berring, "Deconstructing the Law Library," 1390–1400.

31. ABA Standards for Approval of Law Schools, Standard 606, Collections, and Interpretation 606–2 (2010/11), at http://www.americanbar.org/content/dam/aba/migrated/legaled/standards/2010–2011_standards/2010–2011abastandards_pdf_files/chapter6.authcheckdam.pdf. Even the April draft of the revisions to Standard 606 includes this same language. *See* http://apps.americanbar.org/legaled/committees/Standards%20Review%20documents/April%202011%20Meeting/Report%20of%20Subcommittee%20on%20Library.pdf.

32. Intrepretation 606–4 currently permits off-site storage for nonessential materials as long as they are readily available. *See* ABA Standards for Approval of Law Schools, http://www.americanbar.org/content/dam/aba/migrated/legaled/standards/2010–2011_standards/2010–2011abastandards_pdf_files/chapter6.authcheckdam.pdf.

33. Palfrey, "Cornerstones of Law Libraries for an Era of Digital-Plus," 175.

34. *See* generally Robert Darnton, *The Case for Books: Past, Present, and Future* (New York: Public Affairs, 2009).

35. Law firm library print collections have been significantly reduced in size, and most firms rely on very expensive access to digital information. Law firm libraries buy and license content to support just in time legal information needs, not just in case situations. In the future, some academic law libraries may continue to keep large print collections while others, because of their mission, will choose to weed most or all of their print legal works.

36. Anecdotally, we know this to be true in American law schools, but we have few data to back up our claim. *See* the study from Australia where the author found that undergraduates are heavy consumers of electronic materials. Keith Webster, "The Library Space as Learning Space," *Educause Review,* November/December (45:6) 2010 at 1–2, http://www.educause.edu/EDUCAUSE+Review/EDUCAUSEReviewMagazineVolume45/TheLibrarySpaceasLearningSpace/218705.

37. Palfrey, "Cornerstones of Law Libraries for an Era of Digital-Plus," 175.

38. The focus of this chapter is on the law library and the law student. Obviously, other considerations will be examined once we take into account the full array of the members of the law school community who have reason to use a law library's collections.

39. Calvin K. M. Lam and Bernard C. Y. Tan, "The Internet Is Changing the Music Industry," *Communications of the ACM,* August 44(8) (2001): 64.

40. 376 U.S. 254 (1964).

41. The only studies completed that evaluate the trustworthiness and authenticity of legal information have been published by the American Association of Law Libraries. The most comprehensive, current study, State-by-State Report on the Authentication of Online Legal Resources, March 2007, defined an online authentic legal resource as

follows: "An *authentic* text is one whose content has been verified by a government entity to be complete and unaltered when compared to the version approved or published by the content originator. Typically, an *authentic* text will bear a certificate or mark that conveys information as to its certification, the process associated with ensuring that the text is complete and unaltered when compared with that of the content originator. An *authentic* text is able to be *authenticated*, which means that the particular text in question can be validated, ensuring that it is what it claims to be," at 8, http://www.aallnet.org/aallwash/authen_rprt/AuthenFinalReport.pdf. The report makes clear that simply declaring an online legal resource to be official does not mean it is authentic, a fact easier to prove in the print world where paper copies can corroborate the content.An update to this 2007 study was completed in February 2010 and is available at http://www.aallnet.org/committee/ELIAC/Authenticationreportupdates/2009AALLAuthenticationReportUpdates.pdf. See the committee's Web site at http://www.aallnet.org/summit/.

42. Virginia J. Wise and Frederick Schauer, "Legal Information as Social Capital," in *Legal Information and the Development of American Law: A Collection of Essays Inspired by the Contributions of Robert C. Berring* (St. Paul, MN: Thomson & West, 2008), 101, 114–18.

43. An interesting question, outside the scope of this chapter, is whether law libraries will continue to catalog or create local finding tools for the digital content they license and create. If free Web search engines can locate licensed content quickly with appropriate links, why would law libraries create their own records for an online public catalog? At the moment, the free search engines such as Google are not good enough to rely on completely. Too many irrelevant hits are located, and sometimes the needed item is several pages into the search results. This is one of the places we need experienced librarians to help determine what value the library can add to the access of legal information for our users.

44. Dean David Lewis of the IUPUI University Library explains that libraries should move away from purchasing collections (print and electronic) and toward curating unique print and digital collections, particularly the output of the institution's research enterprise. For further discussion of this idea, see David W. Lewis, "A Model for Academic Libraries 2005 to 2025," 10–13, paper presented at Visions of Change, California State University, 26 January 2007, http://hdl.handle.net/1805/665.

45. Joshua Kim, "Library Design," *Inside Higher Ed, Blog U, Technology and Learning,* 10 September 2009, http://www.insidehighered.com/blogs/technology_and_learning/library_design.

46. "SWOT Analysis I: Looking Outside for Threats and Opportunities," in *Strategy: Create and Implement the Best Strategy for Your Business* 1–24 (Cambridge, MA: Harvard Business School Press 2006).

47. An excellent history of the legal publishing industry can be found in Kendall F. Svengalis, *Legal Information Buyer's Guide and Reference Manual* (Westerly, RI: Rhode Island Law Press, 2010), 3–19.

48. For example, BNA has what appears to be an a la carte menu, but in reality it is simply a tiered pricing structure with specific titles at each level that cannot be interchanged. In another example, HeinOnline permits a library to buy various packages of databases, but the content in each is fixed and may not be negotiated differently. The academic contracts for Westlaw and LexisNexis access include a huge amount of content (much of which is of no interest to academic law library users) at a very low price. The academic package is a monolith and cannot be broken; contracts in the private and government sectors are much more segmentable.

49. *See* the homepage for Cambridge Books Online at http://ebooks.cambridge.org/home.jsf.
50. Julie Bosman, "A Limit on Lending E-Books," *New York Times*, Media Decoder, 27 February 2011) available at http://mediadecoder.blogs.nytimes.com/2011/02/27/a-limit-on-lending-e-books/. *See also* Mary Ann Gwinn, "An e-Book Disconnect between Publisher, Libraries," *Seattle Times*, 4 April 2011, B3.
51. Gwinn, "An e-Book Disconnect."
52. For a thoughtful discussion of the role of libraries and vendor e-book licenses, *see* Gregory K. Laughlin, "Digitization and Democracy: The Conflict between the Amazon Kindle License Agreement and the Role of Libraries in a Free Society," *University of Baltimore Law Review* 40 (2010): 3–51.
53. *See* Gwen Gregory, "Ask a Librarian," *Computers in Libraries* (January/February 2011): 33. *See also* Stephen Abram, "Concerns about Technological Fragmentation," *Information Outlook* 15(3) (April/May 2011): 32–4.
54. Geoffrey Nunberg, "Google's Book Search: A Disaster for Scholars," *Chronicle of Higher Education, The Chronicle Review*, 31 August 2009, at http://chronicle.com/article/Googles-Book-Search-A/48245/. *See also* Laura Miller, "The Trouble with Google Books," 9 September 2010, at http://www.salon.com/books/laura_miller/2010/09/09google_books/index/html.
55. *See* Tushar Rae, "E-Books' Varied Formats Make Citations a Mess for Scholars," *Chronicle of Higher Education* (February 11, 2011): A11–12. Of course, in law we have used star paging as a way to be able to refer to the official version of a court's opinion, for example. The online versions of court opinions on Lexis and Westlaw both include star paging to the official version in the commercial versions of the court reporters. Universal (sometimes called vendor neutral) citation form, with references to numbered paragraphs instead of pages, has been vigorously supported by the American Association of Law Libraries and approved for study by the American Bar Association. *See* http://www.aallnet.org/committee/citation/ for further references and links to the AALL Universal Citation Guide, last published in 2002. *See also* http://apps.americanbar.org/tech/ltrc/research/citation/home.html.
56. A recent experience will serve to make this point. The University of Washington School of Law, as with most American law schools, has an e-only student journal, the *Washington Journal of Law, Technology and the Arts*. For several years, they published their content on the law school's Web page in html format with links to authority and other references. When we began to study the process they used for loading the new journal articles, we realized that the conversion to html did not always result in the look the editors were seeking, and they kept finding changes and corrections to make in the text. And even after the "final" version was posted, an endless number of corrections and changes were requested, causing a heavy burden on the law school staff. In a sense, the articles were never done, being subject to changes and tweaks for an unlimited time! Once we decided to host the journal in a digital repository, we needed a better definition for "final" and have moved to adding a final pdf version of each article, which is also the format in which they are now published. *See* http://www.law.washington.edu/wjlta/ for abstracts, and for the full text, *see* http://www.law.washington.edu/wjlta/issues/201100603.pdf. But *see* Richard A. Danner, Kelly Leong, and Wayne V. Miller, "The Durham Statement Two Years Later: Open Access in the Law School Journal Environment," The adoption of the Uniform Electronic Legal Material Act by the National Conference of Commissions of Uniform

State Laws in 2011 has been enthusiastically endorsed by AALL. *See* current status and a link to the final language at, http://www.uniformlaws.org./Act.aspx?title=Electronic Legal Material Act. *Law Library Journal* 103 (2011): 39, 47–50.

57. See the AALL Web site for the various reports and studies that have been done on this subject since 2003, at http://www.aallnet.org/summit/.

58. For example, in the state of Washington, the Code Reviser's office publishes the *Washington State Register*, the chronological publication of state regulations. Recently, they discontinued the print version, but they have declared the electronic version on the Web site to be official. However, the register is not yet authenticated. Here is their statement: "Washington State Register Official Publication Statement. The Statute Law Committee declares that the publication of the Washington State Register on the Code Reviser's Web site is the official publication of the register. The Code Reviser's Office maintains and will continue to maintain a file of every document ever filed with the Washington State Register. When asked to certify a document, the Code Reviser will certify a copy of the original filing." *See* http://www.leg.wa.gov/CodeReviser/Documents/officialstatement.htm.

In contrast, *see* the disclaimer on the Washington State Supreme Court Web site related to their court opinions:

> "Disclaimer. **Published Opinions**. This database contains slip opinions. Slip opinions do not necessarily represent the court's final decision in the case since they are subject to reconsideration, modification orders, editorial corrections, and withdrawal. The official reports advance sheets and bound volumes supersede the slip opinions."

See http://www.courts.wa.gov/opinions/?fa=opinions.recent.

59. Nicholas Carr, "Is Google Making Us Stupid?" The Atlantic.com, July/August 2008, at 6;, available at http://www.theatlantic.com/doc/print/200807/google.

60. Barbara Bintliff, "Context and Legal Research," in *Legal Information and the Development of American Law: A Collection of Essays Inspired by the Contributions of Robert C. Berring* (St. Paul, MN: Thomson West, 2008), 79, 95.

61. Perhaps students will even choose something called the Built-in Orderly Organized Knowledge (BOOK) so humorously described in a 1962 *Punch* magazine article. Terry Martin, professor of law and law librarian at Harvard Law School, revived this tongue-in-cheek piece in his excellent essay, "From Ownership to Access: Standards of Quality for the Law Library of Tomorrow," *Law Library Journal* 82(1990): 129, 141–3; *see* also Kim, *supra*, note 45, and Courant, "Future of the Library in the Research University," in *No Brief Candle* 21–27.

62. *See* generally Bintliff, "Context and Legal Research."

63. *See* "SWOT Analysis I: Looking Outside for Threats and Opportunities," 1–24.

64. Richard A. Danner, Kelly Leong, and Wayne V. Miller, "The Durham Statement Two Years Later: Open Access in the Law School Journal Environment," *Law Library Journal* 103 (2011), 39.

65. *See* Svengalis, *Legal Information Buyer's Guide.*

66. Stephen G. Nichols, "Co-Teaching: The Library and Me," in *No Brief Candle*, 28–34.

67. *See* Ronald Collins and David Skover, Chapter 1, this volume.

68. Andy Havens and Tom Storey, "The Future of Publishing: Libraries and the Changing Role of Creators and Consumers," *NEXTSpace* no. 16 (August 2010): 4–9.

69. Kate Wittenburg, "The Role of the Library in 21st-Century Scholarly Publishing," in *No Brief Candle*, 35–41.

70. *See* the prototype for the casebook of the future from the Center for Computer-Assisted Instruction (CALI) Web site, available at http://www.cali.org/elangdell.

71. *See* Darnton, *Case for Books*.

72. Michael Kelly, "Cornell University Library Takes Stand against Non-Disclosure Agreements," Library Journal.com, March 23 2011, http://www.libraryjournal.com/lj/home/889820–264/cornell_university_library_takes_stand.html.csp.

73. *See* AALL Vendor Relations activities, available at http://www.aallnet.org/vendorrelations/vendorliaison-faq.asp.

74. Recently, in the state of Washington, law librarians have been working closely with the Code Reviser's Office to lobby for authentication and permanent public access before the state moves to a digital-only environment for the state's important legal publications. The conversations have educated both sides about the questions of trustworthiness of legal information in the digital world. A bill is pending before the state legislature that was the product of compromise. Some legal titles will still be available in a tangible print form. An added benefit is that the librarians directed the state to a source for a digital version of the historical state session laws, which are now on the Web site free of charge. See also note 41 for AALL activity related to authentication.

75. Courant, "Future of the Library in the Research University," in *No Brief Candle*, 21, 27.

76. *See* Darnton, *Case for Books*, 77.

77. *See* the alliance Web page for links to their studies and other relevant projects, at http://www.aallnet.org/committee/lipa/.

78. *See* "Berkman Center Announces Digital Public Library Planning Initiative," 13 December 2010, http://cyber.law.harvard.edu/newsroom/digital_public_library.

79. Not all of these digital collections are free, but many are. *See* their Web site at http://www.hathitrust.org/about.

80. For example, the Gallagher Law Library has worked over time to preserve and make accessible an important work on the Washington State Constitution. Working with a faculty expert in this subject, we reprinted *The Journal of the Washington State Constitutional Convention 1889, with Analytical Index*, ed. Beverly Paulik Rosenow, in 1989, including an unpublished collection of newspaper articles about the state constitutional convention in 1899. Today, we are working with the same faculty member to create a research guide and database, linking to important digitized content as a one-stop shop for anyone who is interested in our state's constitution. This kind of project, combining the expertise of faculty with the expertise of law librarians, is a way to preserve important legal content, but also to make it accessible in multidimensional ways. *See also* Lewis, "Model for Academic Libraries."

81. *See* Courant, "Future of the Library in the Research University."

82. *See* Bintliff, "Context and Legal Research."

83. *See* Lankes, "Turn Right at the Obelisk"; *see* also Jake Carlson and Ruth Kneale, "Embedded Librarianship in the Research Context: Navigating New Waters," *College and Research Libraries News* 72(3) (March 2011), 167.

84. *See* Palfrey, "Cornerstones of Law Libraries for an Era of Digital-Plus," 177; Mathews, *Marketing Today's Academic Library*.

PART III

Reforming the Curriculum through Digital Course Materials

8

Law School 2.0

Course Books in the Digital Age

David C. Vladeck

A. THE PROBLEM WITH LEGAL EDUCATION AND LEGAL
EDUCATIONAL MATERIALS

I think it is only fair that I begin this chapter with an acknowledgment that I approach this topic – the future of law school course books – with a perspective that may differ significantly from that of my coauthors, most of whom are distinguished scholars who have spent the majority of their careers in the academy. Although I have taught at Georgetown Law in one capacity or another for more than twenty years, I have never been anything more than a part-time scholar. Most of my career has been spent as a litigator, mainly at a public interest law firm, then as a clinical teacher at Georgetown, and now at the Federal Trade Commission. I have thus not only straddled the divide between the academy and practice, but also straddled a line that divides the faculty at many law schools (though not Georgetown) – the line between classroom teachers and clinicians. At Georgetown, I run a clinical law program that focuses on civil rights and civil liberties litigation, but I also teach conventional classroom courses, including civil procedure, federal courts, and administrative law.

As a clinician, and a longtime public interest (now government) litigator, I have helped train many recent law school graduates in the art of practicing law. That experience has driven home to me both the strengths and the weaknesses of conventional law school education. At the risk of gross oversimplification, law schools do a good job teaching students legal doctrine and reasoning. By the time students graduate from law school, they generally can identify core legal issues, engage in research and analysis to determine the applicable law, and construct (and deconstruct) legal arguments. In other words, law schools teach students to "think like lawyers," and they do that well. One reason that they succeed in that endeavor is that today's course books are all about teaching students how to engage in legal analysis and reasoning.

But law schools and today's course books do not teach students how to *be* lawyers. Most students graduate from law school unprepared to practice law and need some form of apprenticeship to acquire basic practice skills. Indeed, when training new lawyers, I am constantly struck by how little they know about legal practice – not just the technical nuts and bolts, but the basics, from understanding ethics rules, the formation of a lawyer/client relationship, and the need to maintain client confidences to fundamental doctrinal points, such as the relationship between federal and state law or the potential benefits (and risks) of pleading a case in tort rather than in contract. They lack many of the skills – apart from legal analysis and reasoning – that legal practice requires, including, just to name a few, dealing with clients, gathering facts, conducting investigations, solving problems, drafting legal documents, negotiating with opposing parties, and honing and presenting arguments.[1]

Law schools are responsible for this educational gap. Even those that pride themselves on the richness of their clinical offerings (as does Georgetown) can offer most students only one opportunity to take a clinical course. Apart from that one course, and maybe a trial practice or negotiation course, skills training for students ordinarily is gained, if at all, mainly from summer jobs and externships. These are worthwhile endeavors, to be sure, but they are separate and apart from the students' law school training.

So what does this general complaint about law school pedagogy have to do with course books? A good deal, for two related but distinct reasons. My first and most basic concern about today's paper course books is their single-minded focus on teaching doctrine through the case method. The problem is that *course* books remain, by and large, *case*books, focusing mainly on the law as articulated in appellate court opinions. My second concern is that even if course books morph beyond casebooks to be more inclusive, and to address our modern administrative and transactional state, they still need to be further expanded to integrate practice-based skills training as well. The dominance of casebooks in doctrinal training at law schools can be traced back to Christopher Columbus Langdell's invention in the 1870s and 1880s, when he was dean of Harvard Law School. Since then, law schools have generally relied on the case method to teach students doctrine, legal analysis, and reasoning through a structured classroom dialogue led by the professor. No lawyer who has ever seen *The Paper Chase* will forget Professor Kingsfield's inquisition of his students as he forces them to confront the complexities of *Hawkins v. McGee*, better known as the "hairy hand" case.[2]

Relying on close examination of legal doctrine by having students read and then dissect appellate cases in class undoubtedly made sense in the days when Dean Langdell walked the halls of Harvard Law School. And that probably was true in the heady days of *MacPherson v. Buick* when Judge Cardozo and the New York State Court of Appeals were bringing about significant doctrinal changes through common law adjudication. But much has happened since then. The New Deal, the rise of the administrative state, and the Court's focus on textualism as the dominant mode of statutory construction have added complexities to the law not adequately addressed by the case method.

Make no mistake: The case method is still an essential teaching tool. Students must learn to parse cases. Much of the "law" lawyers deal with is judge-made or judge-articulated law. So I am by no means a critic of the case method. I am a critic, however, of feeding law students a diet consisting almost exclusively of the cases that they must digest and reconcile with other cases. Case analysis is not the only analytical tool that is required to "think like a lawyer." Today's law students also need to be taught to engage in sophisticated statutory analysis, navigate their way through the labyrinth of the regulatory process, and understand modes of interpreting legal documents – from contracts, to tariffs, to treaties.[3] Moving on to my second concern, I emphatically reject the notion that skills training is something separate from doctrinal teaching. In my view – which is based on my experience as a teacher/practitioner – the best way to teach doctrine is to have students use it, not just as part of the classroom dialogue, but in practice. I regularly integrate skills training into the classroom courses I teach. But it seems unlikely that today's paperbound course books, limited in length, size, and weight, can be expected to achieve that integration.

These critiques are nothing new, of course. The American Bar Association recently changed its accreditation requirements for law schools to require significantly more skills training.[4] And the Carnegie Foundation for the Advancement of Teaching recently issued a report, *Educating Lawyers: Preparation for the Profession of Law*, criticizing conventional legal training's sole emphasis on doctrine and its relative inattention to skills training and professional exploration. While the report accepts the use of what it calls the "case-dialogue" method of legal instruction to teach legal analysis and reasoning, it urges law schools to move beyond this method and enrich law school offerings by (a) integrating skills training to develop core competences and (b) deepening the exploration of social and ethical issues that pervade lawyering. The report makes clear that this enrichment should not be implemented just through new courses. Rather, the goal should be to embed skills training and role exploration into the core curriculum.[5] Today's course books do not fit within this new vision for law school teaching.

B. THE PRAGMATIC ADVANTAGES OF DIGITAL COURSE BOOKS

1. *General Considerations*

Fortunately, I think that there is a serendipitous convergence between the need to fine-tune our approach to legal education with the stark reality that, like it or not (and I suspect that many of my law professor colleagues are in the "not" camp), the leather-bound, back-breakingly heavy course books we know and love are an endangered species doomed to certain and reasonably swift extinction. They are doomed to become relics for many reasons. One is substantive. Law changes rapidly; print books can only be revised once every few years, whereas digital books can be revised any time a significant development occurs. A second is ecological. What sense does it make to clear-cut acres of forest to print books, particularly when they need to be revised on a regular basis? A third is economic. Printing books is very expensive; that is not so with digital books, which can be updated quickly and inexpensively. And a fourth involves convenience; books are a burden to lug around, and law students are no different from the millions of others who are accustomed to assimilating information online on lightweight laptops, Kindles, Ipads, and other electronic readers. Why carry around a backpack loaded with thirty pounds of books when one can carry a laptop or an Ipad at a tenth the weight?

Still another practical reason for migration to digital course materials is pedagogical. Digitization holds the promise of freeing teachers from the rigidity of general purpose course books. Virtually all professors feel the need to adapt whatever book they choose for their own pedagogic purposes. Although course books generally try to provide a comprehensive overview of the applicable doctrine through case law, they inevitably embody the choices and reflect the vision of their authors. Digital course books will free professors to tailor the materials to their own pedagogical needs, both by adding noncase materials omitted by the course book authors, and, equally important, by subtracting material the professor does not intend to cover.

Digital course materials can thus offer flexibility and choice. Law school teachers will be able to configure course materials in ways that will combine the best of today's course books – carefully selected and edited cases that illuminate doctrine while providing helpful and provocative commentary – with material that reflects the professor's own teaching style and conception of the subject matter. Moving to digital course books will also serve as a counterweight to the unwritten but universal rule that a professor who directs students to buy a casebook adds readings, problem sets, and other materials at his or her peril. Students bridle at having to pay for a course book and then being saddled with significant amounts of supplementary materials. As I envision the digital course book of the future, it will be sufficiently flexible and open-ended that the distinction between the material supplied by the authors and that added by the course instructor is essentially invisible to the students. What they will see, and learn from, is a single, coherent set of instructional materials.

But the migration to digital course books will not, indeed, cannot, displace or diminish the need for scholars to continue to assemble them, as scholars have done since the days of Dean Langdell. The digital course books of the future will be built on the same foundation as today's paper course books. Scholars will still have to develop the architecture for teaching doctrine. And they will still have to identify the key materials, edit opinions and other source material, provide commentary, pinpoint those areas that remain unsettled or in flux, and, above all else, strike the delicate balance of ensuring that the materials are sufficiently challenging to engage students but not so challenging as to be inaccessible. To be sure, the media will be different and more pliable, but the basic building blocks will be familiar.

2. *Personal Applications*

I want to supplement this general description of the pragmatic advantages of digital course books with some personal reflections on how such materials would affect my own teaching.

First, my ability to supplement published material with my own would be an important step forward. I have problem sets that I integrate into conventional classroom courses by making pdfs available on the law school's intranet and by distributing paper handouts. The burdens of doing so – on me and the students – limit the amount of problem sets I can use in any one course. Being able to integrate my materials seamlessly into a course book prepared by other scholars would enable me to add more noncase materials that I think are important for students to study.

Adding noncase materials can enliven and enrich course offerings. For instance, the audio files of Supreme Court arguments are now readily available on the Internet (at www.oyez.org). Integrating digital files of such arguments can really bring a case to life and expose students to the dynamics of actual Supreme Court arguments. Having students read briefs can also deepen their understanding of cases. Many students make it through the first two years of law school without reading a brief. Why is that? Is the academy so court-centered that it dismisses out of hand the role advocacy plays in shaping the law? I think that briefing often matters a great deal, and exposing student to the work product of lawyers – and not just judges – is important for many reasons. And video materials are now widely available and can easily be integrated into digital course materials. As one example, I would certainly have civil procedure students view a few minutes of a videotape of a real deposition in preparation for discussing depositions in class. Beyond giving me the practical means to integrate other materials better, developing new digital platforms would better enable me – and other teachers, of course – to share course materials with students and colleagues (either for free or for a fee).

One of my responsibilities at Georgetown is to codirect a clinical program that handles civil rights and civil liberties litigation. The course includes a two-hour weekly seminar that focuses on developing litigation skills, from client interviews, to complaint drafting, to discovery, to motion practice and appeals. There is no course book that fits this curriculum, so I generate the course materials myself. But each semester I fine-tune these materials to update them and to make them relevant to the cases we are handling that semester. Distributing these materials is done through the school's intranet system, which, as discussed before, is capable of distributing only pdfs, not text files. This means that students cannot adapt these materials, cannot annotate them, and cannot take notes on them. Although I can distribute them digitally, most students end up printing them out. And because the materials are updated frequently, I have to remind myself each semester to send them to colleagues who are interested in them but teach at other schools.

Ideally, a digital platform would be able to make this material available in text form to students and colleagues without burdening the teacher with the responsibility of sending copies to each user. Since technology has developed platforms used for similar purposes outside academia, I am hopeful that law schools may soon acquire similar capabilities.

Last, but hardly least, I would like to see the development of a digital commons for course materials – especially digital course books. I recognize that there are important intellectual property rights at issue (and I am willing for the commons to have pay-as-you-go features). The scholars who labor to prepare course books and then update them regularly merit our collective thanks and surely deserve to be compensated for their efforts. But I would like a commons to develop that permits teachers to select portions of course books and cobble together course materials by integrating published materials with materials selected by the teacher. For instance, I would be happy to use one of several civil procedure books, provided that I could add a new introduction, set forth an introductory fact pattern, add a few cases that pose current problems, and include skills exercises that involve drafting pleadings, initiating discovery requests, and conducting negotiations.

I would also take advantage of being able to decide to exclude material that will not be covered in the class. For example, I teach federal courts using Hart & Wechsler and I am devoted to the book.[6] But face facts. This redoubtable classic is now more than sixteen hundred pages long. No one can cover the whole book in a single semester (indeed, it is not clear that one person can even *carry* the book, given how outsized it has become). All of us who use the book edit by addition and subtraction. My hope is that technology will permit us at some point to use this book, and others like it, as menus that offer teachers choices about what to cover; permit us to add and subtract material; and enable us to make the book conform to our choices about how to teach our students doctrine and how that doctrine is used in law practice

C. THE SUBSTANTIVE ADVANTAGES OF DIGITAL COURSE BOOKS

Convenience and flexibility, however, are only the beginning of the advantages that digital course books offer. My submission, consistent with the problems I identified in the first part of this chapter, is that the shift from paper course books to digital ones will have a seismic but ultimately beneficial impact on legal education. Law teachers should embrace and advocate for this change for pedagogical reasons. In this section I develop in somewhat more detail what to me are the major justifications for giving up our professorial love affair with paper and moving to digital course materials.

As I see it, there are three such reasons. One is to facilitate the integration of skills training into the teaching of doctrine. A second is that digital platforms can aid teachers in promoting collaboration among students. A third consideration is that law students need to be challenged to think through what it will mean to practice law. Does it matter what clients the lawyer chooses to represent? Where do conceptions of "justice" fit in? What are lawyers' obligations to society? To the courts? To their community? These are questions largely unaddressed by today's course books, but fundamental to legal education.

1. *Skills Training*

As I made clear earlier, one serious flaw in conventional legal education is that doctrinal training crowds out skills training. Making matters worse, some law schools maintain the fiction that skills training is something apart from doctrinal teaching, to be addressed, if at all, through clinical programs, skills-centered courses (like negotiation and trial practice), and externships. For that reason, most discussion about skills training envisions *adding* skills-based courses to the curriculum. I have no objection to this approach. But I think that the notion that skills training is distinct from doctrinal teaching is dead wrong. In my experience, it can be, and often is, a key to understanding theoretical material. To give students a foundation in *using* doctrine (as opposed to memorizing it), I supplement course books with extensive problem-based handouts. And the longer I teach the more problem sets I use. In my view, the best way to learn doctrine is to use it, not just as part of the classroom dialogue, but in practice.

To give just one example: I could not teach civil procedure by using a conventional course book that employs only cases and commentary to illuminate complicated doctrinal issues like personal jurisdiction, *Erie*, and issue and claims preclusion. There are many civil procedure course books that do a fine job in laying out this doctrine, and I would not want to teach civil procedure without one. Teaching civil procedure from a course book alone is thus like asking students to assemble a complicated jigsaw puzzle without providing them a picture of what the puzzle is supposed to look like. None of the civil procedure course books that I have seen tries to give students that picture at the outset of the course, no doubt because their authors assume that, at some point during the course, the mosaic will come into focus.[7]

The other problem stems from the first; understanding the issues conceptually rarely translates into practical knowledge that is of use to the students when they start to practice. They may leave law school knowing what a complaint is and the purpose filing a complaint serves. But that knowledge translates poorly, if at all, when the quondam student is asked, often at some early point in his or her career, actually to draft a complaint. I know. When I ask new lawyers to draft a complaint, most stare back in horrified silence. They have no idea what a complaint looks like, what it should contain, or even how to go about thinking through the steps a lawyer might take to draft it.

The better approach, I think, is to start with the picture and then examine the pieces that compose it. I use a problem set to set the stage for that examination.[8] To enable students to envision the totality for themselves, I begin the course by giving them a fact pattern based on a very simple tort case (no knowledge of torts is required, though) that can be used to raise every issue we then cover in class – from personal jurisdiction to subject-matter jurisdiction, pleading rules, basic discovery, alternative dispute resolution, summary judgment, *Erie*, choice of law, burdens of production and proof, preclusion rules, appellate review, and the like.

I do not let students look at the casebook or the federal rules. Instead, I push them to write their own set of rules to govern the resolution of the dispute. That discussion, of course, entails an examination of the considerations that go with each decision: How should the injured party give notice to a potentially responsible party? Should the parties be required to try to resolve the matter informally before beginning an adversarial proceeding? What should the adversarial process look like? What information should the parties exchange? Who should decide which party is right? There are process-versus-efficiency trade-offs that need to be discussed, and some rules will inevitably favor one party over the other. But in relatively short order the class resolves these problems and formulates its own set of rules, which, not surprisingly, often look a good deal like the federal rules. Once the class understands that rules are intended to work together and embody tradeoffs that, when examined together, are supposed to be fair to all, we then turn to the course book.

This initial exercise is not the end of my problem-based approach, however. Throughout the course, I supplement the course book with problem sets that are intended to link classroom discussions about doctrine with skills training. I have students draft complaints, answers, and interrogatories, all based on the simple tort case we started with. All of this supplemental work – rudimentary skills training – strongly reinforces the students' understanding of the key doctrinal points. After all, how can students learn what a "pleading" is if they have not seen one? How can they understand the advantages and pitfalls of interrogatories or the theory underlying Rule 30(b)(6) (interrogatories directed to organizations) if they have not read some? Will they truly understand claims and issue preclusion without having drafted complaints and answers? And why should not students at least view a video of a deposition, if for no other reason than to end the mystery about what a deposition is really like?

The upshot of all of this is that one of my goals is to think about reconfiguring the course book to make it useful for skills training.[9] As any law professor knows, using problem sets as a supplement to a course book can be a logistical nightmare. At Georgetown, I have as many as 115–120 students in a first-year civil procedure course and 90 or more students in federal courts. Typically, I post handouts on an intranet site run by the law school and accessible only by students and faculty. Because the handouts are available only in a pdf format, students cannot take notes on them or integrate them into other materials. Many students respond to this limitation by printing out the supplementary materials, tying up printers, wasting paper, and duplicating effort. Often the handouts refer to cases, statutes, news articles, or other reference materials, which are also downloaded and printed out by many students. And of course I bear the burden of drafting the handouts, converting them to pdfs, posting them on our intranet site, and then printing out a batch of the materials for students who, for one reason or another, fail to look at the intranet site before class.

Digital course books could resolve the logistical problems that now stand as deterrents to integrating skills training into conventional courses. With a digital course book, I could choose where to insert my problem sets into my syllabus, and all the materials would be available to students from the beginning of the course. Because they would be in a digital format that presumably would allow students to underline and annotate the text, there would be far less need to download and print out reams of material. And, as I will explain, the convenience of a digital platform would encourage students to collaborate more freely on the skills component of the course, another important goal.

2. *Encouraging Collaboration*

Collaboration is a value too often neglected in law school, notwithstanding that law generally is practiced collaboratively. To be sure, we all know lawyers (and law professors) we would be happy to see hermetically sealed off in their offices. But good lawyers know that their work product improves when they work with colleagues. That is one reason why lawyers form firms and why we have appellate courts composed of multiple judges. Even law students understand this; they collaborate on their own by quickly forming study groups to help them assimilate the flood of information that inundates them from day one of law school.

But law teaching – and law school grading – is highly individualistic. Students prefer that; they are reluctant to risk their grade on the performance of a team. They understandably want to be judged on their own performance. But collaboration is a critical skill for practicing lawyers, and law schools need to teach students how to collaborate effectively, not just with colleagues, but also with lawyers representing adverse parties.

One example makes this point. When I teach civil procedure, early in the semester I have students draft a simple complaint in the tort case we use as a template. Few if any students have ever seen a complaint, and I do not make one available. I do point students to Rules 8 and 10 of the Federal Rules of Civil Procedure, which spell out the essential elements of a complaint in some detail. But the students' anxiety is palpable. To dampen the anxiety, I assign students to small groups (I pick the groups at random to force them to work with others whom they likely do not know) and make it clear that the exercise will not be graded unless the group clearly blows off the assignment. None do. The students are required to meet at least once, and they are each required to sign the complaint. Although the complaints are not generally works of art, most of them meet the technical pleading requirements, and many are quite good. There is no question that this exercise reinforces their understanding of pleading doctrine and helps them learn basic drafting skills. That is clearly to the good. But equally important, students learn that collaborating in small groups can improve the overall quality of the work product, and they learn a good deal about the dynamics of working in a group – all valuable lessons.[10]

Although I think that this and similar exercises are critically important to enriching the students' understanding of doctrine, they are difficult to administer without a digital platform, and that is a disincentive to using them.[11] At present, they result in a deluge of paper, which I have to sort through and manage. And all I see is the students' final product. It would be extremely useful to see the progression of student drafts: where the students got off course, what tangents they took, and how they got back on track. Looking at the drafting history would give me insights that would help me better understand what the students were thinking, what they understood, and what stumped them. A digital platform would also make this exercise easier for the students. Some students are proficient in using document-sharing programs that allow for multiple authors to be working on the same draft, but many are not. For them, working through this relatively simple problem with fellow students presents serious logistical problems. Having a digital platform that enabled them to work collectively on a single draft, to track changes, and to permit me to review their work would make the skills training in this exercise far easier.

Moving to a digital environment, which facilitates the use of problem sets, would not only help students develop a much richer understanding of the materials, but also be an extremely effective way to teach them how to collaborate. Practicing lawyers are required to collaborate with people they do not know, yet their work depends on finding some way to cooperate for a common end. That is the essence of law practice, and there is no time better to start learning it than the first year of law school.

3. *Understanding Professionalism*

For reasons I cannot fathom, law schools do a particularly poor job teaching students about the profession they have chosen to enter. There is little or no discussion of how lawyers choose whom they represent and the consequences that flow from that choice. Most students go to law school for one or more of a constellation of related reasons: the lure of an intellectually challenging job, the hope of financial security, the luster of a professional career, and perhaps the idea that a law degree will enable them to engage in public service. But they rarely have a concrete understanding of what lawyers do and the choices they have to make.

These are issues rarely discussed in law schools, and if they are, they are generally relegated to an elective course on the legal profession that is bypassed by most students. Because I have observed generations of law school graduates grapple with these problems, it is clear to me that these are questions better posed and addressed in an academic environment, where reflection is the norm, not in a law office, where competing pressures almost invariably win out. But law schools rarely challenge students to examine their assumptions about what being a lawyer really means. Seldom do they undertake a probing examination of the role that lawyers play in society, the choices that lawyers have to make in terms of how they spend their working lives, and how the institutions that provide legal services (big, medium-size, and small firms; legal service providers; government agencies; public interest organizations) operate.

The content of law school course books is part of this general failure to confront questions relating to the legal profession. To take one example I care deeply about, these books rarely identify the achievements of the legal services, civil rights, and public interest segments of the bar as a way of showing students that significant changes in the law generally do not occur by happenstance, but rather through the efforts of lawyers – very often lawyers who have chosen career paths other than corporate law. As a friend of mine put it, the books fail to reflect the "nobility" of the profession. Students read *Brown v. Board of Education*, *NAACP v. Button*, *Goldberg v. Kelly*, *Matthews v. Eldridge*, *Roe v. Wade*, *INS v. Chadha*, *Goldfarb v. Virginia*, and *Virginia State Board of Pharmacy v. Virginia Citizens Consumer Council, Inc.*, without any classroom exploration into the question why these cases were brought as test cases by dedicated, public-spirited litigators in an effort to reshape the law.[12]

Does it make sense to learn about the school desegregation or death penalty cases without any appreciation of the role the National Association for the

Advancement of Colored People (NAACP) Legal Defense and Educational Fund played in those efforts? Should students read the landmark due process cases without an understanding of how the strategy that led to their presence in court was developed by legal services lawyers? How can students understand the significance of *Roe v. Wade* without a broader appreciation of the struggle for reproductive rights in the United States? For example, test case litigation that my former office, Public Citizen Litigation Group, handled brought about many dramatic changes in the landscape of separation of powers jurisprudence, administrative law, and the regulation of the legal profession.[13] Textbooks address the Litigation Group's cases at length, but they make no mention of its role. Why not? These are obvious questions, but law schools do not address them, leaving students the poorer for their lack of understanding about how the profession works, and how and why significant changes to the law occur. Digital course books will be no panacea for this problem. But their flexibility will enable professors who think that these are important issues to add them at the right moment: that is, at the same time students are studying a particular case to learn its doctrinal import. Changes in the law can be brought about not just by lawyers who work for firms or public interest organizations; sole practitioners too are often engaged in cutting-edge legal work. For this reason, when I teach *Connecticut v. Doehr* (a Supreme Court case invalidating Connecticut's prejudgment attachment statute on due process grounds) in civil procedure, I take a few minutes to explain to students that this landmark case was litigated by a solo practitioner in Connecticut with an enviable record before the Court. It is important for students to understand that engaging in precedent-setting litigation is not the exclusive domain of big firm or public interest practitioners.

In a similar vein, when I teach *Virginia Pharmacy Board* in a First Amendment seminar I teach occasionally, I require students to listen to the oral argument (available through the Oyez project), to read the key briefs (now available on Westlaw and Lexis), and then to discuss why the plaintiffs – represented by public interest lawyers intent on creating protection for commercial speech – litigated the case on the basis of a "right to receive information" theory instead of a more conventional "right to speak" First Amendment argument. Were they worried about the consequences of arguing that corporations have free speech rights? If so, why? Were their concerns well founded? A decade ago the burden was on me to compile the briefs and make them available to the students. The Internet has made it easier to ask students to get the source material on their own. A digital platform that seamlessly integrated these materials would be even better and would allow me more control over the course materials that I use to go beyond doctrine and explore the unseen undercurrents that often shape the law.

D. CONCLUSION

The move to digital course materials is already under way. Publishers are already offering teachers digital supplements to course books and other material that is intended to complement conventional course materials. My vision certainly takes account of an ongoing role for publishers, just as it recognizes that there have to be financial rewards to entice already busy scholars to take the time and effort to compile course books. We all benefit from their considerable effort, and they too are entitled to benefit as well.

But I hope that the move to digital platforms also permits greater sharing among law teachers. We need a digital commons to facilitate that sharing within the academy. And we need to find better ways to expose law students to the practicalities of lawyering, not just legal theory. In my view, the joy of lawyering – and yes, I think that lawyering can be joyful – is working with others to pursue a common goal, and learning to perform a craft collaboratively and well. A theoretical grounding is, of course, essential. But there is much more to being a lawyer than understanding theory. And moving away from the course books of the past, toward a more flexible set of course materials that draw from different media, is a step in the right direction.

NOTES

1. Some may be surprised that I see fact gathering as a skill overlooked in law school, because so much attention is given to the manipulation of facts as part of the Socratic dialogue. Students do learn that even a subtle, modest change of the facts can dramatically change the way a legal rule is applied. But facts are the stepchild of legal education because, apart from courses in evidence, scant attention is paid to the way facts are acquired and what makes an assertion of fact a "fact" in the eyes of the law. Students wrongly leave law school thinking that facts are found through discovery, but most lawyers use other tools to develop as much factual material as they can in ways other than formal discovery. And fact gathering is as basic a lawyering tool as they come. In one of the seminars I teach as part of my clinic, I ask the students (all in their third year of law school) how they would go about proving the facts of a simple automobile accident case. They are stumped. Most students gravitate toward the discovery tools they covered in class. Others are just clueless. Rarely does a student have even a clue about how to find witnesses. And to be fair to the students, my class is the first time in law school they are called on to determine how one gathers facts to prove a case.
2. The case, of course, is *Hawkins v. McGee*, and its use in *The Paper Chase* is discussed extensively in the Carnegie Foundation's Report as a memorable, and effective, illustration of the case-dialogue method. William Sullivan et al., *Educating Lawyers: Preparation for the Profession of Law* (San Francisco: Jossey-Bass, 2007), 48–9 (the Carnegie Report).
3. This is hardly an original critique, and I make no claim otherwise.

4. *See* Standard 302(b), ABA Standards for Approval of Law Schools (2010–2011), at http://www.americanbar.org/content/dam/aba/migrated/legaled/standards/2010001E2011_standards/2010001E2011abastandards_pdf_files/chapter3.authcheckdam.pdf). This standard provides: "(b) A law school shall offer substantial opportunities for:

 (1) live-client or other real-life practice experiences, appropriately supervised and designed to encourage reflection by students on their experiences and on the values and responsibilities of the legal profession, and the development of one's ability to assess his or her performance and level of competence;
 (2) student participation in pro bono activities; and
 (3) small group work through seminars, directed research, small classes, or collaborative work."

5. The unacknowledged irony is that law schools were developed to replace, or at least augment, the practice of legal apprenticeship as the gateway into the profession. The Carnegie Report recognizes that law schools ought to integrate into their curriculum aspects of the lawyer-apprentice relationship. But the report does not address whether states ought to consider returning to an apprenticeship route to bar admission, an option that deserves thought given the enormous barrier to entry law school tuition imposes.

6. Richard H. Fallon, Jr., Daniel J. Meltzer, and David L. Shapiro, *Hart & Wechsler's The Federal Courts and the Federal System* (Westbury, NY: Foundation, 6th ed., 2009) (the book has 1,514 pages in text and indices, plus 119 pages of tables and other introductory materials, making it a whooping 1,633 pages).

7. As odd it at may seem, many civil procedure books begin with *Pennoyer v. Neff.* I believe that starting a course by forcing first-year students to read *Pennoyer* is cruel and unusual (it certainly is punishment). Perhaps the authors of these books think that reading *Pennoyer* is an important rite of passage for law students. It may be, but it is quite a cold bath to take on the first day of class.

8. The problem I use is based on one initially developed by Professor Alan Morrison when he was teaching at New York University Law School. Professor Morrison is now the Lerner Family Associate Dean for Public Interest and Public Service Law at George Washington University Law School.

9. I realize that there are books that take a stab at this approach. There is, for example, a civil procedure book that uses a celebrated case as a template for teaching the entire course. The book incorporates the pleadings, briefs, and discovery materials the lawyers involved in the case actually used in the litigation. I have never used this kind of book, in part because I think that focusing on an exceptional case can obscure for students the fact that the case they are studying was, in fact, exceptional. I worry that approach gives students the wrong impression about what real run-of-the-mill litigation is like.

10. They also learn the difference between pleadings and motions, a lesson generally lost on most lawyers, who use the terms interchangeably. *See* Rule 7, Fed. R. Civ. P.

11. I once gave my civil procedure class a negotiation project to teach collaboration with lawyers representing adverse parties and to make clear to students why settlements typically occur close to trial – after parties have discovery and thus a better appreciation of the strengths and weaknesses of their case and their opponent's case. A negotiation is, after all, one form of collaboration. The lawyers have to work together to see whether there is a mutually agreeable solution that avoids one imposed by an adversarial proceeding. And the ability of lawyers to collaborate while championing the interests of their client is

an important one that law schools should help develop. The case involves three parties – the parents of a boy injured when his bicycle fell apart and the seller and manufacturer of the bike. The case also poses some tricky strategic questions – should the plaintiff try to divide and conquer the defendants? Should the defendants try to stick together? Or should they try to settle quickly and cheaply and let the other defendant bear the risk of a large judgment? I assigned two students to represent each party and gave each party its own set of instructions. I weighted the scenario so there was a path to settlement, and around two-thirds of the teams settled. The students loved the exercise and I think got a lot out of it. But the assignment entailed the students' submitting a paper reporting on several stages of the negotiation – the opening offers, where the students ended up, and a brief explanation of the dynamics of the negotiation. From my standpoint, although the exercise was a teaching success, it was a logistical nightmare. As I explain later, I think that a paperless, digital platform might be better suited for exercises like this.

12. This is but one example. The same point could be made to discuss the business community's efforts to reshape the law of punitive damages or expand the scope of regulatory preemption – campaigns orchestrated with some success by the U.S. Chamber of Commerce. There are many illustrations to this point, and many involve law reform efforts that are not litigation based. For instance, the largely successful campaign to create and keep federally funded legal services programs alive has been waged by the legal service bar. The effort to change class action procedures, through the enactment of the Class Action Fairness Act, was brought about by the business community. My point is that behind any significant change in the law is an interest group that favors that change, yet that important fact is often overlooked in law school teaching.

13. *Clinton v. New York City*, 524 U.S. 417 (1988); *Raines v. Byrd*, 521 U.S. 811 (1997); *Metropolitan Washington Airports Authority v. Citizens for Abatement of Aircraft Noise, Inc.*, 501 U.S. 252 (1991); *Mistretta v. United States*, 488 U.S. 361 (1989); *Bowsher v. Synar*, 478 U.S. 714 (1986); *INS v. Chadha*, 462 U.S. 919 (1983) (Separation of Powers); *Public Citizen v. Department of Justice*, 491 U.S. 440 (1989); *Young v. Community Nutrition Institute*, 476 U.S. 974 (1986); *INS v. Chadha*, 462 U.S. 919 (1983); *Public Citizen v. FTC*, 869 F.2d 1541 (D.C. Cir. 1989); *National Grain & Feed Ass'n v. OSHA*, 866 F. 2d 717 (1989); *In re Int'l Chemical Workers Union*, 830 F.2d 369 (D.C. Cir. 1987) (Administrative Law); *Goldfarb v. Virginia State Bar*, 421 U.S. 773 (1975); *Virginia State Bd. of Pharmacy v. Virginia Citizens Consumer Council, Inc.*, 425 U.S. 748 (1976); *Zauderer v. Office of Disciplinary Counsel*, 471 U.S. 626 (1985); *Wieder v. Skala*, 80 N.Y. 2d 628 (1992); *Edenfield v. Fane*, 507 U.S. 761 (1993) (Regulation of the Professions).

9

The New Course Book and the New Law School Curriculum

Edward Rubin

It would be difficult to find any field where there is a closer connection between teaching materials and pedagogical methodology than law. The printed casebook nearly defines the traditional approach to legal education.[1] When C. C. Langdell initiated that approach,[2] his first step was to compile a casebook; as it turned out, that book was his only significant scholarly work. When he began his first class with his pathbreaking command – "Mr. Abbot, state the facts" – he was referring to the facts of a case that appeared in his book.[3] The intervening 140 years, during which the basic contours of Langdell's approach have remained unchanged in most American law schools, have left the dependence of that approach on the law school casebook unchanged as well, as Ronald Collins and David Skover note in this volume's opening chapter.[4] A printed volume that consists primarily of court decisions still constitutes the central teaching tool of virtually every first-year course and most large or standard upper-class courses as well. Students still treat the casebook as defining the course's basic coverage and will grouse and mutter if significant amounts of supplementary material are assigned. Final examinations are still designed to test mastery of the material in the casebook, students still prepare for those exams by outlining the cases, and both they and the professor regard the casebook as an essential means of reaching the pedagogic holy grail of learning to "think like a lawyer."[5]

During the past twenty years, however, law school casebooks have become obsolete. The advent of the personal computer and the Internet has changed the way in which people in our society, and particularly people the age of law students, access and process information, as John Palfrey and Gregory Silverman discuss in their contributions to this volume.[6] It may seem somewhat chimerical to observe that the materials used in legal education are twenty years out of date when the basic law school curriculum is more than one hundred years out of date. Since Langdell devised that curriculum, we have seen the decline of the common law on which the curriculum is based, the dominance of the regulatory government that the curriculum fails to acknowledge, the development of social science that the curriculum generally ignores, and the advent of new learning theories that the curriculum implicitly rejects. If law schools can soldier on, oblivious to these momentous changes in governance, knowledge, and pedagogy, there seems to be no particular reason to think that they will be troubled by a further change in information retrieval and processing. The apparent charm of an educational method that was designed shortly after the Civil War will not be eliminated by one further change. In fact, it may be increased, the way the romantic appeal of candles increased when fluorescent lights began to replace incandescent bulbs.

To be sure, every social transformation creates the possibility of institutional change, even if attempted reforms based on prior transformations have shattered against the adamantine rigidity of the status quo. There is, moreover, some reason to think that this particular transformation may be different. When students first arrive at law school, they generally do not know that common law is in decline, that the American legal system is essentially administrative, that social science is the preferable model for legal analysis, and that progressive education has replaced the Greco-Roman model that still prevailed in Langdell's day. They will not learn these disconcerting facts, at least not in any systematic, comprehensive way, until they have begun practicing law themselves, and perhaps attended a few parent-teacher conferences at their children's elementary schools. But they will be acutely aware that they are being given teaching materials that, from their perspective, are antediluvian, that they are lugging around heavy course books filled with materials that they can generally access in less than five seconds on the same lightweight device that they all use to take their notes and write their course assignments. Their awareness may well render the advent of the Internet, personal computers, cell phones, and related technology the one change that even law schools will be unable to ignore. Perhaps the effect may not appear until these children of the digital age become the majority of the legal professoriate, but perhaps it will occur sooner, when the students begin looking at law professors who assign a book full of reprinted cases as they would look at a driver's ed teacher who showed up riding on a horse.

This chapter will explore the possibilities of the digital revolution for changing the law school curriculum. Part A outlines three particular areas where modern legal education is outdated and that might be modernized through digital materials – the limitation of legal education to common law and judicial decisions, its failure to follow contemporary pedagogic practices, and its continued reliance on inductive reasoning. Part B suggests the way that digital materials could implement this modernizing function. First, they might expand the range of primary materials to statutes, regulations, and contracts, and to exemplary and supplementary materials, thereby overcoming the excessive focus on judicial decisions. Second, digital materials might increase the amount of interactivity in legal education, thereby facilitating the experiential learning that contemporary educators recommend and replacing the inductive method with a more modern, hermeneutic approach. Finally, Part C considers the concerns that several observers, specifically Heidegger and Husserl, have expressed about the consequences of modern technology and explains why those concerns are inapplicable to law school educational materials.

A. THREE OBSOLESCENCES OF CURRENT LEGAL EDUCATION

Among the almost innumerable obsolescences in the law school curriculum,[7] there are at least three that the digital revolution might address directly. The first, noted by every contributor to this volume in one way or another, is the range of materials that law school courses use. In choosing to rely on primary sources, rather than the treatises that had dominated European legal education for the preceding six or seven centuries, Langdell achieved a major conceptual breakthrough, fully consistent with the developments in pedagogic theory that would occur in the following decades. The fact that he relied almost exclusively on judicial opinions, generally at the appellate level, was unfortunate but understandable. At the time he instituted his curriculum at Harvard, common law, which can be defined as judge-made law, still dominated our legal system, particularly at the national level. Federal legislation was a rarity,[8] and even state statutes, which were more extensive, left the basic contours of the law to the judiciary. Moreover, judicial decisions were readily available, being published at the government's expense, and could be used free of charge and without obtaining permission, as Anthony Reese's contribution explains.[9] Decisions were also marvelously indexed, using the best available information-processing technology of the day, allowing their cross-references and interconnections to be readily traced by both teacher and student.

Despite its many virtues, Langdell's exclusive reliance on judicial decisions as primary source materials had serious limitations. The rise of the administrative state was virtually equivalent to the replacement of common law by statutes and regulations. At the same time, the advent of empirical social science taught, or at least should have taught, that deep, extensive networks of legal relationships flourish outside the officially established process for resolving disputes. Contracts and leases that memorialize these relationships are negotiated, drafted, implemented, and revised by lawyers who are assiduously trying to avoid judicial intervention, very often according to well-developed industry norms that rarely surface in decided cases.[10] The main reason why the legal academy did not extend Langdell's use of primary source materials into these additional realms was probably laziness, but a subsidiary explanation lies in legitimate concerns about the obtaining of these materials. Statutes and regulations can be copied as freely as judicial decisions, but they were often ferociously difficult to find and indexed so poorly that both students and scholars had to rely on the nicknames that appeared in the United States Code's

USCA's Table of Popular Names. The hearings that constituted their essential leg-islative history were often not indexed at all and could be found only in universities that had achieved the exalted status of possessing a "depository library," something these universities sought as eagerly as medieval European cities sought archbishop-rics. Contracts and leases presented even greater difficulties. Many were proprietary documents that could not be obtained or reproduced or were locked in law firm files and difficult to access. Even those that were public, such as union contracts or stan-dard form contracts for specific industries, were rarely published and often available only from law firms with no particular incentive to release them. The same could be said of many litigation documents such as complaints, answers, interrogatories, transcripts, and settlement agreements that could provide additional information about the basis of judicial decisions. In addition, as Reese points out, these materials are at least potentially protected by copyright law.[11]

As a result of these limitations, Langdell's use of materials, a pathbreaking inno-vation when initially instituted, became a ritualized distortion of reality, preserved by reliance on the threadbare excuse that judicial opinions, on their own, could teach students to "think like a lawyer." This approach's many champions overlooked the fact that the students were supposedly being taught to think like lawyers with-out the benefit of any materials that were produced by lawyers and were instead studying materials produced by people in a position that only a few law students would ever occupy and that virtually none would occupy – in contrast to European countries, ironically – for twenty or thirty years. The point is obvious and readily discerned by outside observers. The business people who regularly employ attorneys are often perplexed to discover that law students never learn about the statutes and regulations that control the legal landscape of every American firm, that they take a course called "Contracts" without ever reading a contract, and that they receive no systematic exposure to basic litigation practice.[12] It would appear, in fact, that the reason someone really needs traditional legal training is to accept these facts without astonishment. Perhaps that is what defenders of the traditional approach mean by "thinking like a lawyer." After all, as Thomas Reed Powell supposedly said, "if you can think about something that is related to something else without thinking about the thing to which it is related, then you have the legal mind."[13]

The second source of obsolescence that can be remedied by the digital revolution should be equally apparent. This is the advent of progressive or learner-centered education, the general approach developed by G. Stanley Hall and John Dewey,[14] confirmed experimentally by Jean Piaget,[15] and now the basis of modern pedagogic methodology at virtually every level from prekindergarten to medical school. Its essential insight is that education is not properly regarded as a means of training the rational mind, the way the ancient Greeks believed, but rather as the succes-sive acquisition of mastery.[16] One conclusion to be drawn from this realization, as noted by a number of contributors to this volume, including Peggy Davis, Gregory Silverman, and David Vladeck,[17] is that students are more likely to learn through experience, rather than by simply being given information. In other words, they "learn by doing," a particular emphasis of Dewey's.

Although Dewey was certainly one of the most original thinkers in the history of education, this particular position is actually more of a reminder than a discovery. Throughout the Middle Ages, apprentices learned their trade by working alongside a master and succeeded to that status by producing their own product, the so-called masterpiece.[18] At a more advanced, or at least abstract, level, academic students almost always earn their Ph.D., and often their M.A., by producing a scholarly work in their field, not by simply taking an exam to show that they are familiar with other people's scholarship. For a variety of reasons, many parts of the educational system had lost track of this intuitive insight and resorted to memorization, drill, and written examinations by the nineteenth century.[19] Dewey and his followers simply restored what people knew or should have known about the learning process. Modern neuroscience now confirms it, having discovered "mirror neurons" in a person's brain that only respond to the sight of someone else performing an activity after the person has performed that activity herself.[20] In short, we now know that learner-centered education is the most effective approach and that mastery is generally achieved by experiential education, where the learner is given the opportunity to perform the task in question, rather than merely hearing a description of it.

An educational strategy of this kind is more difficult, and more expensive, to implement than reciting facts and examining the students' acquisition of them. It has therefore encountered resistance from educational institutions, and no institution has been more resistant than law school. Of course, most legal educators know, somewhere deep inside their own collection of neurons, that experiential education is the most effective kind. But they have been reluctant to act upon this insight for the very good reason that they are rewarded for producing research, not teaching students, and for the very bad reason that they simply do not want to change. Instead, therefore, law schools have created a rather extensive second tier of teachers, almost always of lower status and often not included in the ranks of the professoriate at all, to provide experiential education – first-year writing instructors, clinical professors, simulation teachers for trial advocacy and moot court, and, most remotely, practicing lawyers who supervise student externships. What they have not done, however, is to find a means of integrating the most effective educational approach into the regular classroom instruction that their ladder (tenure and tenure-track) faculty provides.

It might be objected that the give and take of the law school classroom, the notorious Socratic method, is a form of experiential learning. In some sense, that is true; it is certainly more lively and engaging than a unilateral lecture by the professor.

Langdell, who was very smart, probably intuited the value of experiential learning and did his best to implement it, given the resource constraints and conceptual limitations of his era. But by the time a few more decades had elapsed, it should have been apparent to legal educators that the Socratic method more closely resembled a liminal ritual than true experiential learning.[21] After all, where in the so-called real world, that is, the world outside law school, does anything like it occur? Appellate advocacy is the obvious candidate, but as the development of moot court programs, with their written briefs and carefully prepared arguments, suggests, the resemblance is remote. And even if we were to concede that the Socratic method, or any other form of case-centered classroom dialogue, gives students experience with appellate arguments, what about the 95 or 99 percent of legal practice that involves other modes of action: contract drafting, contract negotiation, statutory interpretation, statutory drafting, interpretation and drafting of regulations, motion practice, discovery, trial practice, and so forth? Learning by doing does not require that the educational program duplicate real world situations, but it does demand that students have some significant exposure to the kinds of experiences that they will confront in the field for which they are being prepared.

The third source of obsolescence is more abstract, but equally important. Langdell's method is based on the idea that students, by reading and analyzing cases, can discern the underlying principles of common law. Those principles do not appear in any official source and, in fact, are generally not written down at all in systematic fashion. They appear in treatises, but typically as a means of reconciling the cases that the treatise describes and that constitute its major focus. Moreover, as noted previously, treatises are not used as a teaching tool in standard law school courses. While it is not considered cheating to refer to them, the expectation is that students will learn a process by which they can discern the underlying principles of common law without relying on external assistance. The principles do in fact appear in commercial summaries and outlines, but these are systematically disparaged by law professors, and students are often cautioned against using them to prepare for course exams. In short, if we probe the meaning of the think-like-a-lawyer slogan, we are likely to conclude that it resides precisely in the ability to perceive the underlying, vaguely articulated principles of common law by examining the opinions in specific cases.

This relationship between specific cases and general rules has a long and distinguished pedigree in Western thought. It is essentially Aristotle's category of inductive reasoning; rather than beginning with the general principle and deriving, or deducing, specific applications from it, one begins from a set of applications and induces the general principle from which they are derived.[22] Thomas Aquinas relies on the same idea in his effort to identify the attributes of God. He distinguishes between a propter quid argument, which directly comprehends God's essence and derives His attributes from that understanding, and a quia argument, which observes God's effects in the natural world and reasons backward to a partial understanding of His essence.[23] Since propter quid arguments are impossible for human beings, St. Thomas says, we are compelled to rely on quia arguments, beginning with specific cases and discerning the force behind them by induction. The very same idea informs Kant's category of judgment, which he contrasts with pure reason; in areas such as aesthetics, we must begin with specific examples and induce general principles such as beauty from their attributes.[24]

During the course of the nineteenth and early twentieth centuries, however, this approach to reasoning was seriously challenged. Hegel's dialectic suggests the possibility of a more organic mode of thought, focused on the generation of ideas rather than the discovery of regularities.[25] At about the same time, Schleiermacher and his followers developed the hermeneutic circle as an approach to interpreting a text.[26] To understand each part of a text, one must know its relationship to the whole, but knowledge of the whole is only gained through an understanding of each part. True understanding, therefore, requires a continual interaction between the parts and the whole. Edmund Husserl, the founder of phenomenology, combined these themes, translating interpretive theory into a general epistemology that replaces categorization with interaction.[27] As he states in his first introduction to phenomenology, "knowledge begins with experience and remains within experience."[28] This could be taken to favor inductive methodology, as Aquinas does for theology and Kant does for aesthetics, but that would simply reassert the distinction between deduction and induction. In fact, Husserl is denying the distinction; his view is that general principles and specific phenomena are both part of experience. There is no qualitative difference between them. The interactive approach that Schleiermacher developed for the interpretation of texts thus applies to knowledge of any kind. In order to understand anything, we must both observe specific cases and abstract some aspects of those cases into general rules. We can only do so by going back and forth between the principles and their particular embodiments or applications. This oscillation is not a merely literary method, according to Husserl, but a general account of human understanding.

The relevance of these insights to legal education is that reading legal texts cannot be treated as a purely inductive process, an examination of specific cases in order to discern in-dwelling general principles. Rather, it is an interactive process in which the general principles of law inform the interpretation of specifics at the same time that the specifics combine to constitute the general principles. Proponents of traditional education might be inclined to question this in the case of common law on the ground that the general common law principles are only comprehensible through specific cases, a sort of propter quid argument against the direct perception of the principles themselves. But, as noted previously, common law is no longer the dominant or even primary source of rules in our modern legal system; our current system is primarily statutory and regulatory. Any method for reading legal texts that fails to account for statutes and regulations is hopelessly out of date, and any method that fails to account for contracts, leases, and settlement agreements is artificially delimited. With respect to all these other types of legal materials, the totality – the general level of the hermeneutic circle – is available in definitively written form, just as the full text of the novel, play, or poem is available. The only way to make sense of such texts is to oscillate between generality and specificity as hermeneutic analysis suggests. These considerations reveal that the common law is really a particular and idiosyncratic variant within our legal system. One might speculate that the unwillingness of judges to state its principles in definitive terms represents an effort on their part to retain control, and that the unwillingness of law professors to articulate those principles for the students, or even to assign them the Restatements, springs from a similar desire – "hiding the ball," as Lawrence Cunningham and Peggy Davis describe in their contributions.[29]

B. HOW DIGITALIZATION CAN REFORM THE CURRICULUM THROUGH EXPANSION AND INTERACTION

Digital materials can provide a direct solution to these obsolescences of legal education. They can end the obsolescence regarding the range of materials by expanding the curriculum. They can end the obsolescence regarding educational theory and interpretive theory by making the mode of instruction more interactive. In doing so, they should serve as a catalyst and medium of curricular reform. While the converse – namely, that certain educational reforms cannot proceed without digital materials – is not really true, it is worth considering. As a number of the contributors to this volume, including Matthew Bodie, Ronald Collins and David Skover, Lawrence Cunningham and David Vladeck, point out, most law professors cannot be expected to generate their own materials.[30] Unless they are unusually motivated or have found some way for curriculum development to count as research for both their home institution and the legal academy in general, they simply do not have time to develop new materials.

To be sure, this situation does not demand digital materials because it is possible to produce printed materials that use statutes, regulations, contracts, and leases as primary source materials; to integrate experiential learning into classroom instruction by redeploying faculty teaching resources; and to employ a hermeneutic approach to texts the same way that it was accomplished in the nineteenth century. Nonetheless, digitalization can greatly facilitate each of these advances. It offers such distinctive advantages, in fact, that it may finally reverse the burden of proof argument that has so often been leveled against curricular reform efforts. Instead of being able to insist that they need not change while the existing approach is "work-ing" (a concept that is generally left undefined),[31] legal educators may now be obli-gated to explain why they should not change their approach when confronted with such an obviously superior one, supported by obviously superior materials.

To begin with the range of primary sources, the digital revolution will inevitably have two principal effects. The first is to make the traditional course book, a book that consists primarily of edited appellate cases, obsolete. At the time when case-books were introduced, and for the century that followed, they served the crucial function of making the cases that formed the subject matter of classroom instruction available to students. Most of these cases were readily available in court reports, of course, but no student could afford to purchase the hundred or so weighty vol-umes that would have been needed in order to obtain the assigned cases for each course. The law library always had these volumes, as Penny Hazelton describes in her contribution,[32] but no school could afford to purchase more than a few copies of each series, and this limitation would obviously have created enormous access problems for the hundred students in a typical first-year class.

In addition to making the assigned cases readily available to students, the case-book authors edited the cases, and careful editing became one of the arts of book authorship. For the most part, however, the editing is an artifact of the printed form in which the cases were made available; unedited cases simply take up too much space and would recreate the problem of unwieldy, expensive materials that the casebook solved. Admittedly, it can be argued that the editing saves the students time, but that saving is at the expense of teaching them to find the relevant discus-sion and skim the unnecessary details – skills that lawyers need, particularly when a client is paying them by the hour.

It is the Internet, of course, that renders the collection of cases that constitute the bulk of the traditional law school course book obsolete. Law students are now able to obtain the text of almost any case online in less than fifteen seconds. The length of the case has absolutely no effect on either its accessibility, which is total, or its cost, which is zero. If the professor really wants to edit the case for the students, instead of telling them what to look for and letting them learn how to find it, she can always post the case to a Web site and highlight the desired sections. For the most part, how-ever, the prepared materials that law professors use can be replaced by a list of cita-tions, and students will soon begin asking why they are being asked to pay hundreds of dollars for the privilege of toting around heavy volumes rather than simply having a hyperlinked syllabus for each of their courses sent to them by e-mail or posted on their professor's Web site.

But the obsolescence of collected cases, and even edited cases, is certainly not an argument against the value of teaching materials for law students. On the con-trary, it opens a vast range of possibilities for expanding the curriculum by using primary sources that have previously been overlooked or underemphasized in legal education. Statutes and regulations are perhaps the most obvious omission from the primary materials that law students are assigned. They are now our dominant sources of law; every student will need to be able to read them in order to practice, and a considerable number will practice in areas where there is little else. Another essential body of primary source material that law students should learn to read and understand consists of contracts, leases, and similar transactional materials; about a third of the typical law school's graduates will work exclusively with such materials and will rarely, if ever, read a case. Many of these materials are much more difficult to locate on the Internet than judicial decisions. Statutes can be located as readily as cases, but finding one's path through a regulatory thicket to the relevant agency's rules is a skill that needs to be specifically taught. Contracts may present still greater difficulties. With some exceptions, such as published standard form contracts in particular industries, these materials are proprietary and, as Tony Reese points out in his contribution,[33] may be protected by copyright. They must be located by the professor if they are to be made available to students. It is thus more justifiable to include them in prepared materials that are sold to students than judicial decisions, which are essentially effortless to access.

It is also more justifiable to sell students prepared materials that present statutes, regulations, and contracts in edited form. Statutes are much more difficult for students to read than cases, in part because they are verbally dense, in part because they are not written in the narrative form to which students have become accustomed from reading nonlegal materials, and in part because they are pasted together by innumerable legislators, legislative staffers, and interest group representatives in an effort to achieve a compromise, rather than being written by a single judge. In addition, modern statutes can be formidably long; the two major enactments of the Obama administration, dealing with health care and financial services,[34] each run more than one thousand pages, which is beyond the skimming capacity of even the most talented law students. Regulations are still more in need of editing than statutes. Skimming a regulation for the relevant sections, unlike skimming a case, is a task that only a well-trained specialist can perform.

The same is true for many contracts, particularly the long form contracts that lawyers are called upon to negotiate, draft, and interpret. Like statutes, they are densely written, lack a narrative structure, and are often a pastiche of different people's efforts in order to embody compromises. Indeed, the standard form contracts used in a particular industry may resemble statutes in both function and form: They establish governing rules for a large number of actors in a variety of situations and must therefore be sufficiently lengthy and complex to serve that function. Standard form contracts provided to consumers by a single seller are sometimes written by one person, and always by one side, but they are often written to be difficult to understand. Thus, the likelihood is that most long form agreements will also need to be edited before they are palatable to, or even digestible by, students.

To be sure, the types of materials that define an expanded curriculum can be, and indeed should be, presented to students in printed course books. They do not require a digital format. The point, however, is that they are likely to survive transition to a digital format in a way that judicial decisions will not. With respect to cases, all that the student in the digital era needs is the name of the case; she can easily find the decision and read it on her own. To be sure, the supplementary material – comments, questions, and problems – will still be of value, but the casebook's basic function of supplying primary source material will no longer be needed. This is not true for the new types of primary sources in an expanded curriculum. To summarize, regulations are more difficult to locate, and contracts may not be available unless supplied by prepared materials; in addition, statutes, regulations, and long form contracts all need editing in order to be comprehensible to students. Thus, as we move into the digital era, the value of prepared material will increase if these additional materials become part of the curriculum.

There are, moreover, other types of materials, and uses of materials, that can only be presented to students in digital form. These uses can be described as exemplary and supplementary, and the types of materials flow from these uses. By long tradition, cases have been taught through a close reading of their language, an approach that is certainly facilitated by the argumentative and analytic style in which they are written. The denser language of statutes, regulations, and contracts does not lend itself as readily to presentation in this manner. An alternative way to present these materials might be through an exemplary approach, in which the student is invited to read rapidly through ten or twenty related statutes or contracts and asked to observe regularities or differences. The problem in adopting this approach in a printed book is that it tends to increase the length of the book by a factor of 10 or 20. It might be possible to resolve this difficulty by heavy editing, but reducing the material to snippets may defeat the purpose.

A supplementary approach provides the students with the background of the principal text under discussion. For a judicial decision, this would consist of the motions, the briefs, and the discovery materials; for a statute, it would consist of legislative history materials such as prior drafts, committee reports, and statements presented on the floor of the legislature. For a regulation (at the federal level), it would include the notice of proposed rule making that appears in the Federal Register, with its statement of basis and purpose, the comments presented in response, and various background memos and studies prepared by the agency.[35] For a contract, it might consist of the deal memo, prior drafts, or subsequent interpretations or written communications between the parties. Non-textual material could be included as well. Lawyers not only examine witnesses through written interrogatories; they depose them and examine or cross-examine them on the witness stand. Regulators typically examine or inspect the facilities they are regulating, and contract lawyers will often want to see the product, place, or person that is the subject matter of the contract. Moreover, as Ronald Collins and David Skover have pointed out, many of the materials that lawyers use in modern practice, such as video recordings, are themselves audiovisual.[36] In other words, the purely verbal format of traditional teaching materials, perhaps punctuated with a few charts or grainy photographs, is an artificially limited presentation of lawyers' work that can be readily and extensively overcome in the digital age. It can be overcome even more effectively if Matthew Bodie's suggestion for an open source approach to teaching materials evolves, so that supplementary materials can be contributed by all of a particular program's users.

Material of this sort, representing a further expansion of the curriculum, is obviously too voluminous to present in a printed text, except in tiny amounts that do little more than alert the student to its existence. It is also too voluminous for the student to read in detail for every case, statute, regulation, or contract. But if it can be made available to students, it can serve important educational purposes. To begin with, its production is lawyers' work. A judge writes the opinion, but practicing lawyers write the motions, briefs, and interrogatories. Policy makers determine the ultimate shape of statutes and regulations, but lawyers generally produce the majority of the preliminary documents. Business people determine the overall structure of a deal, but lawyers memorialize it and (to take liberties with English) boiler-platify it in a long form contract.

Reviewing material of this sort and finding the relevant portions are also lawyers' work. Students have only a limited amount of time to carry out these tasks, of course, but so do lawyers. Quite often, they must be able to act quickly because a client is paying for their time or a policy maker is waiting for an answer. It can thus be of great educational value to provide the students with a case file consisting of supplementary material. But this approach is clearly impossible with printed materials; the length of a casebook would increase inordinately, not merely by a factor of 10 or 20, as with exemplary materials, but by a factor of 100 or 200. In the digital era, students can readily access this material on the laptops that they now carry to class every day and store it on a flash drive that costs much less than a single course book and weighs so little that it can be used as a key chain ornament. New technology that may be even more powerful and convenient is rapidly becoming available.

The expansion of the curriculum through the quantity of information that can be accessed and stored is only the simplest application of digitalization, of course. A more sophisticated feature of electronic receptacles and the Internet is their interactive capacity. This relates directly to the experiential nature of education that Dewey recognized, its character as the acquisition of mastery rather than the absorption of information. While the traditional approach to classroom instruction in law schools incorporates at least some primitive experiential elements, the written materials are largely limited to one-way communication. Authors make some effort, in the notes following the cases, to reflect the give-and-take interaction of Socratic instruction, as Lawrence Cunningham describes in his contribution,[37] but this is only a pale reflection of an interaction that, as described earlier, is itself a poor substitute for true experiential learning.

Resistance to experiential learning in law school is certainly not theoretically based; the overwhelming majority of educational experts favor this approach, and most law professors know too little about educational theory to frame any countervailing arguments. Rather, the resistance is economic and attitudinal – economic because experiential education requires that faculty members devote more time to interacting with the students, and attitudinal because it requires that faculty members alter their ideas about both instructional strategy and personal status. Digitalization offers a partial solution to the first of these impediments. It allows the interaction process to be automated, so that the faculty member need not interact directly with each of the many students in a typical lecture class. This does not mean, of course, that law professors have been eliminated from the educational process and replaced by machines; the author of the materials must design the protocol by which the interactive process occurs. What it does mean, however, is that, as a result of this design, the classroom teacher has been replaced by the author, just as he has been replaced when he uses a traditional casebook that selects and edits the cases. This replacement is efficient and corresponds to existing educational incentives; the author gets credit with her institution for creating and promulgating course materials, while the classroom teacher is freed of this responsibility and thus able to pursue his own research.

Interactive protocols that make use of digital technology and function as an integral part of the teaching materials can be simple or complex. In the simplest form, students are given a series of multiple-choice questions to answer that move them along a linear progression. For example, after reading a contract in their electronically accessed materials, the students can be asked to draft a contract of their own for a given factual situation. Each step of the process would consist of a multiple-choice question, such as a set of alternative contract terms. There would be only one right answer; students who get the wrong answer would be so informed and told what they did wrong, while students who get the right answer would be told to go on to the next question and, importantly, told what they did right. A more sophisticated program would consist of a branching progression, where the program responds to each choice with a further question based on that choice. Such a program might be designed to recognize more than one right answer, or it might lead the students along a path they incorrectly chose and confront them at a later point with the consequences of their error.

The next stage of complexity, which could be achieved once law professors become familiar with the new technology (or once they die and are replaced by younger people with this familiarity), involves various forms of artificial intelligence. Instead of being given a multiple-choice program for drafting a contract in a given situation, the students could be asked to draft the contract in question themselves. If the facts were sufficiently simple, a sophisticated program might be able to recognize divergences from a preprogrammed optimal contract supplied by the author and point out those divergences to the student. Alternatively, as Gregory Silverman suggests in his contribution,[38] the students might "play" against each other in negotiating the contract, with the digital program providing each side with commentary that was either available or not available to the other side. Obviously, the same approach could be used for drafting statutes, drafting regulations, interpreting statutes and regulations, writing motions, and designing interrogatories. Litigation, because of its structured, adversarial nature, lends itself naturally to game-type approaches where the students play against each other or against the program.

It is crucial to understand, as Peggy Davis and David Vladeck point out,[39] that interactive activities of this sort should be characterized as basic education, not "skills training." Law professors are often scornful of skills training, an attitude that the American Bar Association has only strengthened with its various heavy-handed efforts to impose some pedagogically questionable strategies under that title.[40] But interactive exercises are not intended to teach students how to draft legal documents or conduct litigation. Their purpose is to improve the students' understanding of the primary source material that the course is using. After one has tried to put a goal, agreement, or arrangement into statutory or contractual language, one's understanding of the process becomes much deeper, and one's ability to read real statutes and contracts increases dramatically. The process can be compared to learning the geography of a region; students who have seen that region, walked around it, and know it well enough to have a mental image of the way it looks are likely to learn the material more easily than students who have never seen it. The discovery of mirror neurons, as described previously, lends support to this idea. In another, rather different psychology experiment, chess masters were found to be vastly superior to nonexpert players in memorizing game positions, but no better than average when the pieces were placed randomly, in patterns that could not possibly occur in a game.[41] To requote Husserl, "knowledge begins with experience, and remains within experience."

Conceivably, the availability of digital materials that provide interactive experiences, having partially removed the economic impediment to experiential education, may begin to undermine the attitudinal impediment. Such a shift in attitude might open the door to institutional innovations that would greatly facilitate curricular change. While it is probably unrealistic to expect skills teachers to be granted any higher status in American law schools, it is not unreasonable to expect that ladder faculty might work together with skills teachers to deliver a more coherent course of study to the students. They might also work productively with the library staff who assist students in learning research skills, as Penny Hazelton and John Palfrey suggest.[42] At present, for example, first-year writing courses in most law schools are taught by part-time or temporary faculty. The marginality of these courses, signaled by the lower status of their instructors, and often by pass-fail grading or lower allocations of academic credit as well, produces predictably unsatisfactory results. If digital materials were to increase the perceived value of experiential education, these courses might be integrated into the first-year educational program. Each first-year course could have an interactive component, presented through its digitally based materials, recognized and discussed by the classroom teacher, and monitored by one or several nontenured writing instructors, each of whom would work with small groups of the larger class. (As a specific example, a class of one hundred might be divided into four groups, meeting for three hours with the professor as a whole class and one hour of interactive instruction in groups of twenty-five; one writing instructor could then provide the additional hour for all four groups.) Because the interactive activities are being designed by the author of the teaching materials and already coordinated with them, the writing instructors would be able to assist students with those activities in a manner that was consistent with the objective and style of the course. This human assistance might remove the sense of science fiction that otherwise accompanies the use of artificial intelligence. Instead of functioning autonomously, the digital program for the interactive activities would be explained, guided, and monitored by the writing instructor.

The third obsolescence of legal education that digital materials can address involves its inductive method. As noted, both the philosophic critique of the deductive-inductive distinction and the increasing dominance of positive law cast serious doubt on the continued validity of the inductive approach. The ability of digital materials to resolve the problem resides in an application that is certainly more complex than access, and perhaps more complex than interactivity as well – the use of hypertext links. Hypertext links can implement the hermeneutic circle, the oscillation between part and whole that the modern analysis of textual interpretation has established as the successor to deduction and induction. In essence, they can lead the student reading a primary source to switch levels from specific to general, or general to specific, in the manner that an experienced lawyer in the field would do naturally, without external guidance.

Consider the problem of teaching students to read and interpret a statute. Practicing lawyers with experience in the field can read the statute more easily, even if it is one they have never seen before, because they will understand the way its provisions relate to each other and what their potential effect will be on situations that they have encountered or cases they have dealt with.[43] This conceptual contextualization of the statute can be partially duplicated by hypertext links to legislative history, descriptions of fact situations, decided cases, political commentary, and similar materials. The author of the materials might create a link at the beginning of each provision that calls up an outline of the statute, with the particular provision's place within the statute indicated. Given that statutory texts are often pastiches of different drafts, the functional position of the provision might be better indicated by an outline of the statute's functional structure, rather than its literal text. Obviously, an outline of this sort cannot be generated by the beginning students, but only by the author of the materials. The many other possibilities would include a link to a committee report indicating the purpose of the provision, a link to a dissenting report criticizing the provision, links to selections from law review articles discussing or critiquing the statute, links to fact situations that the provision would govern, and links to cases that the statute overrules or might conceivably overrule. These links could of course be combined with the sort of interactive material discussed previously. Thus, the student might be given a link to a fact situation, then asked by the program to apply the statute to that situation, and then led through a series of steps challenging her conclusions.

Contractual material could be handled in a similar way. Here, the more delimited purposes of the primary document might lead to a more heavily interactive approach. That is, in addition to links to an outline of the contract's structure or to the statutes and cases that the contract is drafted to obey or circumvent, the links might emphasize the fact situations that the contract potentially governs. Interactive material could then be used to focus on the way that lawyers – as opposed to judges – interpret contracts. Since litigation is always a possibility, the lawyer needs to engage in the same type of interpretive process as the judge and understand how the contract might be interpreted by a court. Since litigation is almost always an unfortunate event to be avoided, however, a good lawyer also needs to engage in an entirely different process that assesses what the client should insist on, what it should compromise, and how the provision might be restructured to keep the relationship between the parties functioning.[44] Clients will often regard contracts from an economic, rather than a legal rights perspective. A clearly established contractual right might be relinquished to preserve a more valuable business relationship, or simply because it is cheaper to give up the right than to assert it through litigation. In other words, it is certainly true that considerations of this sort occur "in the shadow of the law," that is, the ultimate judicial interpretation that determines whether a contractual right exists.[45] It is also true, however, that judicial shadows are not the only factor governing the situation. Hyperlinks and interactive follow-ups can explore these lawyers' tasks, often the heart of a transaction practice that is almost invisible in the traditional law school curriculum. Given that law schools are supposed to be training lawyers, not judges, the relative absence from the curriculum of lawyers', as opposed to judges', interpretive tasks is a situation that needs to be corrected.

Hyperlinks would also be valuable in presenting judicial decisions, currently but inexcusably the overwhelming majority of the primary sources to which law students are exposed. Such linkages, in fact, could be seen as the natural format for the note material that currently appears in law school casebooks, with their present format being an awkward forerunner compelled by technological limits, like the steam-powered car or the punch-card-fed computer. To be sure, some of the questions and comments that appear in the notes at the end of the case relate to the overall struc-ture of its argument, but most refer to particular provisions and would be more effec-tive if hyperlinked to the relevant portion of the text. Students can be shown related cases or statutes, asked questions to test their understanding, or provided with com-ments from secondary sources as they are reading the case. If the casebook author or the course teacher believes that the student should read the case through once before dealing with the issues (the implicit educational premise that determines the placement of notes in a traditional casebook), then that instruction, which is entirely consistent with the hermeneutic approach, can be given at the beginning of the case. In fact, the materials can be programmed so that the hyperlinks do not even appear until the student has read the case and answered some questions to indicate that he has done so.

As John Palfrey's contribution recommends,[46] it would seem preferable for well-thought-out educational initiatives to determine the use of technology, rather than having technology catalyze or compel educational initiatives. But because American law schools have been so resistant to change, and so unwilling to think about their educational mission in terms of modern learning theory, the pressure that digital technology is likely to exert should be welcomed. In fact, the possibilities that dig-ital teaching materials offer seem to lead directly to beneficial changes in the law school curriculum more generally. The increased access to legal materials that they provide may finally enable law schools to prepare students to practice law, as Peggy Davis and David Vladeck recommend:[47] to teach the students about lawyers' work as well as judges' work; to recognize that many of their graduates – perhaps the majority – will be transactional lawyers and regulatory lawyers, not litigators; and to acknowledge that, for those who do become litigators, the bulk of litigation practice is not courtroom argument but fact discovery, brief writing, and settlement negotia-tion. The possibilities of interactive materials may enable law schools to teach in a manner that comports with modern learning theory. The possibilities of hyperlinks may enable them to abandon the inductive approach that constitutes an atavism when applied to common law, and a fetish when applied to statutory law.

These possibilities combine in complex and dynamic ways. The new materi-als, representing the expansion of the curriculum, that can be accessed by digital means simultaneously demand and lend themselves to interactive and hermeneutic presentation. Statutes, regulations, and contracts are not only more difficult to read than cases, thus requiring more guidance to the student, but they are also conceived as being subject to continual transformation by the pressure of events in a way that a judicial decision is not. While judicial decisions can be overruled or ignored, of course, each one is regarded as a final product when it is written. In contrast, modern statutes are continuously reinterpreted by regulations and sometimes have no fixed or final meaning until the regulations are adopted. Contracts, as already noted, are regularly reinterpreted, revised, or simply ignored by parties whose primary goals are economic, not legal. In other words, the text of a statute or contract, unlike the text of a decision, is often explicitly intended as a framework for further legal clarification, rather than a final product. The new materials in the expanded curriculum that digitalization will facilitate are also more fluid, as Matthew Bodie and Ronald Collins and David Skover suggest in their contributions.[48] They demand the interactive and hermeneutic approach that the digitalization process will facilitate as well.

C. THE POTENTIAL DOWNSIDES OF TECHNOLOGY

Technology may appear to offer great promise for updating and improving the law school curriculum, but our society is well past the point where it can view technology as an unambiguous good. Our increasing dependence on it, the disadvantages that accompany its benefits, its devastation of our environment, and the fact that its military applications, even in this post–cold war era, could turn everyone into a thin gas in about the space of half an hour, all counsel us to be cautious in lauding or extending it. The question that remains, therefore, is whether the digitalization of the familiar and entirely comfortable printed book that has been central to university education since the Renaissance, and the written word that has been central to it since the Middle Ages, will produce countervailing disadvantages. In other words, will law students lose more than they gain if they demand and receive more up-to-date, technologically sophisticated materials?

The two most influential critiques of technology are from the phenomenological tradition, specifically from the works of Martin Heidegger and Edmund Husserl. To summarize, Heidegger's argument is that technology drains nature of its meaning for us, transforming it into what he describes as a "standing reserve."[49] In other words, it becomes a resource, a certain amount of material for our use, rather than being an all-encompassing reality to which we relate.[50] He describes this as a matter of deep recharacterization of the object in question; technology, he says, is a process that reveals objects as standing reserves. A river can be a god, a pathway, a barrier, or a source of inspiration; once we use technology to build a dam, however, it becomes, for us, so many acre-feet of water, made available for our use, and nothing more. As he says:

> The hydroelectric plant is set into the current of the Rhine. It sets the Rhine to supplying its hydraulic pressure, which then sets the turbines turning... In the context of the interlocking processes pertaining to the orderly disposition of electrical energy, even the Rhine itself appears to be something at our command. The hydroelectric plant is not built into the Rhine River as was the old wooden bridge that joined bank with bank for hundreds of years. Rather, the river is dammed up into the power plant. What the river is now, namely, a water-power supplier, derives from the essence of the power station.[51]

Just as the river becomes a source of drinking water or power, the land becomes agricultural acreage, the forests a source of timber, and the mountains a storehouse of minerals. In fact, Heidegger argues, technology's relentless recharacterization, or enframing, of objects as their instrumental uses exercises its deleterious effect even on its own creations.[52] "Yet an airliner that stands on the runway," he writes, "is surely an object. Certainly. We can represent the machine so. But then it conceals itself as to what and how it is. Revealed, it stands on the taxi strip only as standing-reserve, inasmuch as it is ordered to insure the possibility of transportation."[53] This prescient passage was written before the development of jetways. Now, people often board the airplane, travel thousands of miles, and leave it at their destination without even seeing its exterior; it truly is, for them, just a set of seats that takes them where they are going. The romance of flight, the sense of rising above the clouds on a marvelous machine,[54] has gone the way of our perception of the land as our home, the river as our friend, and the mountains as a threat or challenge.

Nor is this technology's most deleterious effect in Heidegger's view. He goes on to observe that once every object is reduced to a standing reserve, "and man in the midst of objectlessness is nothing but the orderer of the standing-reserve, then he comes ... to the point where he himself will have to be taken as standing-reserve. Meanwhile, man, precisely as the one so threatened, exalts himself and postures as lord of the earth."[55] This again is prescient; governments now measure every feature of their populace, talk about manpower resources, and worry about the demands that an aging population will place on medical and social security resources. We may well ask whether such management of people as resources and statistics is consistent with either human rights or democratic governance. Is it possible that we, while seeing ourselves as "lords of the earth," are in fact being defined by our technological advances in ways that we cannot control and, indeed, in ways that will impair or eliminate any possibility that we can control our most important and fateful perception – our perception of ourselves?

Husserl offers a different, although related critique of technology that has been equally influential. He begins by noting that geometry, which was well developed by the ancient Greeks, represents an idealization of the world that we experience (the "lifeworld" in his terminology). Geometry, however, is limited to the shape of objects, something that can be mathematized directly because one can abstract it into an ideal form, as Plato did. Plato then generalized this insight by arguing that there exists an ideal version of every real world object that enables the mind to recognize that object, a true horse that real horses reflect, as well as a true triangle that we imperfectly represent with materials or drawings.[56] While this notion was enormously important in the development of religion, and specifically Christianity, it led nowhere in terms of technology.

The "European sciences" became distinctive, Husserl argues, when thinkers such as Galileo expanded this process of mathematization by dividing experienced objects into sets of attributes, such as their mass, their motion, and their chemical composition, in addition to their shape or physical appearance. Doing so enabled Galileo to describe motion in mathematic terms because motion was now perceived at the same level of abstraction as geometry, even though the process had to be accomplished indirectly because motion, unlike shape, has no ideal form.[57] Descartes, Galileo's contemporary, mathematized space itself by developing the Cartesian grid.[58] The process necessarily involves focusing on certain attributes to the exclusion of others; in measuring the motion of objects, for example, Galileo ignored their color, even though color is something we immediately observe about an object. As science proceeds, increasing numbers of attributes are treated in this manner; indeed, we can now mathematize color as particular wavelengths of light. In so doing, however, we are not discovering some hidden verity about the object. Rather, we are developing a way of seeing objects, a cultural creation that can be transmitted to others within our society (transmitted intersubjectively in Husserl's terminology). This way of seeing is intrinsically involved with measurement. Husserl's analysis thus led to the contemporary insight that technology drives science as often as the reverse.[59] Our efforts to achieve a particular goal, which we implement as a matter of practice, can lead us to see ways of representing objects in increasingly separate and mathematized parts.

While Husserl's attitude toward science and technology is not as negative as Heidegger's, he does identify a serious problem. In separating, abstracting, and mathematizing objects, we develop a way of seeing that is distinct from, and inconsistent with, the way we actually experience objects – "the surreptitious substitution of the mathematically substructed world of idealities for the only real world, the one that is actually given through perception, that is ever experienced and experienceable – our every-day life-world."[60] This does not mean that science is outside the lifeworld; the lifeworld is our horizon of experience, in Husserl's view, and nothing exists for us outside it.[61] Rather, it means that the scientific or technological perspective becomes part of our lifeworld. But because we can never separate ourselves from lived experience, from a nonmathematical way of seeing, our culturally developed scientific perspective conflicts with lived experience and thus disrupts our sense of meaning and integrity. As he says: "Are science and its method not like a machine, reliable in accomplishing obviously very useful things, a machine that everyone can understand how to operate correctly without in the least understanding the inner possibility and necessity of this sort of accomplishment?"[62] Thus, for Heidegger, the critique of technology is that it drains nature of meaning, turning it into a resource, and ultimately turning us into a resource as well. For Husserl, the critique is that technology creates a way of looking at the world that conflicts with our instinctive way of doing so, thus turning us into conflicted, alienated beings who have difficulty accepting or acting in accordance with the world that we instinctively perceive.

The critiques of technology that Heidegger and Husserl advance have been vastly influential[63] and continue to resonate with us in this era of global warming, putrefying oceans, hyperlethal weaponry, runaway third world urbanization, and increasing first world exurbanization. It might appear, therefore, that their vision, and the many subsequent critiques of technology, would alert us to particular dangers regarding the use of digital material in law school. In fact, however, there are no such dangers. The critique of technology has little to tell us about this subject and offers no reasons not to proceed as quickly as we can along the lines described. The only real danger is that the same forces that have led the legal academy to resist curricular change will seize on this critique to deposit a patina of modernity on an otherwise indefensible commitment to tradition.

The reason why the critique of technology has no particular relevance to legal teaching materials involves the nature of these materials. To put the point in its simplest form, legal teaching materials currently consist of writing, and writing is already technology. It can be described, in fact, as the most radical technology that human beings have ever developed. As Don Ihde points out, most technological devices, no matter how advanced, are designed to improve human perception or manipulation of the natural world. The telescope enables us to see farther than we can with our eyes, the microphone enables us to speak louder than we can with our voices, the automobile allows us to move faster than we can with our legs, and the power shovel allows us to dig deeper than we can with our hands.[64] Thus, their referent remains the natural world, and they are subject to the critiques that Heidegger and Husserl advanced; they turn that natural world into a standing reserve and create a disjunction between our technological and our instinctive perceptions of that world.

But this characterization does not apply to writing. Writing does not involve perception or manipulation of the natural world, but rather relates to human, or intersubjective, communication. The pretechnological version of writing is not seeing, hearing, moving, or lifting, but memory, which, however primeval, is a subjective human capacity. Even without relying on the postmodern critique of "phonocentrism," which asserts that writing is superior to speech,[65] we can say that writing is a means of interpreting or constructing the world, not a means of amplifying it. Perhaps something is lost in moving from an oral to a written culture, as some students of epic poetry contend, but what is lost is already culture, already a separation of human beings from their natural environment. A body of writing is already a standing reserve, a certain amount of information that has been separated from the environment that generated it and stored for human use. It is already an abstraction from the world that we perceive through our senses, a symbolic representation that has no direct relationship to what it represents.

The radical nature of writing as a technology can be appreciated by comparing its mode of instrumentation to that of other technologies. When we use a telescope, we see an image. It is an image of something we could not possibly see on our own, but it is essentially something that we would see if we had better eyes. Moreover, we see the image with our eyes, just as we see objects naturally, with technologically unaided vision; the telescopic image is thus simply an enhanced form of seeing. When we drive a car, we move much faster than we could on our own, but the controls make the car do the sorts of things that we do when we actually are moving on our own, although more slowly; turning the steering wheel moves us from side to side as we would move if we were running; pressing the accelerator or the brake makes us speed up or slow down. Even highly sophisticated instrumentation has this quality. A spectroscopic image of a star is something we cannot possibly see, even for a nearby object, but it is still a form of seeing. We are simply seeing things that are beyond the resolving power of our vision, rather than beyond its spatial range. And once the instrument creates the spectroscopic image for us, we still must see it with our eyes, as we do an ordinary object.

Writing is completely different because the instrument – words on a page – has no relationship to what it describes or presents.[66] Consider the following sentence: "There were snowy mountains in the distance." While the sentence reliably calls up a particular image, it bears no physical relationship to that image. It is not a picture of snowy mountains, not a schematic representation of them, not a representation of some image we could not formulate with our sense organs. It is a set of black marks on a white background (more generally, a set of marks on a contrasting background), an ordered arrangement of thirty-six shapes, or more precisely, seventy-four straight and curved lines. Moreover, the same types of shapes, the same straight and curved lines, can call up completely different images if rearranged. We are dealing, in other words, with a technology that, even in its earliest form, before the invention of the printing press, to say nothing of the personal computer, is entirely abstract. Writing is a tool; in moving from written words on a page to electronic signals appearing on a screen, we are not moving from a freely flowing river to a reservoir created by a dam, but from an earth-filled dam to a poured concrete dam. We are not moving from perceiving something with our senses to describing it with mathematics, but from describing it with algebra to describing it with calculus.

This is not to suggest that we cannot make comparisons between different forms of technology or frame arguments why a simpler technology may be preferable to a more advanced one. Rather, the point is simply that in making such comparisons and arguments with respect to writing, we cannot invoke a critique of technology itself. We need to think, in other words, of comparisons within technology, the choice between one mode of technological representation and another. If we favor an earlier technology, such as the printed word over the electronically transmitted one, we are not getting back to nature, or retrieving authenticity, but rather arguing about the disadvantages of specific technological advances.

Michael Heim has advanced precisely such an argument.[67] Writing before the advent of the Internet, he argued that the word processor degrades the quality of written work; in effect, it represents more modern, but inferior technology. Instead of crafting well-formulated prose, taking care to deploy language in an artful and reflective manner, a person using a word processor is engaged in a rapid, slovenly, and formulaic process, the cut-and-paste mentality that John Palfrey ascribes to modern "Digital Natives."[68] The text becomes overly malleable; errors can be instantly corrected, paragraphs shifted from one place to another with the mere touch of a button, whole passages imported from another document. A. E. Housman reported his sustained effort searching for a single word to describe the view from Bredon Hill (the word he ultimately hit upon was "colored" in the verse "Here of a Sunday morning, / My love and I would lie, / And see the coloured counties, / And hear the larks so high, / Above us in the sky").[69] The word processor creates a pace of composition that makes such efforts seem quaint at best, obsessive at worst, and a waste of time in any case.

Heim's critique is powerful; one wonders whether it is correct. Are there other reasons, perhaps related to the decline of privilege, why belles-lettres has lost its appeal? Is he comparing the apple of the past's great literature with the prune of the modern world's pragmatic discourse? Does the word processor destroy the euphony of language or merely preserve and broadcast quotidian documents that would previously have been consigned to the fire or the outhouse? Whatever the answer to these questions may be, the fact is that his critique does not apply to legal prose, which is inherently pragmatic rather than expressive. A novelist can choose eloquence over imprecision and gain a reputation for profundity as well as eloquence by doing so;[70] the lawyer who makes the same choice when drafting a contract is committing malpractice. Significantly, Heim uses the term "boiler-plate" in his condemnation; this image, with its heavy technological associations, is in fact particularly linked to legal documents, but its application to that context long precedes the development of the word processor.

The same pragmatic purpose governs educational materials. Few instructional manuals can be praised for their felicitous prose or their elegant construction, but they cannot be criticized for the lack of it either. That is simply not their role. Like legal documents, they are designed for pragmatic purposes, and their value depends on their ability to achieve those purposes. When we combine the inherent instrumentalism of legal documents with the inherent instrumentalism of instructional materials, the result is a type of writing that is simply not intended to be the well-crafted, eloquent, and elegant prose whose demise Heim attributes to the word processor. If the author of instructional materials in law wants to give the students examples of well-written legal arguments – briefs or secondary sources, for example – she can certainly do so, but that cannot possibly represent the major part of any law school course, or the major part of the materials provided for such a course. Just as the critique of technology in general cannot be coherently applied to the shift from writing to word processing, the critique of word processing as a degraded form of writing cannot be applied to legal materials or instructional materials, and certainly not to instructional materials in law.

In fact, at least with respect to both legal materials and educational materials, and certainly to the conjunction of the two, Heim's argument can be reversed. We can say that digital texts are the culmination of writing. Better still, we can say that the invention of both writing and printing looked forward to the digital text, that these advances were achieved with the digital text as their ultimate goal, and, indeed, their inherent purpose. Writing and printing aspire to record human thought, after all, but human thought is associational, not linear. It was not until the advent of electronics that the lambency, the flexibility, and the multilayered interconnectedness of thought could be captured in permanent and communicable form: that a means could be found to trace the rapidly branching and bifurcating pathways that our minds pursue in learning or problem solving. The idea that printing, which precedes electronics by hundreds of years, and writing, which precedes it by thousands, would aim toward this development may seem counterintuitive. But as Heidegger tells us, the essential meaning of human inventions is not always revealed at the time of their discovery. "All coming to presence, not only modern technology, keeps itself everywhere concealed to the last. Nevertheless, it remains, with respect to its holding sway, that which precedes all: the earliest. The Greek thinkers already knew of this when they said: That which is earlier with regard to its rise into dominance becomes manifest to us men only later."[71]

Resistance to the idea of electronic teaching materials, then, reduces to a sort of nostalgia, an affection for tradition based on familiarity. This is certainly not an insignificant instinct. Academics, as a general rule, love books; many law professors have had the experience, when house hunting, of being shocked at the small number of books that even educated professionals possess, and of anxiously informing their real estate agent that the cost of installing another three hundred linear feet of shelving will need to be factored into the price of the home. Most members of the legal academy remember the thrill of seeing their first article in print, and even senior ones get at least a mild surge of pleasure when that brown box filled with the reprints of their most recent article arrives. But nostalgic idiosyncrasies of this sort cannot be a justifiable basis for resisting a technological change that offers educational benefits for the students. It is one thing to insist that the research function is as important a part of the academy as teaching, or that theoretical and ethical considerations are as important a part of the educational process as pragmatic skills. But it is another thing entirely to resist educational change on the basis of personal predilections or peccadilloes. If there is an argument to be made against the use of modern technology in legal education, it must be made in educational terms.

That argument will be difficult to make because the use of electronic materials represents progress. The critique of technology has made "progress" an ambiguous term in our modern world. Too often, it refers to the despoliation of nature, the eradication of an indigenous culture, or the ruination of a small town's commercial center by Wal-Mart. Before we naively or aggressively describe some change as progress, we must specify the dimension along which the alleged advance occurs and justify the valorization of that dimension over others where that same change might lead to a decline. But, as discussed previously, the use of electronics for law teaching materials is progress because it occurs along exactly the same dimension as the technology that it displaces. The law school casebook is not nature; it is simply the human artifact that represented the best available technology for the transmission of information at the time that American legal education was developed. There is no justifiable reason why we should not continue to rely on the best available technology, why we should not continue to make progress in the mode of education that society entrusts us, and pays us, to provide.

NOTES

1. *See* Elizabeth Mertz, *The Language of Law: Learning to "Think like a Lawyer"* (New York: Oxford, 2007), 84–96; William Sullivan et al., *Educating Lawyers: Preparation for the Profession* (San Francisco: Jossey-Bass, 2007), 47–86 (Report by the Carnegie Foundation for the Advancement of Teaching); Russell Weaver, "Langdell's Legacy: Living with the Case Method," *Villanova Law Review* 36 (1991): 517.
2. Lawrence Friedman, *A History of American Law* (New York: Simon & Schuster, 3rd ed., 2005), 466–72; William La Piana, *Logic and Experience: The Origin of Modern Legal Education* (New York: Oxford University Press, 1994), 55–78; Robert Stevens, *Law School: Legal Education in America from the 1850s to the 1980s* (Chapel Hill, N.C.: University of North Carolina Press, 1983), 35–50.

3. For a detailed description of Langdell's teaching method, *see* Bruce Kimball, "'Warn Students That I Entertain Heretical Opinions, Which They Are Not to Take as Law': The Inception of Case Teaching in the Classrooms of the Early C. C. Langdell, 1870–1883," *Law & History Review* 17 (1999): 57.

4. *See* Ronald K. L. Collins and David M. Skover, Chapter 1, this volume.

5. *See* Mertz, "The Language of Law," 207–24.

6. *See* John Palfrey, Chapter 5, this volume; *see also* Gregory Silverman, Chapter 6, this volume.

7. For my views on other obsolescences, *see* Edward Rubin, "What's Wrong with Langdell's Method and What to Do about It," *Vanderbilt Law Review* 60 (2007): 609.

8. *See* Brian Baloch, *A Government Out of Sight: The Mystery of National Authority in Nineteenth Century America* (New York: Cambridge University Press, 2009); Thomas McCraw, *Prophets of Regulation* (Cambridge, MA: Belknap, 1984), 1–77; Stephen Skowronek, *Building a New American State: The Expansion of National Administrative Capacities, 1877–1920* (Cambridge: Cambridge University Press, 1992).

9. *See* R. Anthony Reese, Chapter 3, this volume.

10. *See* Lisa Bernstein, "Private Commercial Law in the Cotton Industry: Creating Cooperation through Rules, Norms, and Institutions," *Michigan Law Review* 99 (2001): 1724; Ian MacNeil, *The New Social Contract: An Inquiry into Modern Contractual Relations* (New Haven: Yale University Press, 1981); Stewart Macaulay, "An Empirical View of Contract," *Wisconsin Law Review*, 1985 (1985): 465; Stewart Macaulay, "Elegant Models, Empirical Pictures, and the Complexities of Contract," *Law & Society Review* 11 (1977): 507.

11. *See* Reese, Chapter 3, this volume.

12. *See*, e.g., Lawrence Friedman and Stewart Macaulay, "Contract Law and Contract Teaching: Past, Present, and Future," *Wisconsin Law Review* 1967 (1967): 805.

13. Lon Fuller, *The Morality of Law* (New Haven: Yale University Press, rev. ed., 1964), 4.

14. *See* John Dewey, *Democracy and Education: An Introduction to the Philosophy of Education* (New York: Macmillan, 1929); John Dewey, *Experience and Education* (New York: Touchstone, 1938); John Dewey, *The Child and the Curriculum and the School and Society* (Chicago: University of Chicago Press, 4th ed., 1956); John Dewey, *The Way Out of Educational Confusion* (Cambridge, MA: Harvard University Press, 1931); G. Stanley Hall, *Aspects of Child Life and Education* (New York: D. Appleton & Co., 1921).

15. Jean Piaget, *The Grasp of Consciousness: Action and Concept in the Young Child*, trans. Susan Wedgewood (Cambridge, MA: Harvard University Press, 1976); Jean Piaget, *The Origins of Intelligence in Children*, trans. Margaret Cook (New York: International Universities, 1952); Jean Piaget, *The Child's Construction of Reality*, trans. Margaret Cook (London: Routledge & Kegan Paul, 1955).

16. See Lawrence Cremin, *The Transformation of the School: Progressivism in American Education, 1876–1957* (New York: Vintage, 1964); Merle Curti, *The Social Ideas of the American Educators: With a New Chapter on the Last Twenty-Five Years* (Totowa, NJ: Littlefield, Adams, 1978); Patricia Graham, *Progressive Education from Arcady to Academe: A History of the Progressive Education Association* (New York: Teachers College, 1967); Herbert Kleibard, *The Struggle for the American Curriculum, 1893–1958* (New York: Routledge, 2nd ed., 1995)

17. *See* Peggy Cooper Davis, Chapter 10, this volume; *see also* Silverman, Chapter 6, this volume; *see also* David C. Vladeck, Chapter 8, this volume.

18. Steven Epstein, *Wage Labor and Guilds in Medieval Europe* (Chapel Hill: University of North Carolina Press, 1991); Barbara Hanawalt, *Growing Up in Medieval London: The Experience of Childhood in History* (New York: Oxford University Press, 1993), 129–72; Ruth Karras, *From Boys to Men: Formations of Masculinity in Late Medieval Europe* (Philadelphia: University of Pennsylvania Press, 2003), 109–50.

19. The opening of Charles Dickens, *Hard Times* (London: Penguin, [1854] 1985), with its peroration by the remorseless schoolmaster Thomas Gradgrind ("Teach these boys and girls nothing but Facts. Facts alone are wanted in life."), in part for the benefit of the new teacher, Mr. M'Choakumchild, provides an unforgettable depiction of this attitude toward education.

20. Giacomo Rizzolatti and Corrado Sinigaglia, *Mirrors in the Brain: How Our Minds Share Actions, Emotions and Experience*, trans. Frances Anderson (Oxford: Oxford University Press, 2008); V. S. Ramachandran, *The Tell-Tale Brain: A Neuroscientist's Quest for What Makes Us Human* (New York: W. W. Norton & Co., 2011), 117–35, 123–35.

21. See Victor Turner, *The Ritual Process: Structure and Anti-Structure* (New York: Aldine De Gruyter, 1995); Victor Turner, *Dramas, Fields and Metaphors: Symbolic Action in Human Society* (Ithaca, NY: Cornell University Press, 1974), 231–70.

22. Aristotle, "Posterior Analytics," in *The Works of Aristotle*, trans. G. R. G. Mure (Chicago: Encyclopedia Britannica, 1952), 95–137.

23. Thomas Aquinas, *Summa Theologica*, trans. Fathers of the English Dominican Province (Notre Dame, In: Christian Classics, 1948), 12, 48–59 (Ia Q2, Art. 2, 1a Q 12).

24. Immanuel Kant, *Critique of Judgment*, trans. J. H. Bernard (New York: Hafner, 1951).

25. G. W. F. Hegel, *The Phenomenology of Mind*, trans. J. B. Baillie (New York: Harper & Row, 1967).

26. Friedrich Schleiermacher, "Foundations: General Theory of Art and Interpretation," in *The Hermeneutics Reader*, ed. Kurt Mueller-Vollmer (New York: Continuum, 1985), 73–96; Wilhelm Dilthey, "Schleiermacher's Hermeneutical System in Relation to Early Protestant Hermeneutics," trans. Theodore Nordenhaug, in Wilhelm Dilthey, *Selected Works*, vol. IV (Princeton, NJ: Princeton University Press, 1996), 33–228.

27. See Edmund Husserl, *Ideas: General Introduction to Pure Phenomenology*, trans. W. R. Boyce Gibson (New York: Collier, 1962); Edmund Husserl, *Experience and Judgment: Investigations in a Genealogy of Logic* (Evanston, IL: Northwestern University Press, 1992).

28. Husserl, *Ideas*, 45 (emphasis omitted).

29. *See* Lawrence A. Cunningham, Chapter 4, this volume; *see* also Davis, Chapter 10, this volume.

30. *See* Matthew T. Bodie, Chapter 2, this volume; *see* also Cunningham, Chapter 4, this volume; Ronald K. L. Collins and David M. Skover, Chapter 1, this volume; Vladeck, Chapter 8, this volume.

31. *See*, e.g., Patrick Hobbs, "Guidelines for Quality Legal Education across the Globe," *South Texas Law Review* 43 (2002): 727; William Reynolds, "Back to the Future in Law Schools," *Maryland Law Review* 70 (2010): 101. As long as law schools control admission to the bar, Druidic incantations would "work." But the argument that the traditional curriculum works in any deeper sense is generally based on mere repetition of the claim. It cannot explain why about two-thirds of modern practice – regulatory and transactional law – is almost completely ignored in the first-year curriculum, and why the remaining one-third – litigation – excludes the litigation practices that constitute the vast majority of lawyers' work.

32. *See* Penny Hazelton, Chapter 7, this volume.
33. *See* Reese, Chapter 3, this volume.
34. Patient Protection and Affordable Health Care Act of 2010, Pub. L. 111–148, 124 Stat. 119 (2010), as amended by the Health Care and Education Reconciliation Act, Pub. L. No. 111–152, 124 Stat. 1029 (2010), to be codified in 42 U.S.C.; Dodd-Frank Wall Street Reform and Consumer Protection Act, Pub. L. 111–203, 124 Stat. 1376 (2010), to be codified in 12 U.S.C.
35. For a detailed description of the process, see Jeffrey Lubbers, *A Guide to Federal Agency Rulemaking* (Chicago: American Bar Association, 2006). Because of its pragmatic orientation, this book provides a good guide to the kinds of written materials associated with a regulation.
36. Ronald Collins and David Skover, "Paratexts," *Stanford Law Review* 44 (1992): 509.
37. *See* Cunningham, Chapter 4, this volume.
38. *See* Silverman, Chapter 6, this volume.
39. *See* Davis, Chapter 10, this volume; *see* also Vladeck, Chapter 8, this volume.
40. *See* American Bar Association Section of Legal Education and Admissions to the Bar, *Legal Education and Professional Development: An Educational Continuum* (Chicago: American Bar Association, 1992) (McCrate Report).
41. The original work was carried out by the Dutch chess master Adrian de Groot; *see Thought and Choice in Chess* (The Hague: Mouton, 1965). For subsequent analysis of the issue, *see* William Chase and Herbert Simon, "Perception in Chess," *Cognitive Psychology* 4 (1973): 55; Fernand Gobet and Gary Clarkson, "Chunks in Expert Memory: Evidence for the Magical Number Four ... or Is It Two?" *Memory* 12 (2004): 732. Chase and Simon's theory is that experts retain information in "chunks."
42. *See* Penny Hazelton, Chapter 7, this volume; *see* also John Palfrey, Chapter 5, this volume. As they note, this function becomes more important for library staff as the need to maintain a print collection decreases.
43. This is the nature of expertise, the general field into which the studies of chess masters belong. *See*, e.g., John Anderson, ed., *Cognitive Skills and Their Acquisition* (Hillsdale, NJ: Lawrence Erlbaum, 1981); K. Anders Ericsson, Neil Charness, Paul Feltovich, and Robert Hoffman, eds., *The Cambridge Handbook of Expertise and Expert Performance* (New York: Cambridge University Press, 2006).
44. *See* Bernstein, "Private Commercial Law in the Cotton Industry"; MacNeil, *New Social Contract*; Macaulay, "An Empirical View."
45. The phrase is from Robert Mnookin and Lewis Kornhauser, "Bargaining in the Shadow of the Law: The Case of Divorce," *Yale Law Journal* 88 (1979): 950.
46. *See* Palfrey, Chapter 5, this volume.
47. *See* Davis, Chapter 10, this volume. *see* also Vladeck, Chapter 8, this volume.
48. *See* Bodie, Chapter 2, this volume; *see* also Collins and Skover, Chapter 1, this volume.
49. Martin Heidegger, "The Question Concerning Technology," in Martin Heidegger, *Basic Writings*, trans. William Lovitt (New York: Harper & Row, 1977), 287–317.
50. Regarding attitudes toward nature through premodern Western history, see Clarence Glacken, *Traces on the Rhodian Shore: Nature and Culture in Western Thought from Ancient Times to the End of the Eighteenth Century* (Berkeley: University of California Press, 1976); Roger Sorrell, *St. Francis of Assisi and Nature: Tradition and Innovation in Western Christian Attitudes toward the Environment* (New York: Oxford University Press, 1988); Raymond Williams, *The Country and the City* (New York: Oxford University Press, 1973).

51. Heidegger, "Question Concerning Technology," 297.
52. *See* Collins and Skover, "Paratexts" 510–11, n. 5.
53. Heidegger, "Question concerning Technology," 298.
54. The element of romance was certainly present for early aviators. *See*, e.g., William Leary, *Aerial Pioneers: The U.S. Air Mail Service 1918–1927* (Washington, DC: Smithsonian, 1985); Antoine de Saint-Exupery, *Night Flight*, trans. Stewart Gilbert (New York: Signet, 1945). It was romantic for passengers as well, but also quite uncomfortable, two features that may be necessarily related. *See* R. E. G. Davies, *Airlines of the United States Since 1914* (Washington, DC: Smithsonian, 1972), 41–53, 508–29; T. A. Heppenheimer, *Turbulent Skies: The History of Commercial Aviation* (New York: John Wiley, 1995), 196–226.
55. Heidegger, "Question Concerning Technology," 308.
56. Edmund Husserl, "The Origin of Geometry," in Edmund Husserl, *The Crisis of the European Sciences and Transcendental Phenomenology*, trans. David Carr (Evanston, IL: Northwestern University Press, 1970), 353 (appendix VI).
57. Husserl, "Crisis of the European Sciences," 23–59.
58. Husserl, "Crisis of the European Sciences," 60–5.
59. *See*, e.g., Bruno Latour, *Science in Action: How to Follow Scientists and Engineers through Society* (Cambridge, MA: Harvard University Press, 1988); Michael Polanyi, *Personal Knowledge: Towards a Post-Critical Philosophy* (Chicago: University of Chicago Press, 1958).
60. Husserl, "Crisis of the European Sciences," 48–9.
61. The image of a horizon is from Gadamer, a follower of Heidegger. *See* Hans-Georg Gadamer, *Truth and Method*, trans. Garrett Barden and John Cumming (New York: Crossroad, 1988), 217–25, 267–74.
62. Husserl, "Crisis of the European Sciences," 52.
63. *See*, e.g., Jacques Ellul, *The Technological Society*, trans. John Wilkinson (New York: Vintage, 1964); Herbert Marcuse, *One-Dimensional Man: Studies in the Ideology of Advanced Industrial Society* (Boston: Beacon, 1964); Langdon Winner, *The Whale and the Reactor: A Search for Limits in an Age of High Technology* (Chicago: University of Chicago Press, 1988). All these authors are also influenced by Marxism, but their approach to technology and its relationship to nature follows Husserl and Heidegger. Their view has become so well established it can seem inevitable, but it in fact a specific perspective. Other approaches, often by American writers who have been less influenced by phenomenology, can be identified. *See*, e.g., Henry Adams, *The Education of Henry Adams: An Autobiography* (New York: Book League of America, 1928), 474–98 (technology as determining the pace of human history); Lewis Mumford, *The Myth of the Machine*. Vol. 2, *The Pentagon of Power* (New York: Harcourt Brace, 1970) (technology as a means of human self-definition).
64. Don Ihde, *Technology and the Lifeworld: From Garden to Earth* (Bloomington: Indiana University Press, 1990), 72–80.
65. Jacques Derrida, *Writing and Difference*, trans. Alan Bass (Chicago: University of Chicago Press, 1978); Jacques Derrida, *Positions*, trans. Alan Bass (Chicago: University of Chicago Press, 1981)
66. Ihde, *Technology and the Lifeworld*, 80–108.
67. Michael Heim, *Electric Language: A Philosophical Study of Word Processing* (New Haven: Yale University Press, 1987).
68. *See* Palfrey, Chapter 5, this volume.

69. Laurence Housman, *My Brother, A. E. Housman: Personal Recollections Together with Thirty Hitherto Unpublished Poems* (Port Washington, NY: Kennikat Press, 1965), 102–3.
70. So can popular music writers, as anyone who listens to modern indie rock can attest. *See* Weird Al Yankovic, *Smells Like Nirvana*, http://www.sing365.com/music/lyric.nsf/smells-like-nirvana-lyrics-weird-al-yankovic/f87ad8210a9640ac4825690e0020db4a.
71. Heidegger, "Question Concerning Technology," 303.

Casebooks, Learning Theory, and the Need to Manage Uncertainty

Peggy Cooper Davis

Law students' principal texts have shifted and evolved over time as the legal academy has absorbed progressive education's principle of learning by doing – or through practice. This chapter traces that evolution, emphasizing both the relevance of progressive theories of education to professional training and the complexities inherent in following progressive education's prescription of teaching law by having students practice using it. The lessons of the history I will trace are the following:

1. Law is, as proponents of legal realism famously claimed, the dynamic and indeterminate product of human interaction.
2. Law's dynamism and interactivity make the progressive principle of learning by doing particularly appropriate for training legal professionals.
3. Practice in using the law is discomforting, for it requires that we accept, and try to manage responsibly, law's indeterminacy.
4. Interactive media facilitate student comprehension and acceptance of the interactive character of lawyering and the indeterminate character of law.

The evolution of law school texts can be quickly summarized. The earliest U.S. law schools[1] are said to have relied principally on expert compilations or statements of the law that I will refer to generically – and somewhat loosely – as treatises. In the beginning, students read treatises, and law professors reportedly recited or described the contents of these treatises in the law school classroom. The iconic law school text shifted in the late nineteenth century from the treatise to what we know as the casebook – books that collected the original texts of judicial opinions (and later of statutes)[2] for students to analyze on their own and in class discussion.[3] Critics complained that judicial opinions are not "cases" themselves but fragments from the late stages in the development of cases,[4] and some authors began to include trial transcripts, exhibits, and other documents for students' consideration.[5] But the focus of the casebook continued to be the judicial opinion, and collections of judicial opinions continue to be called casebooks. Casebook formats evolved to include more and more elaborate collections of commentary and background materials (the "Cases Materials" format) and, in some cases, to include problems that students were asked to solve in light of assigned cases and materials (the "Cases and Problems," or "Cases, Problems, and Materials" format). More recently the problem model has expanded to include complex simulated case files that students fill out with their own work product (in the form of documents – office memoranda, pleadings, agreements, briefs, interview reports, etc., and transcribed or taped interviews, arguments, negotiations, etc.). In this simulation model, cases and commentary on cases are largely left for students to find on their own, and students' filled-out case files become texts for collaborative evaluation and critique. In the simulation model, not only do students learn in the process of doing, but their own work product becomes a principal text for their study.

The textbook genres described previously are rarely discussed in terms of pedagogical theory. Indeed, as with most graduate and professional school teachers, law professors have not worried much or written extensively about pedagogy. Nonetheless, if we review the shifts and combinations among treatises, casebooks, and case files, we can see that law school texts have, in fact, been informed by pedagogical theory, even though that theory has been underdeveloped and rarely articulated. As the following examination of each genre will show, law school texts have consistently evolved in accordance with the tenets of the so-called progressive schools of education to emphasize learning by doing, learning through collaborative practice, and learning to develop expertise rather than simply collect knowledge. They have moved from materials designed to transmit knowledge of the law to materials designed to support mastery of the lawyer's art. They have moved, that is, from materials that seemed to convey reasonably certain truths to materials that seem to do nothing but pose questions.

A. THE TREATISE

The function of the treatise was – and is – to report principles that have been distilled by legal scholars from statutes and judicial opinions. Students in the era of the treatise were not required to read the justices' opinions in *Pennoyer v. Neff* or *International Shoe Co. v. Washington*. A treatise would simply tell them that through these cases "the conceptual basis of state jurisdiction [shifted] from territoriality and physical power to contacts between the defendant and the forum state and fairness." Learning in this way, students would not have to puzzle out in different contexts the ambiguities of "contact" or the determinants of "fairness."

When treatises were law schools' principal texts, education was seen as a transmittal process. Interpretation seemed the province of the professors and of the scholarly senior practitioners who authored treatises and presented lectures. The work of the law student was to internalize authors' and professors' scholarly wisdom with the thought that s/he would be prepared to recall and apply that wisdom to future clients' circumstances. The academy was the source of knowledge, and the student was the vessel into which that knowledge was poured.[6] All of this began to change with the invention of the casebook.

B. THE CASEBOOK

The core function of the casebook is to reproduce for students the texts of judicial opinions, usually at the appellate level, usually edited to highlight particular issues and delete matter thought to be extraneous to those issues, and usually ordered to track the development of lines of doctrine. Casebooks were invented in or about 1870 as Christopher Columbus Langdell (and some of his colleagues and contemporaries) transformed legal education from the passive study of legal principles that could be found in scholarly treatises to active, "Socratic" discourse about the meanings and possible applications of official enactments and judicial pronouncements. With this development, primary sources – constitutions, statutes, and, most prominently, judicial opinions – became the law student's basic texts, and interpretation became the law student's basic task. Internalization and recall remained essential, however. Students had to know the facts, procedural circumstances, rationales, and results of cases. Treatise reading also remained important, for it gave students background knowledge of how experts interpreted and explained doctrinal developments. But this knowledge was no longer the ultimate goal of professional training. It was the foundation from which students could practice the skill – or art – of using the law in new circumstances to serve the interests of a client or a cause. Instead of being given rules to learn, students were called on to ponder new mixes of precedent and circumstance and argue for, or against, fresh readings of doctrine. The implicit (and sometimes explicit) assumption was that lawyers needed to be trained to go beyond recalling and reciting the law to participating in giving it meaning.

The shift in legal education from passive rule learning to active and interpretive practice coincided with – and was part of – the rise of what came to be known as "progressive" education. A key component of progressive education was learning by doing. Students who learn sums, multiplication tables, and the formulae of algebra, geometry, calculus, and trigonometry are able to apply that learning in order to add, multiply, divide, and calculate the results that mathematical formulae yield. They can report memorized associations and perform prescribed operations. But they do not necessarily understand what they are doing. That is why there is a consensus among educators that students need to "play" with concepts rather than simply apply them.

As did European children's classrooms grounded in the work of Johann Heinrich Pestalozzi, Friedrich Froebel, Edward Seguin, and Maria Montessori, the Langdellian classroom involved learning by doing. Just as Froebel designed toys, puzzles, and games that led children to visualize and play with mathematical concepts, Langdell crafted hypotheticals that led law students to conceptualize and manipulate legal principles. Langdell's Socratic method was in harmony with progressive theories of education championed in the United States by Francis Parker, John Dewey, Charles Eliot, and a transported Maria Montessori, all of whom urged that, as Pestalozzi once put it, the "aim of ... teaching was to develop the children's own powers and faculties rather than to impart facts," and all of whom, in one way or another, believed that students learn naturally and well when they follow their curiosity to engage in playful problem solving.

In addition to learning for mastery and learning by doing, the progressive school encouraged learning through collaboration. The psychologist Lev Vygotsky, whose work was also a foundation for progressive education, taught that people learn to make and do things through the collaborative discourse and effort involved in trying to make and to do. This kind of learning is social rather than solitary. It depends on the process of exchanging ideas, language, and tools.7

Collaborative learning by doing is particularly apt for professional training for at least two reasons. It is, in part, the process by which experts display and report technical knowledge to their less expert, and often junior, collaborators. It is like, but more structured than, the apprenticeship model under which lawyers and members of other highly regulated professions were trained in the past. But it also involves more than merely handing down developed skills. As more and less experienced professional collaborators pursue their projects, they sometimes innovate. They replicate tested techniques and products, but they also fashion new techniques and products and acquire new knowledge. Practicing doctors reclassify diseases and discover new treatments. Practicing architects and engineers modify their understandings of what it is possible to build. Practicing lawyers struggle to apply established rules in new (and often unanticipated) circumstances. As do children playing with mathematical concepts, aspiring professionals need to do more than learn and apply rules and formulae. They need to understand what they are about and to think critically about alternative courses of thought and action. This kind of understanding and critical thought enables creativity and innovation. It also enables career-long professional growth and the advancement of the practitioner's discipline and art. We might say that it enables progress.

Imagine post-Langdellian law students working from the texts of statutes and judicial decisions to understand what the law might require in an arguably novel hypothetical situation. Imagine the dialogue among teachers and students as they struggle together to fashion arguments on each side of the question and to reach a resolution. You can perhaps see how participating students' analytic and rhetorical skills would sharpen as they construct, argue, and weigh competing interpretations of ambiguous texts.

But you might also imagine a need to return to the treatise. Remembering 12 times 8 is more efficient than conceptualizing it. Like anxious parents whose children are being taught "new" math, anxious law students are impatient for answers. When a hypothetical has been posed for deliberation, they might wonder whether the situation posed in the hypothetical has been considered by an authoritative court or addressed by a learned treatise writer. They might then read ahead in search of a case that raises and answers the professor's hypothetical question. Or they might go out and buy a treatise. Or borrow someone's notes from a prior year. Worst case, they will go out and buy an overly simplified treatise or hornbook. Whichever path students in post-Langdellian Socratic classes take, they can and will at times skip the work of pondering and arguing the outcome of each hypothetical in favor of searching for a canned answer (or, in the case of the more sophisticated student, for a predigested set of arguments on each side of the question). Students who do this might remain in a pre-Langdellian pedagogical environment, reading and remembering rather than working actively to solve problems. But this is not necessarily so. A student armed with knowledge of prior attempts to resolve a doctrinal question may be enabled to think actively – and creatively – about how the question should be (or should have been) resolved. Whether students read for answers or read critically will depend to a large extent on how professors conduct their Socratic questioning. If professors solicit and applaud nothing more than simple repetitions of case outcomes or treatise writers' rules, their students will go to class prepared only to recite. If, on the other hand, professors solicit and applaud argument and critical commentary, their students will go to class prepared to reason and to engage with other students' reasoning.[8]

It appears that Langdell, who is said to have authored the first casebook, took the latter course, demanding students' active reasoning from and engagement with the cases he required them to read.[9] He certainly did not intend that the treatise be abandoned. His conviction that law students should attempt to sort out for themselves the meanings and implications of judicial decisions did not require him to deny the value of scholars' disquisitions on what those texts might mean. Indeed, Langdell was himself hard at work on a treatise on contract law as he developed his pioneering casebook on contracts.[10] He may have hoped that when he asked his students to interpret an important contracts case, the students' responses would reflect and test the judgments of the best treatise writers.

We can see, then, that the casebook has not replaced, nor should replace, the scholarly treatise. The casebook has served to make students active and progressive learners by giving them analytic and interpretive work to do, and the treatise has become a resource rather than the ultimate object of study. The future holds opportunities to use new media and technology to devise more efficient and effective ways of packaging, updating, and delivering the legal knowledge that treatises contain. As we shall see, however, the more important task will be to improve on Langdell's dialogic, casebook method by facilitating and complicating the Freubellian play with which law students discover knowledge on their own and construct new knowledge.

C. CASES AND MATERIALS

1. *Looking beyond the Judicial Opinion*

In response to criticism that the so-called case method, with its focus on judicial – and usually appellate – opinions gives students an inadequate understanding of law or of lawyers' work, some casebook authors have expanded the notion of a case to provide, with respect to some matters, other parts of judicial records, such as trial or argument transcripts, pleadings, or exhibits. These additional case materials expand a student's field of vision so that s/he sees beyond opinion writers' descriptions of adjudicated controversies to consider how those controversies arose and were presented for decision. This broader field of vision can give students a richer understanding of legal process. In addition – and perhaps more important – it can complicate students' sense of the determinants of judicial decision making by revealing the extent to which outcomes are the result of advocates' strategic or rhetorical choices as well as – or perhaps instead of – the result of pure analysis. With this revelation, it becomes apparent that the lawyer's art involves strategy and persuasion just as it involves reasoning from legal knowledge. It also becomes apparent that lawmakers' decisions can be the result of judgment as much as – and sometimes instead of – the result of reasoning from legal knowledge. We might say that this is the first step in taking an outside view of legal process rather than restricting one's gaze to the language and logic of official texts.

Looking beyond the process of reasoning from legal knowledge can be unsettling to students and to professors alike. It is possible to trust that reasoning from legal knowledge will lead to results that are necessarily correct, if not necessarily just. And a "correct" result is difficult to fault. On the other hand, reasoning in response to an advocate's strategic moves or persuasive powers robs us of any assurance of correctness – or of justice – and leaves a feeling of uncertainty. This uncertainty arouses anxiety that the more accomplished, or the more richly funded, or – worst of all – the least scrupulous lawyering can usually win the day. It is perhaps for this reason that so-called skills training is segregated and devalued in the legal academy.

This kind of training is thought to emphasize methodology rather than substantive law, and we have no appetite to teach or learn how to "work the system." We would prefer to keep our eyes on the law and our faith in the possibility of a correct result.

The critique of "skills" training that I have just described is, of course, flawed. I will address its flaws presently, but it is necessary first to describe the materials beyond the official records and particular histories of cases that are typically included in what has come to be known as a casebook. Doing so will reveal additional sources of scholarly anxiety about the teaching of lawyering as opposed to the teaching of law.

2. *Looking beyond the Case*

Casebook authors typically provide supplemental materials to aid or structure students' interpretive work. As a result, casebooks are typically titled "Cases and Materials" on some area of law and contain various combinations and quantities of extrarecord information. This extrarecord information can be divided into two prominent categories: 1) Many authors supplement judicial opinions with treatise excerpts and other interpretive commentary so that student readers can consider the interpretive conclusions of legal scholars and other experts. 2) Casebook authors also include factual accounts or research literature that might inform students' own interpretive conclusions.

Student resort to treatise excerpts, law summaries, and other commentary has been addressed earlier. Whether it occurs because students do independent research or because commentary is structured into a casebook, it can threaten experiential learning by providing answers to questions students should ponder on their own. But, as with the student who takes initiative to discover treatises and other commentary independently, the student provided with commentary can, and should, be encouraged to use it to deepen, rather than to substitute for, his or her own analysis of primary sources. Moreover, the inclusion of commentary enables authors to select for their readers commentary that is scholarly and balanced rather than summary and conclusive.

To say that Cases and Materials texts offer commentary and supplementary documents to aid in the interpretation of law's original and official sources is to broaden again the student interpreter's field of vision. Students of law may now look beyond *both* statute or judicial pronouncement *and* the record and immediate circumstances of a case to see the wide range of considerations a decision maker may entertain in interpreting a law. This raises one of law's most vexing questions: Upon what kind of material may a decision maker legitimacy rely in making an interpretive choice?

3. *The Problem of Uncertainty*

To limit or expand the range of appropriate references for legal interpretation is to accept – or to posit that a decision maker might accept – a particular theory of legal interpretation. It is to choose, for example, among the *textualist* belief that a law means exactly what it says, the *originalist* belief that a law means what its authors intended it to mean, or the *functionalist* belief that a law has – or should be read to have – the meaning that would best serve the function that lawmakers intended it to serve (or that it *ought* to serve).

Imagine a world in which all decision makers are strict textualists who believe that the proper meaning of a law is fully expressed by its language. In such a world, interpretation of a newly enacted law should require no more than the text of the law and, perhaps, materials about common or accepted language usage. Similarly, parsing the meaning of a statute that had been interpreted by a court of ultimate jurisdiction would require no more than the text of that court's decision. Imagine instead a world in which all decision makers are strict originalists who believe that the proper meaning of a law depends on the intentions of those who made it. In such a world, consistency would require that a decision maker's interpretation of enacted law be found in evidence of the lawmakers' opinions at the time of enactment, and interpretation of a controlling opinion would be properly aided by evidence of what the deciding judge or judges meant to say. If all decision makers were functionalists and believed that laws should be interpreted so that they served the social function they were meant to (or ought to) serve, then interpretation would be properly influenced both by evidence of the lawmakers' goals and by evidence of the law's actual or predictable efficacy.

In the real world, decision makers are almost never "pure" textualists, or originalists, or functionalists. One can think of cases that would test the ability of any decision maker to hold strictly to any one of these positions. How would a textualist fix the meaning of a sign directing drivers to "proceed at a reasonable speed"? How would a contemporary originalist fix the sign's meaning if it was posted when there were no motorized vehicles? How would a functionalist fix the meaning of the sign if it were posted in error? Most decision makers are eclectic when they choose (or fall into) interpretive theories, and not all decision makers work from – or seek to work from – the same mixes and versions of those theories. Moreover, we know that judges are susceptible to being unwittingly influenced by factors that should, under their espoused theory of interpretation, be irrelevant.

It follows that lawyers should be trained and prepared to argue from text, from lawmakers' intent, or from function and to make judgments about which sort – or combination – of arguments and evidence will be effective in any given situation. Casebook authors have, for the most part, taken this eclectic stance and offered materials relevant to laws' literal terms, their original intent, and their functionality. Thus, one might find in a casebook dictionary definitions or sociolinguists' essays about the meanings of terms, one might find documents that express or suggest lawmakers' intentions, and one might find studies relevant to the predictable social effects of alternative constructions of a law.

To acknowledge all of these interpretive aids is to see that each may support a different interpretation of a law's meaning. The definition of the words "quiet" and "zone" do not tell me whether I am permitted to hum. A "quiet zone" may have been established by a committee whose reports and other documents reveal that its members had different notions about how quiet people passing through the zone had to be. And empirical studies are unlikely to determine whether a strict or a lenient reading of the "quiet zone" rule will establish over time an intended or desirable atmosphere. Moreover, to attempt to use these aids in concrete cases is to see that each type can, in some circumstances, support a variety of interpretations. Different advocates will define the word "quiet" differently, different advocates will cite different passages from the committee's minutes, and competing experts will say competing things about enforcement rigor and social behavior.

This second excursion beyond the pages of opinions and other official texts intensifies the disquiet of uncertainty. When the entire record of a case could be considered, it became apparent that particular circumstances of litigation, like practitioners' strategic choices, might be outcome-determinative to the extent that they affect what and how much decision makers will know and what authority they will acknowledge. We now see that outcome-determinative variation can also result from the kind of interpretive theory a decision maker holds and the kind of interpretive evidence and argument practitioners' offer.

If students must factor in variations in strategy, resources, and knowledge and then factor in variations in decision-making philosophies, how can they imagine that there is a single, predictable, and correct answer to a legal question? And if there is no such answer, what is the object of Socratic dialogue? If I am preparing to be grilled in a civil procedure class, do I need to know the correct interpretation of *Erie v. Thompkins*? Will a treatise or hornbook statement of its holding serve me adequately? Is my professor seeking answers? Or does the professor want me to appreciate how a probably ambiguous result flowed from interactions among parties, advocates, and decision makers in a particular set of personal, institutional, social, cultural, and political circumstances? Should I be searching for truth or undertaking a critical analysis of interests, philosophies, norms, contingencies, and moves?

There has been abiding controversy about whether, when Langdell enshrined the case method, he thought he was engaging in – or engaging his students in – quests for absolute legal truths or studies of the social construction of rules.[11] This controversy was richly complicated by the work of the legal historian Andrew Chase[12] and of Langdell's painstaking biographer, Bruce Kimball.[13] The evidence now available suggests that Langdell wavered uncomfortably between the two poles, as many legal scholars do today: As an answer-seeking mortal, he craved definitive truths, but experience and sophistication led him to see legal pronouncements as provisional responses in transitory circumstances.[14]

In the early decades of the twentieth century, the legal realist school of scholars shook the academy by announcing that a sense of uncertainty about the meaning of law or about the answer to a legal question was appropriate. Law, they claimed, is indeterminate. This claim immensely complicated legal interpretation and legal theory, but it proved hard to dispute. Scholars, like their students, were able to look beyond the neat logic of judicial opinions to a sea of contingencies that might have influenced those opinions. Indeed, it was not long after the realists announced their claim that respected, mainstream scholars could say (admittedly with some exaggeration) that "we are all realists now." Still, uncertainty remains disquieting, and the disquiet prevents us from following the pedagogical implications of the realist insight. Few among us speak clearly or coherently to our students about indeterminacy, and many of us postpone the discussion until students have been entrapped by illusions of certainty. Postrealism's critical legal theorists deepened mainstream legal scholars' disquiet over uncertainty by suggesting that in addition to being undeterminable by fixed principles, legal outcomes are – or can be – determined by influence, interest, and bias. This added the insult of impure motives to the injury of unpredictability and further motivated us to cling to the reassurance that accompanies believing that legal outcomes are "correct" in some verifiable way.

4. The Pedagogic Response to Uncertainty

If we treat the choice between a quest for absolute truth and a study of social construction as philosophical, we may debate it endlessly without agreement. But the pedagogic issue is practical rather than philosophical. We want to know what beyond the text and the internal logic of a case students need to know or understand. The wise strategy of "backward design"[15] counsels that the desired result of a learning experience be established *before* that experience is designed. In other words, before we construct a learning experience, we should know what we want students to gain from it. Let us remain agnostic about whether any given legal pronouncement might be true or eternal and simply ask what students should know about it.

What we think law students need to know depends on what we understand to be the purpose of law school training. Perhaps surprisingly, this is something about which legal academics seem to disagree. The overwhelming majority of law students go on to participate in the creation, interpretation, and enforcement of law. They become practitioners, administrators, legislators, adjudicators, and adjudication facilitators.[16] Most of us who teach law students aspire to prepare them to assume these roles, albeit as novices. There is, however, a competing view – expressed most frequently by faculty members who see (or wish to see) law schools more as research facilities and less as professional training grounds. This competing view is that law schools should concentrate on teaching legal doctrine and theory, as practice skills are ephemeral and best learned on the job. In this formulation, legal doctrine presumably means the best contemporary statement of official rules governing a subject area. The contents of an ideal treatise, perhaps? The meaning of legal theory is more ambiguous; often it seems to mean hypotheses about how a subject area or category of human activity is best governed (e.g., a cost-benefit or social welfare theory of torts). At other times it seems to refer to hypotheses about lawmaking and legal process. We might take the theories of interpretation described previously as examples of what legal academics refer to when they talk about this second kind of "theory."

There are few who doubt that law schools should teach both doctrine and theory of the kinds I have described. However, we who strive to make our students practice-ready argue, following education theorists of the progressive school, that doctrine and theory are best understood in context. This is true, we sense, even for those who intend to teach and to engage in theoretical analysis rather than to practice law. When we say this, we are, in effect, rejecting the theory/practice dichotomy. We are resisting the compartmentalization of legal education into "what" and "how-to" chambers. We are resisting sharp distinctions between "academic" and "clinical" training.

Those who disagree argue that things should at times be broken down into learnable parts; that those who teach law and theory best are not necessarily equipped to teach practice skills, while those best equipped to teach practice skills may have little expertise in theory. What contestants in this argument miss is that the Rubicon has already been crossed, and Christopher Columbus Langdell led the crossing. *When law students began practicing the work of interpretation, they began learning the work of practice.* For this reason, authors of Cases and Materials texts do not choose a theory of interpretation to advance but offer materials to support arguments that might be made to decision makers who embrace a variety of theories. Students have not entered law school to learn a jurisprudential faith (although they may have one or decide to adopt one). They have entered to prepare themselves to predict the judgments of, and to be advocates before, decision makers of every faith. A practitioner may not be agnostic about how laws *should* be made and interpreted, but a successful practitioner must work with the fact that laws *are* made and interpreted in interactions among people who hold a variety of views about the making and interpretation of laws. The same can be said of a skillful scholar.

Recognition that laws and lawmakers are not controlled by any single theory makes controversial the casebook author's choice of materials as interpretive aids, for many selected materials will seem inappropriate to those who hold particular theories of interpretation. A textualist, for example, may protest inclusion of stories about the parties' social or economic or personal circumstances on the ground that they are not legally relevant. If the sign says, "No Vehicles," what does it matter that the occupant of a motorized wheelchair is therefore unable to enjoy the park?[17] In certain circumstances an originalist might do the same. If the sign was posted in response to an automobile accident, what does it matter that a toy truck makes a hideously loud noise?

This is an appropriate moment to return to the problem caused by segregating law and theory, on the one hand, and practice, on the other. When we have made students active interpreters of *law* and acknowledged that advocates and decision makers are not bound by a unifying *theory*, we gain a new appreciation of the centrality of *practice*. We see that no one of these elements can be fully grasped unless the other two are also considered.

To recap: We have seen that the earliest law school courses were focused principally on teaching doctrine or the meaning of law itself. Each subsequent step in the evolution of course materials expanded law students' horizons. The casebook empowered law students to practice the art of interpretation on their own. With this, right answers ceased to be offered from the law professor's podium. When the "cases" of the case method were expanded to include the official and historical record beyond the judicial opinion, the law student's universe was opened to a fuller understanding of the facts and circumstances of a case and to matters of strategy and methods of persuasion. With this, legal decision making began to seem to depend on the contexts of deliberation as well as on practitioners' effort and skill. The cases and materials model for law school texts raised the question of what secondary and extralegal materials students should consult if they were to be seen as interpreters of law and not just receptacles for legal knowledge. This expanded students' horizons beyond litigation controversies to offer broader knowledge about personal, political, and social context and the guidance of the human sciences.

D. CASES AND PROBLEMS

Is there a logical next step in the development of texts for training lawyers? I believe that there are two: making texts of students' practice experiences and offering texts that address the methods by which students enact those experiences.

The casebook serves to frame discursive learning experiences as much as it serves to transmit information. It provides the original sources whose meaning professors and students will debate in the classroom, as well as commentary and materials that enrich classroom debate. As law school text authors absorbed this idea, they began to offer, in addition to commentary and enrichment materials,

problems for students to ponder after they had read the original source materials
of statutes and case law. With this move, casebook authors relieved professors
who assigned their texts of at least some of the responsibility for structuring class
debate, and a Cases and Problems model emerged. Whereas students had typically been surprised in class by the hypothetical scenarios and problems they had
to confront, the problem method gave them the opportunity to think through at
least some questions in advance. The practice of giving students problems prior
to their class performances is preferable pedagogically because each student who
prepares for class can try to apply what s/he has read. On the other hand, law
professors often substitute or mix in surprise questions, either on the theory that
lawyers must be trained to "think on their feet" or because discussion leads organ-
ically to unanticipated issues.

It is possible to construct problems for students that have a definitive answer key.
Similarly, it is possible to organize a Socratic discussion in which all questions are,
in educators' jargon, inauthentic – questions for which the questioner already has in
mind a fixed answer. But the best cases and problems texts – as do the best Socratic
teachers – minimize or avoid these fill-in-the-blanks questions and regularly pose
genuine questions that require students to anticipate the next development in a
line of doctrine or to confront a scenario that confounds what seemed in other circumstances to be a sensible rule. Here too, then, uncertainty reigns, and students
worry, as Langdell's students worried nearly a century and a half ago, whether their
professors know any law and why, if they do, they will not simply "teach" or tell it
to them.

E. SIMULATIONS – STUDENT WORK AS TEXT

Education theory may tell us that people learn best by doing, and we may or may
not be persuaded. But in law, what is done – and how it is done – is all there is to
learn. There are theories from many disciplines that will help us to assess lawyers'
and decision makers' strategic, rhetorical, and policy choices, both prospectively
and retrospectively. But there is no grand theory that will allow us to deduce how
participants in a free and open society will in the future arrange their affairs and
resolve their disputes. Only the scattered few who cling to outmoded claims of legal
certainty would argue otherwise.

The case method permitted students to study and to practice interpreting the
opinions issued at the end of a litigated matter or motion and to test the relevance
of those opinions to new matters. Cases and materials gave students materials, both
within and outside the records of cases, that might inform their interpretive practice.
Cases and problems gave students contexts for interpretive practice. The simulation
model turns students' own work into the text. It gives them concrete and complex

problem scenarios and asks that they do what needs to be done to resolve a legal matter. It then takes what was done – students' memoranda, videotapes of meetings, arguments, outcomes, and coparticipant reactions – as text for critical study. Law, theory, and practice join as strategic, rhetorical, ethical, and policy choices are analyzed and alternatives are considered. Students become more sophisticated, both about doing law and about what law is.

The texts that are given to students for simulations differ radically from the casebook. When students engage in simulations, primary and secondary sources are for the most part *not* provided but left for students to find through their own research. Faculty who supervise simulations must understand the primary sources upon which students in role are most likely to rely, but these sources (and secondary sources interpreting or explaining them) are materials for a teachers' manual rather than for student consumption. What students need is a set of materials that will place them convincingly in role and give them the information and guidance they need to carry out a lawyering task.

The professional skill of practicing or rehearsing in role is initially awkward for many law students. In time they will see that suspending disbelief in a simulation – suspending one's knowledge that the work is not "real" or that it does not fully "count" – is as natural and as essential for a professional lawyer as dedicated training is for a professional athlete or dedicated rehearsal is for a professional actor. But the adjustment process is facilitated to the extent that information and direction are provided in role. For this reason, it is best that student materials be provided in the form of a simulated case file and through oral or written communications from simulated supervisors, clients, officials, and other interested parties.

To be effective, simulations must both encourage students to be reflective and function at the "growing edge" of the students' abilities. What is required to achieve these pedagogic goals is a case file that does at least four things:

1. *It lays the foundation for fact development.* Each simulation will begin with a set of given facts. Some of these will be buried in documents. Others will be in the role assignment memoranda for persons (students, teaching assistants, or actors) playing the client, supervisor, official, witness, or some other party. In either case, they are for the student to find in careful document review and interviewing.

2. *It poses one or more debatable legal questions.* Good simulations, as do most matters for which people need sophisticated legal representation or counsel, involve questions of law that can be answered or argued more than one way. They involve interpretive choices that are likely to be made differently by different thoughtful students. Legal indeterminacy is, then, at the heart of a well-designed simulation.

3. *It assigns students one or more tasks that require a) developing and integrating facts and b) analyzing and applying law in order to c) solve a problem or achieve a goal.* Thoughtful development and interpretation of facts, skillful research and penetrating interpretation of law, strategic integration of law and fact, and mindful problem solving are the central lawyering arts. Practicing them raises skill levels and at the same time deepens understanding of how they interconnect to shape a legal culture.

4. *It structures and sequences students' progress through the assignment (or through a set of assignments) to assure that they are working reflectively and at the growing edge of their abilities.* Practice alone does not make perfect; repetition does not assure improvement. The most important component of a simulation is critical reflection on one's choices, and the most important benefits of the process of practice and reflection are the expansion of skills and the enhancement of critical judgment.

As I have already mentioned, a good simulation needs to generate student work that is both reflective and at the "growing edge" of a student's ability. The first requirement may be more readily perceived in the preceding discussion, but the second requirement is just as important to experiential methodology. The progressive learning methodologies most famously promoted in the United States by John Dewey are supported and illuminated by the work of Lev Vygotsky. Vygotsky saw learning as a social process in which people work collaboratively with others – usually more expert others – to do things that they could not do on their own. We can imagine that for each person there is a category of things s/he is unable to do, a category of things s/he is able to do with help, and a category of things s/he can do on her own. Novices learn as they work with others to do things they could not do on their own, and eventually the things they work on are edged into the category of things they are able to do on their own. Vygotsky called the place between what one has mastered and what one can master with help the zone of proximal development;[18] following Bruner, I refer to it as a student's "growing edge."[19] Successful simulations are sequenced – with one another and with other kinds of learning experiences – to assure that students are not working by rote or aimlessly but are working for growth.

The case file materials described earlier cannot be properly presented in a bound book format, for simulation materials should be both individualized and sequenced. The overall design of simulation materials should be modifiable so that their challenges can be tailored to suit the preferences of professors and the goals of the varied courses for which they will be used. Modifiability is desirable for any published teaching materials, but it is especially important that simulation materials be adaptable to jurisdictions and to the sizes and time constraints of different courses. The rigidity of a bound volume is especially problematic for simulation materials, for they invariably need to be tailored to the evolving needs and progress of different groups of students and, ideally, to the needs and progress of individual students. Simulation materials should, of course, be individualized for students working in different roles. Students working as advocates for a side or as parties, information sources, or decision makers can not work effectively or credibly if they are all exposed to the same facts and responding to a common set of directions. Just as important, simulation materials must be *modifiable in sequence, rather than all at once.* A simulation should present students with challenges that are responsive at critical points to their own strategic choices and to the strategic choices of students working in different roles. If at all possible, simulation materials should also be responsive to particular students' developmental progress. Individualization and responsiveness of these kinds are compromised by the use of bound, or even of printed, materials.

Case materials are not all that students need for a successful learning experience in simulation work. A simulation requires the exercise of a variety of skills, and students are entitled to guidance in developing those skills. It is often in a simulation that the skill of legal analysis is most explicitly broken down into its functional parts and methodological guidance is offered so that students have a clear sense of what they are doing and how they might go about doing it more expertly. In the careers of many law students, it is *only* in simulation and clinical courses that the often neglected skills of fact development, interviewing, counseling, and formal and informal advocacy are broken down functionally and explicitly developed. Since the need for students to use – and opportunities for them to develop – these skills will recur throughout the stages of a simulation and across the simulations of a course, guidance for developing them is best provided in electronic format so that it can be hyperlinked to simulation materials and referenced repeatedly and as needed. Electronic formats also permit guidance that is not limited to written instruction but can include demonstrations and interactive exercises. Since fact development, interviewing, counseling, and formal and informal advocacy are interactive, they are best developed when students can interact easily and then record and review their interactions. Electronic formats not only facilitate interactions but also allow their recording, annotation, and repeated review.

F. MANAGING THE UNCERTAINTY

The increasingly experiential approaches to law teaching that I have described highlight uncertainties that can be, as we have seen, disquieting on several levels. They expose litigation and legislative histories in ways that highlight the uncertain effects of circumstance, strategies, and choices. They focus on alternative reasonable interpretations of the law rather than on correct interpretations. They expose lawyers and judges as moral agents making interpretive choices rather than announcing fixed principles. The disquiet generated by exposure of these uncertainties has, I think, inhibited experiential learning's acceptance and development in the law school setting. Some critics of experiential methods for training lawyers argue that students should not be confused by what they see as a constant harping on uncertainty when so much in law is fixed and clear. Others worry that frank discussion of alternative theories of interpretation carries worrisome "C[ritical] L[egal] S[tudies] overtones."[20] Critiques of this kind are sometimes made with respect to first-year courses on the ground that beginning students need to be oriented by some amount of learned doctrine. Later, these critics argue, with some law under their belts, students can engage more responsibly and more comfortably with the idea of indeterminacy. In their first year of study it can only confuse them.

The difficulty with this approach is that it instills a more profound confusion than frank discussion of uncertainty could ever arouse. Students typically enter law school with the fervent belief and faith that their mission is simply to learn the law. Dissonance is created when they endlessly debate reasonable alternative statements or interpretations of various laws in Socratic classes. But the faith survives because they are also convinced that their futures will depend importantly on whether they know enough black letter law to score well in each of their courses on a single, final, time-limited examination in which knowledge often seems to matter more than judgment. Too often the result is a cognitive splitting; students know at some level that law is indeterminate but speak and act as if it were fixed and certain. Alas, some of their professors display the same kind of cognitive splitting as they expound upon cases' subtle vagaries yet then, without explanation, give their students only short answer and multiple choice exams or only ask fill-in-the-blanks questions during what professes to be Socratic dialogue.

The form and substance of course materials also contribute to students' tendency to think and work as if law were rigidly fixed. Coping with the fluidity and unpredictability of simulation case materials and with colleagues' varied judgments and interpretations of fact and law helps students to see law as the living, interactive, and changing thing that it is rather than as a fixed code. This lesson of indeterminacy is instinctively grasped in the kind of give and take that is possible in electronic formats, for these formats easily permit – and often require – responsiveness to competing and ever changing opinions and interests.

Law students are intelligent adults. We who teach them need not treat indeterminacy as if it were, in the words of one of my colleagues, "law's dirty little secret." Our students can absorb the idea that laws are the products of public and private commerce and of human discourse, decision making, and compromise. They can simultaneously understand, without dissonance or confusion, that laws can and usually do have both generally agreed-upon and patently absurd constructions. They can accept that some agreed-upon constructions should be learned yet still appreciate the need to master and constantly critique the process of construction. If taking in all of this is confusing, then students need to be confused. The alternatives are to deny professional choice by maintaining a delusion of certainty or adjusting to cognitive splitting. Both alternatives are unpleasant, because both hide the need to take, and the possibility of taking, moral and civic responsibility for the professional choices one inevitably makes. As Lon Fuller argued in his illuminating 1958 debate with H. L. A. Hart,[21] to deny uncertainty and choice is to suspend judgment, and the consequences range from absurdity to atrocity: If we commit to a clear, fixed meaning for the law that says "No Vehicles in the Park," we risk closing the park to children's tricycles or to the fire truck that might save an occupied and burning puppet theater.

NOTES

1. This description applies to formal, school-based legal education, not to the apprenticeship training that was common and legally adequate before the development of law schools and law school accreditation.
2. I refer here to statutes and regulations, as well as to cases, as primary sources of law. In the nineteenth century, before the extensive codification of common law and the rise of the administrative regulatory state, cases were a nearly exclusive focus of legal study.
3. For more detailed accounts of this history, *see* Anthony Chase, "The Birth of the Modern Law School," *American Journal of Legal History* 23 (1979): 329; Bruce A. Kimball, *The Inception of Modern Professional Education: C. C. Langdell, 1826–1906* (Chapel Hill: University of North Carolina Press, 2009). *See also* Peggy Cooper Davis, "Desegregating Legal Education," *Georgia State University Law Review* 26 (2010): 1271, 1271, 1275–8, and authorities cited therein.
4. *See* Jerome Frank, "Why Not a Clinical Lawyer School?" *University of Pennsylvania Law Review* 81 (1933): 907.
5. *See*, e.g., Richard Lempert, Samuel Gross, and James Liebman *A Modern Approach to Evidence: Text, Problems, Transcripts, and Cases* (St. Paul, MN: West, 3rd ed., 2000) (using transcripts in the teaching of evidence); Jack Friedenthal, Mary Kay Kane, and Arthur Miller, *Civil Procedure: Cases and Materials* (St. Paul, MN: West, 4th ed., 2005) (using case files in the teaching of civil procedure).
6. For a vivid description of this knowledge-dispensing view of education, *see* Paulo Freire, *Pedagogy of the Oppressed*, trans. Maya Bergman Ramon (London: Continuum Publishing, 1970).
7. I use the term "tool" broadly to include, for example, the forms a police officer or social worker might fill out or the classification systems by which legal sources are referenced.
8. *See* Peggy Cooper Davis and Elizabeth Ehrenfest-Steinfeld, "A Dialogue about Socratic Teaching," *New York University Review of Law and Social Change* 23 (1997): 249.
9. Kimball, *Inception of Modern Professional Education*, 147–60.
10. *Id.*, 102.
11. *See* Carrie Menkel-Meadow, "Taking Law and _____ Really Seriously: Before, During and After 'The Law,'" *Vanderbilt Law Review* 60 (2007): 555, 561–4; *see also* Edward

Rubin, "What's Wrong with Langdell's Method, and What to Do about It," *Vanderbilt Law Review* 60 (2007): 609, 631–5 (arguing that Langdell viewed law as a fixed system, like a pre-Kuhnian natural science); Davis, "Desegregating Legal Education," 1279.

12. Chase, "Birth of the Modern Law School."

13. Kimball, *Inception of Modern Professional Education.*

14. Davis, "Desegregating Legal Education," 1288–9.

15. See Grant Wiggins and Jay McTighe, *Understanding by Design* (Upper Saddle River, NJ: Prentice Hall, 2005).

16. Of all employed graduates from the class of 2009, approximately 55.9 percent work in private practice, 13.5 percent in business, 11.4 percent in government, 8.7 percent as judicial clerks, 5.7 percent in public interest, and 3.5 percent in academia, with 1.4 percent employed in an unknown category. Of the business jobs, 28.9 percent require bar passage. Overall, 81.4 percent of the jobs held by the class of 2009 require bar passage. National Association for Law Placement, "Class of 2009 National Summary Chart," accessed 8 March 2011, www.nalp.org/uploads/NatlSummaryChartClassof09.pdf.

17. *See* H. L. A. Hart, "Positivism and the Separation of Law and Morals," *Harvard Law Review* 71 (1958): 593; Lon Fuller, "Positivism and Fidelity to Law: A Reply to Professor Hart," *Harvard Law Review* 71 (1958): 630 (*The Hart v. Fuller Debate*).

18. Lev Vygotsky, *Educational Psychology* (Boca Raton, FL: CRC Press, 1997).

19. *See* Jerome Bruner, *Actual Minds, Possible Worlds* (Cambridge, MA: Harvard University Press,1986), 77.

20. Correspondence within the Special Committee to Report on the Lawyering Program (12 November 2009, 11:47 a.m.) (on file with the author).

21. *Hart v. Fuller Debate.*

Index